Beyond 2020

Part of the American Council on Education Series on Higher Education
Susan Slesinger, Executive Editor

Other titles in the series:

Community Colleges on the Horizon: Challenge, Choice, or Abundance
edited by Richard Alfred, Christopher Shults, Ozan Jaquette, and
Shelley Strickland

Out in Front: The College President as the Face of the Institution
edited by Lawrence V. Weill

Minding the Dream: The Process and Practice of the American Community
College)
by Gail O. Mellow and Cynthia Heelan

Higher Education in the Internet Age: Libraries Creating a Strategic Edge
by Patricia Senn Breivik and E. Gordon Gee

American Places: In Search of the Twenty-First Century Campus
by M. Perry Chapman

New Game Plan for College Sport
Edited by Richard E. Lapchick

What's Happening to Public Higher Education?
Edited by Ronald G. Ehrenberg

Lessons from the Edge: For-Profit and Nontraditional Higher Education in
America
by Gary A. Berg

Mission and Place: Strengthening Learning and Community through Campus
Design
by Daniel R. Kenney, Ricardo Dumont, and Ginger S. Kenney

Portraits in Leadership: Six Extraordinary University Presidents
by Arthur Padilla

College Student Retention: Formula for Student Success
edited by Alan Seidman

Building the Academic Deanship: Strategies for Success
by Gary S. Krahenbuhl

Teacher Education Programs in the United States: A Guide
compiled by ACE/AACTE

The Entrepreneurial College President
by James L. Fisher and James V. Koch

Speaking of Higher Education: The Academic's Book of Quotations
by Robert Birnbaum

What Business Wants from Higher Education
by Diana G. Oblinger and Anne-Lee Verville

Beyond 2020

Envisioning the
Future of Universities in America

Written and Edited by Mary Landon Darden

Published in partnership with the

Rowman & Littlefield Education
Lanham • New York • Toronto • Plymouth, UK

Published in partnership with
the American Council on Education

Published in the United States of America
by Rowman & Littlefield Education
A Division of Rowman & Littlefield Publishers, Inc.
A wholly owned subsidiary of The Rowman & Littlefield Publishing Group, Inc.
4501 Forbes Boulevard, Suite 200, Lanham, Maryland 20706
www.rowmaneducation.com

Estover Road
Plymouth PL6 7PY
United Kingdom

British Library Cataloguing in Publication Information Available

Library of Congress Cataloging-in-Publication Data

Darden, Mary Landon, 1952–
    Beyond 2020 : envisioning the future of universities in America / Mary
Landon Darden.
        p. cm.
    "Published in Partnership with the American Council on Education."
    Includes bibliographical references.
    ISBN-13: 978-1-60709-073-1 (cloth : alk. paper)
    ISBN-10: 1-60709-073-2 (cloth : alk. paper)
    ISBN-13: 978-1-60709-075-5 (electronic)
    ISBN-10: 1-60709-075-9 (electronic)
    1. Education, Higher—United States—Forecasting. I. American Council on
Education. II. Title.
    LA198.D37 2009
    378.73—dc22   2008046965

⊗™ The paper used in this publication meets the minimum requirements of
American National Standard for Information Sciences—Permanence of
Paper for Printed Library Materials, ANSI/NISO Z39.48-1992.
Manufactured in the United States of America.

To my husband, hero, and inspiration,
Robert F. Darden III

Contents

List of Figures and Tables ix

Acknowledgments xi

Introduction xiii
by Mary Landon Darden

1 Overview of the Future University Beyond 2020 1
with James J. Duderstadt

2 The Presidency of the Future University 13
with Stephen Joel Trachtenberg

3 Significant Continuing and Emerging Issues Facing
Tomorrow's University 25
with Claire Van Ummersen, Helen Astin, and William Underwood

4 Future Legal Issues 47
with Robert C. Cloud

5 Students of Tomorrow 63
with Alexander W. Astin

6 The Evolution of International Higher Education 77
with H. Stephen Gardner and Vivian Bull

7 Technology Today and Tomorrow 99
with Jay Box

8 University Libraries of the Future 113
with James G. Neal

9   Financing the Future of Higher Education   123
    with Randy Livingston and H. Stephen Gardner

10 Advancement in the Future University   137
    with Ronald D. Vanden Dorpel

11 Continuing Education, Workforce Training, and
    Lifelong Learning   147
    with Andrew L. Meyer

12 Higher Education Marketing   157
    with Karen Fox

13 The Future Physical Plant   165
    with John Carmody

14 Partnerships of the Future University   175
    by Nancy L. Zimpher

15 University Governance Beyond 2020   191
    with Larry Gerber and Daniel McGee

Conclusion   209
    by Mary Landon Darden

About the Writer and Editor   219

Figures and Tables

FIGURES

6.1. Population, Age Sixteen to Fifty-nine, by World Regions,
1950–2050   85

TABLES

6.1. Student Mobility: Top Receiving and
Sending Countries, 2005   79

6.2. Foreign Students in the United States, 1970–2006   80

6.3. U.S. Study-Abroad Students, 1970–2005   81

6.4. GMAT Examinations, 2006–2007   84

6.5. School Enrollment Rates, 2005   85

Acknowledgments

Special thanks to:

Robert F. Darden III
Dr. Robert C. Cloud
Dr. Ann McGlashan
Susan Slesinger
Paula Moore
Bernard Rapoport
Dr. Michael Cady
Dan Barkley
Rachel, Mark, and Asa Menjivar
Van Darden
Marcla Sue Ellison
Bill Hair
Dr. Stan Madden
Dr. Deborah Johnston
Dr. Rosalie Beck
Dr. Georgia Green

Dr. James Williamson
Larry Brumley
"The Heretics"
The Round Table
John Wilson
Carol Hobbs
Pattie Orr
Mimi Zylinski
Seventh and James
Book Contributors
Book Contributor Support Staff
Patti Belcher
The *Scholars of Practice* Educational
   Administration Doctoral Program at
   Baylor University
The American Council on Education

Introduction
by Mary Landon Darden

Academia traditionally moves with glacial deliberation to organize, ponder, assimilate, and eventually disseminate information. This is a good thing. A careful examination of issues, facts, problems, theses, and opportunities has enabled academia to generally avoid the pitfalls of knee-jerk reactions and ill-advised plunges. And therefore, it abides.

This is because academia is in the information business. It succeeds or fails in both the quality of the information it collects, synthesizes, and distributes as well as the speed with which that transfer takes place.

But as the world has progressed with increasing acceleration from the Machine Age to the Information Age, that measured, even plodding approach can place administrator, faculty member, and student alike at a potentially dire disadvantage.

To move into this brave new world, the academic animal needs additional tools. What's ahead? Forewarned, of course, is forearmed. Armed with knowledge, the future stands not as another barrier, but an unparalleled opportunity.

Serving as a college administrator for a decade and subsequently completing a doctorate in higher education administration has made me acutely aware not only of the great opportunities for higher education in the future, but also of how vast and complex the field of higher education administration is, and that the university itself is moving into the future at such a rapid pace that even thorough preparation for the top leadership positions is not enough to guarantee success. Being a successful university leader is somewhat like executing an intricately choreographed series of challenging swim strokes in perfect form while swimming through a stormy sea. It is constantly shifting, difficult and dangerous. It requires great skill, endurance, agility, and practice. And there is little or no room for error.

Recognizing this extreme challenge juxtaposed with rapid change, it has been my heart's desire to interview some of the best known and accomplished leaders in the specific fields of higher education administration to find out how they navigated these waters so successfully. I wanted to know what is likely to change in the next few decades and beyond, and how administrators can best prepare for success amidst these changes. If these great scholars and leaders—including more than a half-dozen university presidents—didn't know the answers, I did not know who would. It was an enormous privilege to choose the topics, discuss them with the contributors, and compile their input into a one-of-a-kind how-to book on preparing and administrating for the future university.

The chapters in the book, save for the independently written chapter on partnerships, were based on interviews that I conducted with the chapter experts. Three of the interviews were conducted in person and the rest were via telephone. I selected the interviewees primarily based on their experience and success in their particular disciplines. I drafted the chapters, provided an opportunity for review and feedback, and made the final edits and changes to the chapters.

The voices in the chapters are mainly those of the interviewees themselves. However, while attempting to preserve their unique voices, I used my "writing voice" to help blend the chapters and lend a bit more of a uniform flow to the finished manuscript.

The tone of the book is a bit more relaxed and informal than many academic books. The contributors are mostly well-known and highly respected scholars and administrators who are also devoted public servants. I wanted the reader to have a sense of who these people are personally and feel as if they were receiving unfiltered, one-on-one information and advice from these accomplished and caring leaders. I believe that their personalities, demeanor, passions, and priorities provide additional insight into the things that matter most in successful leadership. Each interview was inspiring, information-dense, and most provided a sense of hope, optimism, and at times even excitement about the future of the university.

The book's organization is intended to gradually move the reader from more general, overall, macro topics to more specific areas. I placed governance at the end because I believe that, in the end, governance and ethics are about how we treat each other on the most micro of all behavioral levels, person-to-person. Governance may also be highly impacted by a single individual, particularly by a president. When I completed the interviews for this chapter, I was left with the feeling that the values expressed are vital to the success of not only the university, not only to the successes and failures of each individual, but also collectively to all of humanity.

The title, *Beyond 2020*, was selected for several reasons. Success in the future university will require near perfect 20/20 vision; many presidents have named their current university plan "2020"; and the term "beyond" implies that it is perhaps even more necessary for us to see well into the future, rather than be content with what we can in the present.

Fortunately, I found an abundance of vision, experience, successes, and guidance. Many experts even shared potential pitfalls and dangers. In the end, the manuscript covers virtually every major facet of administration and provides excellent insight and advice from outstanding people. I believe *Beyond 2020: Envisioning the Future of Universities in America* will serve as a useful handbook for university board members, presidents, and administrators for years to come. This is a collection of refreshingly frank opinions and observations from people on the front lines, people with the best views of tomorrow. It is a nautical map prophetically detailing how to guide the university past unseen reefs and safely into the future.

I want to thank my contributors for selflessly providing their input, insight, and projections. They exceeded my expectations in painting a picture of the university of the future and providing priceless advice on how to maximize success in that future model. It is my great hope that every current and future university board member and administrator will read this book and benefit from the collected wisdom that has been shared on these pages.

Chapter 1

Overview of the Future University Beyond 2020

with James J. Duderstadt

James J. Duderstadt is president emeritus and university professor of science and engineering at the University of Michigan. He is a well-known author on the future of the university and his books include A University for the Twenty-first Century, The View from the Helm: Leading the American University in an Era of Change, *and* The Future of the Public University in America: Beyond the Crossroads. *He also serves as director of the Millennium Project, a research center concerned with the future of higher education.*

Duderstadt received his doctorate in engineering science and physics from the California Institute of Technology. His interests have spanned a wide range of subjects in science, mathematics, and engineering, including work in areas such as nuclear systems, computer simulation, science policy, and higher education.

Among Duderstadt's numerous national awards are the E. O. Lawrence Award for excellence in nuclear research, the Arthur Holly Compton Prize for outstanding teaching, and the National Medal of Technology for exemplary service to the nation.

Duderstadt has served on and/or chaired many boards, including the National Science Board; the Executive Council of the National Academy of Engineering; and the Commission on Science, Engineering, and Public Policy of the National Academy of Sciences.

Duderstadt is one of the world's best-known writers on higher education administration and the future of the university. His writings have been a guiding

---

This chapter is based on an interview on the future of the university that I conducted with President Emeritus Duderstadt on November 20, 2007, for this book. It presents a multifaceted chart for the highly complex course ahead for universities.

light and a constant inspiration. Duderstadt has become a legend in his own time. It is with deep and humble gratitude that I accept the task of sharing a small part of his great wisdom.

HISTORICAL HIGHLIGHTS OF
UNIVERSITY ADMINISTRATION AND THE PRESIDENCY

The history of higher education informs academia of who we are by reminding us from where and for what we were created. While parts of the mission and purpose of the original higher education institution are still with us today, much has changed.

It is like being the captain of a small vessel on a stormy sea. Each new swell reveals new challenges for pilot and crew alike. But each new wave may also take the ship closer to safety and home.

Since the founding of Harvard and until the mid-nineteenth century, university presidents were pastoral, because the colonial colleges were more concerned with the socialization of young men for leadership roles for the society's elite.

"Lord Rugby said that like the British public school, the role of the colonial colleges was to 'transform savages into gentlemen,'" Duderstadt said. "So, presidents had that headmaster kind of character. They often taught a capstone course, usually on moral development in our institutions."

This long-held approach changed with the industrialization of America, the founding of the public universities, the Land Grant Act, and similar events.

"By the end of the nineteenth century, presidents were leading institutions with not just a hundred faculty and several hundred students, but many hundreds of faculty and thousands of students," he said. "It required management skills beyond simply headmaster skills. By the 1930s and 1940s, many of these institutions were the size of large cities, and presidents began to take on the role not so much as a corporate leader, but more like a mayor, but mayor of very complex heterogeneous communities. That role continued into the 1950s and 1960s."

In the 1970s and 1980s, the internal role of the president, leading this complex organization, turned outward. The president's role increasingly became one of interfacing the university with the outside world, including fund-raising, and interaction with state and federal government. That model continues through today.

"Although people sometimes portray the university president as a chief executive officer, in reality most university presidents are more concerned with the interface between the institution and society than with the internal leadership of its academic programs—which is delegated to the provost—

or its financial activities, which has been the responsibility of the chief financial officer," Duderstadt said. "I think the difficulty with that concept is it pulls the contemporary president further and further away from the core mission of the university, teaching and learning, and that is how universities get in trouble."

MAJOR ISSUES AND EVENTS FOR HIGHER EDUCATION TODAY

Duderstadt has identified a number of reports from the past several years, including the Spellings Commission, in which he discussed some of the current concerns in higher education. "I recently gave the keynote address to the AAU presidents in California," Duderstadt said. "The big fear that the Spellings Commission expressed was *accessibility*—the fact that not enough Americans have the opportunity for higher education today and that this opportunity has become extremely dependent upon socioeconomic circumstance—in sharp conflict with what we are supposed to be as a democracy."

Duderstadt's second concern is *affordability*. Higher education is becoming more and more expensive, in part because it is being increasingly perceived as a benefit rather than a public good. As such, the justification for investing in higher education is less to benefit all society than to provide a benefit to the individual students that participate. This has resulted in higher education dropping further and further down on the public's priority list. As it relates to higher education funding, Duderstadt said that most of the states are now treading water or cutting back the support of higher education. When coupled with the concerns of an aging baby boomer population who will prioritize health care, he said that the situation is not likely to turn around. Ultimately, he believes that students and their parents must be prepared to bear more of the real cost of education.

The third critical issue involving the future of higher education that Duderstadt identified was *accountability*. This issue has received a lot of recent attention from people who want to know how to ensure that universities are accountable to public purpose and to the population it serves. Duderstadt said that an understanding of this issue is the key to public trust and confidence. "There are certain ironies here," he said. "Universities have never been more important, and yet public trust and confidence in those universities is somewhat fragile. Universities need to disclose more about what they do, how they determine their prices, and whether they are actually achieving their educational objectives. Those are the three issues that came out in the Spellings Commission."

But Duderstadt mentions additional critical issues, including *the role of the university in the knowledge-economy*. "That's Thomas Friedman's *The*

World is Flat theme," he said. "This is a knowledge-driven society, where educated people and ideas are the wealth of nations. Universities create both. They create new knowledge, scholarship, and a human capital through education."

A fifth concern on Duderstadt's list is *globalization*, the concept that the world is becoming increasingly more tightly integrated economically and culturally, through transportation and communication technology. In these areas and more, globalization is having a profound effect on higher education. Recent studies show that the majority of students enrolled today in the University of California system are either immigrants themselves or one of their parents is a first generation immigrant. By that standard, UCLA is a global institution. According to Duderstadt, the migration of students and faculty continues, and universities are now establishing branch campuses throughout the world, in China, India, and Europe.

The final theme on Duderstadt's list of higher education issues was one that interested him because he chairs the advisory committee to the National Science Foundation on what is called "cyber infrastructure," which includes computers and networks. "I am becoming more and more convinced that this is a game-changer," Duderstadt said. "When I was president in the 1980s, my university joined with IBM to help the federal government connect a lot of computers. At the time, we called it the 'inter-network.' The problem was it was growing at a rate of about 10 to 15 percent a month, and by the time we spun it off in 1993, people were naming it the Internet. I have seen how technologies can spring out of nowhere and change the world. I think that will continue to happen."

Emerging Important Issues

Today's university presidents will have to address a number of pressing issues over the next decade, some of which, he said, they may not be currently thinking about. One such issue is *demographics*. Most developed nations, including North America, Europe, and parts of Asia, have aging populations, and dramatically decreasing birthrates. Japan's birthrate is only at half the level necessary to replace its population and Europe has fallen below replacement value. Even the United States would be below replacement value except for the rate of immigration.

"What this means is most developed nations in the world are getting old, and older people have different priorities: retirement, health care, safety from crime, national security, and tax relief," Duderstadt said. "Far down the list is the next generation, unfortunately. Whether it is K–12 education or higher education, we are going to go through a generation where deploying tax dollars to provide more educational opportunity is not going to be given much priority. That will be a tough time."

In most of the rest of the world the average population age is below twenty. There are very young populations in Africa, Latin America, and parts of subcontinental Asia and, according to Duderstadt, it is estimated that within the next decade there will be more than 250 million people in the world who will be ready for a college education but there won't be any place for them to attend. "In fact, even to keep up, there would have to be a university the size of the University of Michigan built every few days, and we can't do that," Duderstadt said. "This imbalance between the aging populations that no longer give priority to education and the young developing populations that are terribly frustrated because they don't have the opportunity is going to be something very difficult to resolve."

A second emerging issues theme relates to the *knowledge-economy*. "I think people ought to read Thomas Friedman every few months," Duderstadt said. "Because, although many of us have been warning about this for years, Friedman explains it in a very lucid and compelling way. The world is changing. I was at a presentation by the CEO of General Motors, and he pointed out that more than 60 percent of General Motors' activity is now in developing nations like China and India. America is not where the action is. The action is the 'knowledge pallet.' China already is the second largest economy in the world and we have to find a way to deal with it."

The third theme on Duderstadt's emerging issues list is *global sustainability*. He cited the recent release of the *Synthesis Report*, a comprehensive report compiled by an international group of 4,000 scientists. "They concluded that there is absolutely no doubt whatsoever that humankind is changing the planet," Duderstadt said, "that it is much more serious than most people realize, that we can't deny it anymore, that we are headed for big trouble, and it is our universities that will develop the knowledge and hopefully the educated citizens who will grapple with that knowledge. If we don't, we are *all* in trouble."

It is these kinds of issues, demographics, sustainability, and the knowledge economy, that he believes most modern university leaders will have to work with in the years to come.

Duderstadt said that further downstream, the game changes even more. He said that there is a sense among people around the world now that universities, or entities that look like universities, are beginning to define themselves in global rather than regional or national terms. These entities are sometimes referred to as "universities in the world and of the world." The first is the truly global British Open University, with 350,000 students, which has been followed by the University of Phoenix and the Apollo Group.

Duderstadt said that among the traditional American university systems, MIT was among the first to seriously consider becoming a global university. "That will mean recruiting a student body from the world rather than just from the United States," he said. "Institutions will become global and detach themselves from local kinds of issues and activities. They are the next stage. Along with the state universities, many nations will someday have national and global universities."

Duderstadt's next theme was *lifelong learning*. He said that this was the most important recommendation of the Spellings Commission, and one that was most often overlooked by academics and politicians. "In this knowledge-society with knowledge changing so fast, the shelf life of an education is very short," Duderstadt said. "In my field, engineering, much of what students learn today is obsolete by the time they graduate. People have to understand that they need to continue to learn for life or they will find themselves in the unemployment line. It becomes the responsibility of government institutions to provide those lifelong learning opportunities. If the experience of the twentieth century is repeated in the twenty-first, life spans may be twice what they are today, which means that careers will be twice as long."

From the point of view of the university, Duderstadt said that most people who enroll in programs ten years from now will be adults, not the traditional eighteen- to twenty-two-year-olds. "The idea of having mom and pop pay for Junior to go to college is going to be tough because mom and pop will be in college themselves," he said. "Most of these folks will have jobs, so they won't come to campus. They won't care about fraternities and sororities or residence halls. That changes the paradigm of how you conduct higher education, how you distribute it, and how you finance it."

Duderstadt identified two final issues that he called *game-changers*, one of which is just now on the horizon, and universities are trying to figure out how to grapple with it. It is a new kind of philosophy called *open education resources*. The Open University—as seen with the British Open University—admits all who apply, but enrollees must achieve the university's standards in order to graduate and earn a degree.

But the "open resources" concept goes beyond this. Duderstadt gave the example of MIT, which announced several years ago that it was going to take all of the digital resources underlying its courses—everything from class notes to reading, to actual lectures, to video streaming—and put it all in the public domain on the web for anyone in the world to use. As of September 2008, MIT had all 1,800 of its courses on the web and, at last count, about 3 million students were accessing that information.

"More than 150 other universities are right behind them, all preparing to implement just such a policy," Duderstadt said. "This includes the University of Michigan, which is putting its entire medical school curriculum on the web, primarily for people in Latin America and sub-Saharan Africa where they don't have access to a medical education. The software that is used is being produced through something called *open source software development*, which means that it is also being given away for free."

Duderstadt said that the final part of *open education resources* is the most controversial to some people, but he believes that once they begin to think about it, they will realize the implications. "In 1994, Michigan announced, with four other libraries, that it would allow Google to digitize its entire eight-million-volume library," Duderstadt said. "We didn't think they could do it. They thought they could. Their intent would be to provide full text search to those materials. The other institutions involved were Stanford, Harvard, Oxford, and the New York Public Library. These are heavy hitters when it comes to academic libraries. Google is not only on track, but they are currently scanning 30,000 books each week at Ann Arbor, and will have our entire eight-million-volume library digitized by 2010. Twenty-five of the world's libraries have signed up with Google, and their combined collections are estimated to represent about 60 percent of the books in the world today in about four hundred languages. The entire collection will be full-text searchable within a decade. On the University of Michigan website, anything Google has scanned that is no longer under copyright control will be full-text accessible, and can be downloaded directly." Duderstadt added that UM would also send a printable copy, if needed.

The final theme on emerging issues is what Duderstadt described as "putting everything I've mentioned together." He said that within a decade or two, the majority of the world's population will be interconnected by electronic devices. Most people will be able to interact with one another and have access not just to much of the digitized knowledge of the world, but also to the tools for using that knowledge as more and more universities begin to give away their curriculum online. "It will be a world characterized by universal access to learning and knowledge," Duderstadt said.

Is that what the future of the university is? Duderstadt is not sure. "I think that when you get seven or eight billion people interacting together with access to knowledge, to the Oxford Library in the middle of the Kalahari Desert, you are going to get a completely different kind of civilization," he said. "That will happen certainly during the life span of today's students, and I suspect during the life span of most of us. Those are the kinds of extreme things I am trying to get people to think about."

The end result of these various, often interrelated sets of issues is that higher education is facing a sea-change of almost unimaginable proportions.

POTENTIAL SOLUTIONS TO POSSIBLE THREATS
TO THE FUTURE OF THE UNIVERSITY

"I think that the American paradigm of colleges and universities is almost irrelevant to the rest of the world," Duderstadt said. "The idea of a residential campus is a very expensive form of education, the most expensive in the world. That does not apply to much of the rest of the world. To deal with sub-Saharan Africa or Latin America, we need new paradigms, and probably the most affective paradigm is the British Open University."

The British Open University (BOU) once had a correspondence style of education, but now it is heavily Internet-based. The BOU is at the vanguard, embracing many open-learning techniques and other new educational paradigms.

"The challenge is that the clock is ticking," Duderstadt said. "If young people are aware in many of these developing economies that their welfare, their lives, depends on having advanced education, and they don't have access, that is the hopelessness that drives terrorists. We have a clock ticking, and we are trying to do something about it."

The difficulty is that our learning style involves teachers and students, which works fine if you have a classroom, laboratory, or campus, but that may not be effective in other parts of the world.

Duderstadt said that MIT is finding that their advanced curriculum—which is designed for highly motivated and very intelligent self-learners—is not useable by most people. Therefore, it will be necessary to develop new kinds of pedagogy.

Interestingly enough, Duderstadt also noted that the United States faces problems similar in complexity, but of a quite different nature.

"The Achilles heel of American education is a secondary education where we sadly lag behind much of the rest of the developed world," he said. "Once again, new paradigms of learning for this new net-generation are going to be necessary. New kinds of learning will be necessary because our society is becoming global in a very real sense, even within the borders of our nation. We have four states now that no longer have a particular majority. The concept that minorities will eventually become the majority will probably be true across the United States by the year 2030 or 2040. These new populations learn in much different ways, and the old school paradigms we have are not very effective at providing them learning opportunities."

Duderstadt has written widely on these many issues and affirms that the challenges remain on the higher education journey ahead:

All of these are challenges, and my sense is that—in order to deal with these—first we have to recognize that the status quo is no longer a viable option. It only takes us to the brink, so experimentation is going to become re-

ally important. To try new approaches to learning, new approaches to organizing education, new structures of learning-institutions, and paying for it,
will take investment and some fairly high-risk activities. I view the next
decade or so as a very exciting time in education. I think that if we approach
it as a renaissance or enlightenment-like period in our society, it will not be
very stable. A lot of things will be happening, and if people become educators because they want to be like the people who taught them, they will be in
for a lot of disappointment because it won't work. To enjoy a world in which
there will be a lot of opportunity, challenge, and change, people will find the
next ten or twenty years quite an exciting time.

ADVICE TO THE FUTURE LEADERSHIP IN PREPARING FOR RAPID CHANGES IN HIGHER EDUCATION

In projecting over the next twenty-plus years on the possibilities for higher
education, Duderstadt has a wide range of advice for future administrators
and future university presidents. During his decade as president of one of
the top research universities in the world, both Duderstadt and the University of Michigan became known for riding the crest of the wave of change.

He recommended that the preparation for the leadership roles in tomorrow's university begin early. "Begin as undergraduates," he said.
"Even in a world of continual change, it is important to have a broad undergraduate education that provides the capacity and the desire to continue to learn."

A more difficult question is one of identifying what kind of work preparation administrators need for future higher education. "That is tough, because the target is moving," he said. "The kinds of things you learned in
the past might be relevant for a first job, but much beyond that people will
have to move with the flow, and continue to learn through various kinds
of experiences."

Duderstadt added that the great strength of American higher education
is that it is highly diverse and serves a highly diverse population, and that
this is our contribution to the world, whereas the European view of the
university is what academics would call a "research university." With an
additional year of secondary school, European students theoretically receive the liberal general education before they get to college. Duderstadt
added that European higher education is primarily seen as intellectual. In
the United States, we add another year or two where, presumably, young
people grow up, are socialized intellectually and in other ways. This system is unique to the United States.

Within the United States, Duderstadt emphasized there are a variety of
schools and colleges that deal with these various parts of the equation, including the community colleges, which have student development as

their principal focus and are most similar to what might have been seen in the original colonial colleges. In contrast, the research universities that stress either professional education at the graduate level or research are more typical of European higher education. Not surprisingly, Duderstadt said that these are quite different kinds of institutions requiring quite different kinds of faculty and leadership.

"As people look at administration, they have to figure out which one of those environments they are preparing for," Duderstadt said. "When preparing to lead an independent or community college, or even a comprehensive regional university, there should be more attention to student development, including some of the more novel approaches to the way people are learning. When preparing for leadership in a research university, it is important to first toil in the vineyard. The only way a scholar-to-be can really understand scholarship is by doing it. For those roles, it is important to have an academic background, which means first becoming an academic, and then working up the academic ladder through a series of administrative appointments. An exception to this is taking a staff position, such as in student services, admissions, or financial aid, which requires preparation similar to a business education."

Strategic Planning Recommendations for Administrators and Future Presidents

Duderstadt's first recommendation is to read his book on university leadership: *The View from the Helm*. Based on his lifelong career, the book describes the numerous and varied roles of a university administrator, particularly the president. In it, Duderstadt emphasizes the many characteristics of academic leadership and how it is important to build a team that represents strength across the spectrum.

"Whether it is executive, academic, moral, or political leadership, it is important to recognize that we are good at some things and not very good at others," he said. "My concept is that any of these leadership roles at a significant institution must necessarily be a team activity. After establishing their own strengths and weaknesses, leaders should surround themselves with people who are good in their areas of weakness. Some people are good at politics, while some are good at academic leadership, but would be destroyed if they went up to a state legislature."

Duderstadt said that future leaders must look within themselves, figure out what they are good at, and determine what particular role they are going to play. That will, in part, determine the kinds of institutions they will ultimately serve most successfully.

"Large university systems require people with strong political skills," Duderstadt said. "Other universities are facing the wolf at the door, and need someone that is able to raise a lot of money. Learning how to do fund-raising and financial management can be vitally important."

In smaller institutions, however, he believes that "moral leadership" becomes paramount.

"I was on a task force with the Association of Governing Boards and we identified significant flaws in university leadership today," he said. "Whether it is the demands of the job, the perception of the higher education community, or the manipulation by search and compensation consultants, too many presidents today view their position as the same as a corporate CEO. They become detached from the academic core of the institution's teaching and learning. That is a disaster in many ways.

"Somehow, we have to redefine these roles into one as a *public servant*. It is a *calling*. They should not aspire to make as much money as football coaches. Philosophically, it is a form of personal commitment and sacrifice. Many of my colleagues believe that. It comes back, again, to the fact that people have to recognize that there are diverse capabilities and that they need to understand and figure out a way to balance those."

Finally, Duderstadt reiterated that institutions and societies are diverse and undergoing rapid change. He said that it is possible to plan for some of the ensuing changes, but there is still a great deal that simply cannot be planned for.

Tips for Creating the Perfect Presidential Team

"The first warning is one I heard from a great many people before I became a president: 'For God's sake don't clean house,'" Duderstadt recalled. "Particularly when coming in from outside. These are big, complex institutions. But, even when coming from inside, there is a lot of corporate knowledge contained in the existing leadership team that your predecessor leaves behind that most new people don't have. It is tempting fate with almost certain disaster to replace all those people at once. That doesn't mean not to replace some of them, and over time, if the stay is long enough, replace most of them. The point is that it is not advisable to step on an airplane and replace all the pilots with people who don't know how to fly the plane. That is number one."

Second, Duderstadt said that people have a variety of leadership styles. "Some people lead more like generals and surround themselves with people who will carry out their orders," he said. "That works from time to time, but I never thought the imperial Louis XIV presidency worked very well."

As an engineer, Duderstadt was trained from the beginning about the importance of working in teams and team-building. It is a concept that profoundly shaped his understanding of higher education leadership. "Every leadership role I have been in, I surrounded myself with a team of people I felt were hopefully smarter than I was," he said. "I treated them like peers in the sense that we figured things out together—'How we are going to deal with this,' rather than 'You do this.' That is a style I have worked with all my life because of my background. A lot of people would be very uncomfortable with that, so they have to find out what leadership style they are most comfortable with, and build a team that fits that style. The key to success in these roles is the ability to judge people, their abilities, and to lead them."

He reemphasized that leadership style depends on the individual at the helm—no one can prescribe one particular approach over another.

"I can recommend that leaders build an experienced team, make certain that some of those folks understand enough about the institution so that you don't crash, and don't be threatened by people that are smarter than you are, because there will probably be a lot of them that are," he said.

Presidents who make radical changes generally do not last very long. Duderstadt said this was based on an idea that Burton Clark developed years ago, called the *institutional saga*.

"Institutions that have survived for a long time are built up like a large ocean liner, with a good deal of momentum," Duderstadt said. "They can't turn on a dime. I found numerous examples in higher education and in my own institution, that if you understand that culture, that saga or mythology, and build on it, then you are usually successful. If you don't understand it or you try and change it, you better watch out—because these institutions don't change easily."

As he wrote in his groundbreaking biographical overview on the life of a university president, *A View from the Helm*:

> Today, there is an urgent need to reconnect the university presidency with the academic values and public purpose of higher education, to link university presidents tightly to the institutional saga that animates and shapes the evolution of their institution. The pace and nature of change affecting the higher education enterprise both in America and worldwide in the years ahead will require such strong, informed, and courageous leadership. True, it is sometimes difficult to act for the future when the demands of the present can be so powerful and the traditions of the past so difficult to challenge. Yet such academic leadership will be the most important role of the university president in the years ahead, as we navigate our institution through the stormy seas of a changing world. (Duderstadt, 2007, p. 375)

REFERENCES

Duderstadt, J. J. (2007). *The view from the helm*. Ann Arbor: University of Michigan Press.

Chapter 2

The Presidency
of the Future University

with Stephen Joel Trachtenberg

Stephen Joel Trachtenberg is president emeritus and University Professor of Public Service at George Washington University (GWU).

Trachtenberg is chairman of Korn/Ferry International's North American Education Practice. He writes a "brainstorm" blog for The Chronicle of Higher Education *and has a new book on higher education:* Big Man on Campus: A University President Speaks Out on Higher Education, *which was released in June of 2008.*

Trachtenberg's many publications include Reflections on Higher Education *(2006),* Thinking Out Loud *(1998), and* Speaking His Mind *(1994).*

Among his many honors and awards is the 2008 Allen P. Splete Award for Outstanding Service from the Council of Independent Colleges, the 2003 Albert B. Sabin Institute Humanitarian Award, the U.S. Treasury Department's Medal of Merit, and a number of honorary doctorates from various universities. He was named a fellow of the American Academy of Arts and Sciences in 2002.

Trachtenberg served as the fifteenth president of GWU from August 1, 1988, to July 31, 2007. Prior to that, he was president and professor of public administration for eleven years at the University of Hartford and dean of arts and sciences and vice president at Boston University for eight years. During the administration of President Lyndon Johnson, Trachtenberg was special assistant to the U.S. Commissioner of Education, Department of Health, Education, and Welfare.

This chapter is based on an interview that I conducted with Stephen Joel Trachtenberg on December 22, 2007, for this book.

Trachtenberg earned a Juris Doctor from Yale University in 1962, a master's degree in public administration from Harvard University in 1966, and a bachelor's degree in American history from Columbia University in 1959.

MAJOR HISTORICAL EVENTS IN HIGHER EDUCATION ADMINISTRATION AND THE PRESIDENCY

Institutions of higher education started shortly after the Pilgrims came to America. Massachusetts colony settlers realized that, inevitably, with the passage of time, their pastors were going to die, so they created institutions to make it possible to train future members of the cloth.

Little by little, the institutions took root and, as other disciplines arose, they were incorporated. As we look at the country, we see early Americans going from the east to the west coast and every time they stopped, they set up a little college. So places like Pennsylvania are dotted with small colleges created early in the history of the country. We are a country that is committed to learning.

People did not conventionally think of the United States as a scholarly place, but I think the evidence is to the contrary. In the middle of the Civil War, when the Congress and the president were distracted by the North and South killing each other, Congress nevertheless took the time to pass the Morrill Land Grant Act and establish what turned out to be flagship state universities in all the states. These institutions were designed to educate a practical side of America—to develop engineers, schoolteachers, farmers, and mechanics to be sure we had the capacity to feed and support ourselves. Through history, those institutions matured. The small cottage operations became massive, multibillion-dollar enterprises.

Today, universities may have more than 50,000 students, and a range of disciplines so complex and arcane that the founders never heard of them, and would not know what they were if they came back to life and walked on the campuses.

Perhaps with one exception: the only founder who would recognize his physical university would be Mr. Jefferson, who would probably still recognize the University of Virginia because of its adherence to his architectural vision. In terms of programs, we are teaching astrophysics and other things that did not exist when those early universities were founded. Higher education in this country today is dramatically different in style, shape, commitment, philosophy, and theology.

In its vast diversity, American higher education institutions consist of large land grant state universities; small liberal arts colleges; all-women institutions; institutions that are faith-based, including Catholic, Mormon, Jewish, and a whole assortment of various Protestant sects. We have institutions devoted to technology: MIT, California Institute of Technology; and we have others that are functionally devoted to the essence of the liberal arts: St. John's at Annapolis is driven by the great books. Some institutions like Howard, founded to educate African Americans, and institutions like Wellesley, founded to educate women, both continue that service today. In America, there is a wide range of alternatives so that almost every interest can be served. What we have developed over several hundred years of our history as a republic is a complexity and variety that I think is challenged only by what can be found in the Galapagos.

CURRENT MAJOR ISSUES AND EVENTS FOR HIGHER EDUCATION TODAY

The Importance of Higher Education

Democracy is both the challenge and the problem. We've come to believe, and there is evidence to persuade us, that it's important to have a highly educated populace. This is good for driving both the republic as a political entity and the current that moves educated people up, adding more value to the gross national product. Education enables society to do the things that are necessary in the twenty-first century. There are machines to do the manual work of earlier eras. Building back-roads, digging coal, and working on an assembly line are increasingly historic. Now, people push buttons on machines that have been designed to accomplish those ends.

Basically, work is becoming less ministerial. It is becoming discretionary, and it calls for an articulated intellect and the ability to take data, consume it, and create something new from it. Our goal is to have an educated population. We're not always successful in that.

Access and Funding

Some problems emerge in the elementary and secondary schools where not all students experience equal opportunities and support. But the most daunting concern is one of access: finding the institution of higher education that suits everybody who wants to go and has the ability to benefit from it. There is then the issue of funding those students. In the end, just as we would love to see that everybody in America has health coverage, we would also like everybody to have access to as much education as they can use, given their capacities, strengths, interests, and abilities.

And yet we fall short, for political, economic, and philosophical reasons. Access continues to be an elusive horizon. We walk toward it and it moves away from us, but as a matter of policy, the country is still ideo-logically committed to it and continues the journey. There are numerous ideas on how we move forward, and those are always intentioned.

Additionally, there are the questions of the institutions: How to organize and fund them? What to teach in the classroom? These questions stimulate constant discussion. In the thousands of schools around the country, various curriculums are in place. The single issue that challenges all these institutions is how to pay for their enterprises. Money is the mother's milk of higher education. To feed people, you have to pay for it. To provide any service, you have to find a way to compensate the people who provide the services.

Large universities are indistinguishable from other institutions in our society. They are as much caught in the iron grip of economics as anyone. Whether you are running a luncheonette, an automobile factory, or a university, there is one inevitable truth: if you want to turn on the electricity, you have to pay the electric company. If you want to have something supplied, whether it is books, steel, or laboratory equipment, somebody has to write a check.

Universities are very expensive. They are expensive because they are labor intensive and the material that they consume, computers, journal subscriptions, books, and artistic supplies, all cost money. The question becomes: where does that money come from? Do we expect the students to pay for it? If so, what does that mean for the socioeconomic groupings of the students and universities? Do we expect the state to pay for it? What does that mean for taxpayers? Do we expect business or industry to pay for it? What does that mean for commerce and philanthropy? Maybe all of these, in some measure, contribute. The question then becomes: how is that organized? What implications does it have for our tax laws, and how is this resource distributed? Are poor people going to be given equal opportunities to attend universities?

Education is a key issue on the American agenda. It is impossible to pick up a newspaper almost any day of the week, fifty-two weeks a year, without finding articles raising questions about access to colleges, what is taught in the colleges, and the behavior of students and faculty. One of the reasons that Americans are so concerned about education is that they recognize that if they want to succeed in this country, and want their children to flourish economically and socially, they will need a university education. There are exceptions. We all love to talk about how Bill Gates dropped out of Harvard, but for the most part, we know that if our children drop out of Harvard, they are not going to found Microsoft, and that they are likely to struggle. We want the best for our children. We want them to attend universities for good educations. This is a serious concern for all Americans.

HIGHER EDUCATION OF THE FUTURE

The Role of the Community College

It is as difficult to talk about the future as it is to talk about the past. We don't know enough about either of them. The most unique quality of American higher education, in much the same way that jazz is a uniquely American musical form, is the community college. It is very special. It has the capacity to educate people of post and secondary levels in both theoretical and practical arts. The community college is not as valued as it should be.

In the future, we will discover that the community colleges hold more of the answers for America, for achieving that goal of additional post and high school education, than we have recognized. The community colleges tend to be economical to run, tuitions are conventionally lower, and therefore access is generally greater than in other forms of higher education. They have programs for the hand, heart, and mind. It is possible for somebody to attend a community college, have an economically affordable experience, and come away with a degree that is either terminal or allows them to transfer to a baccalaureate-level institution.

Ultimately, the community college provides an education that allows graduates to earn a livelihood and make a contribution to the economy. These are not trivial things. When we see as clearly as we should the magnitude of the challenge before us in the twenty-first century, community colleges are going to play an increasingly large role in the solution. Community colleges are physically accessible to almost every American across the nation from New York to California, and I think we need to be paying more attention, uplifting them, and recognizing that they are both a gateway and a terminal institution.

Technology

We will see changes in all our institutions as a result of technology, which opens doors and turns the achievement of many academic programs. Conventionally, institutions are place-based. Technology makes it possible for people to adequately earn plausible degrees, if not perfectly, through distance learning. That will occur more and more, particularly with certain kinds of degrees and commodities. As commodities, there is no reason to go from one institution to another. They can be centralized, or at a distance.

I believe there will always be place-based institutions for reasons that may or may not have to do with education—it may be partly a rite of passage and partly to liberate the parents. It's what we do in our society as a transition from being a child under your parents' roof to living on your own. There will be graduate disciplines, which require physical presence, which makes it possible to be in contact with certain kinds of machines, hardware, and technology that simply can't be duplicated throughout the country or that must be centralized in a single place. It's impossible to do all of the research and teaching that is done on some of the big campuses without actually being there.

The Stakeholders and Change

Increasingly the appearance of universities will change just as the population of the country is changing. Demography is destiny. Everybody who will be going to a university twenty years from now is already born. It's possible to figure out who they are and to count them. We discover that if we do this, we see that the population of America is changing. It's becoming more Hispanic, Asian, and African American. Our colleges will become increasingly populated by people of color and that will result in change. Just as bringing in G.I.s after the Second World War changed the sociology of the environment of the university, the way people spent their social time, the kinds of foods they ate, their attitudes, and their values, so the culture of the university will be different a decade or two from now.

Change will be incremental in many ways, dramatic in others. Higher education is a dynamic, living entity, and it will have to become even more flexible and more change-accommodating than in the past. Institutions cannot risk the chance of becoming obsolete, and so universities will simply have to adapt. They're going to do so reluctantly, partly because of the people who are in universities. Even students become tradition-bound very quickly after they enter the institution, and often some of the most reactionary stakeholders in universities are the students. But faculty like the way things are and don't want to change. Alumni want their universities to stay exactly the way they were when they attended. They're always shocked to come back to the campuses and discover some building has been torn down.

Universities are made up of multiple stakeholders: the faculty, alumni, administration, neighbors of the university, parents, students, legislators, and community members. There are many people who think they own the university and have an interest in its outcome. They all want a voice in how it changes. But it will change. Technology, inevitably, will keep driving it to change, and it will survive one way or another.

HOW TO PREPARE FOR ADMINISTRATION AND
THE PRESIDENCY OF THE FUTURE

Read science fiction. In the past, as administrators we've looked for people who are of the academy and who are largely people to shepherd the institutions through. We didn't search for people who were visionaries so much as people who were sound, weren't going to change us too radically, and who would participate in the continuity of the institution, passing on what had been given them to the next generation with some added value. For the most part, being a change agent was not considered a virtue.

Increasingly, we will need leaders who are capable of imagining different kinds of institutions. As the problems and challenges that come to universities increase and become more stark, more different, as we try to do jobs with limited resources, with increasingly grumpy constituencies, we will need skills that we haven't had in the past.

It will not be sufficient merely to obtain a good degree in the classics at the university. Being "one of us" is always nice, but it will not be enough. We need people who are trained in entrepreneurial strengths and skills, but are also politicians, people capable of working with a non-university world and rallying it to the side of the university. We need people who are capable of saying "no" to faculty and students. Saying "yes" is easy, saying "no" is hard. Deciding when to say "yes" and when to say "no" is difficult. We will need people who are trained in management and human relations, because universities are very human institutions. Universities really do need the active participation of all of their members to make them function. In governance, transparency of its management is going to be increasingly relied upon. It is not a job for the faint of heart.

People will have to be courageous to become university presidents and to succeed. There are two kinds of people who want to be university presidents: people who want to "be president" and people who want to "do president." Being president is appealing to somebody who sees the theatrical, the optical roles of a university president. It often includes a big house, being called "Mr. President," and good seats at the football games. There are many ceremonial and joyous occasions. That masks the actual hard work that presidents have to do. Unless an individual is prepared to "do president," which is to work seven days a week; be constantly available; think of the institution all the time; work out alliances with other universities, museums, and corporations, and elementary and secondary schools; and work every minute, then they will not be a good university president.

There is a term in the Christian church, "servant leader," that I think university presidents will increasingly have to be, people who on the one hand are capable of being decision-makers, and on the other hand capable of great humility. Triumphal presidents are more unlikely in the future. There have been great triumphal presidents in the past, but I do not think the model will work as well in the future.

Advice for Future Presidents

Future presidents need to rule "extensively"; they need to know something about the history of the institution that they are involved in running. They need to have a body of skills. Presidents have to be able to do the numbers, to read the budgets, but must always remember that budgets are not financial documents, they are philosophical statements. A budget tells not where the money went, but what the person who developed that budget believed in, because the money will go to where the person in charge believes the money should be spent. While it is necessary to have accountants who keep track of all the beans, the development of a budget is really a visionary statement.

My dad used to say that if you gave him a person's check register he could tell what that person believed in. Studying what people write checks for will tell what they value. That's true of a university as well. The type of new buildings on a campus tells something about what that institution thinks it is and where it's going.

Everyday we see universities announcing new things. A recent example of this was when Harvard announced that it will provide student grants rather than loans. That announcement reveals, in part, what the institution can afford and where it chooses to spend its money. A president has to prepare to make those kinds of decisions.

A president of the future must care immensely about people, while, on the other hand, also be capable of inflicting pain on people. Presidents have to be able to tell people that they are not going to get what they want—that they're not going to be promoted, or they're going to be fired—and they have to do that, presumably, because they have a higher life, which is the institution itself. As I said, being university president is not a job for the faint of heart. It's also not a collection of small skills. It's not enough to have an MBA and know how to run the business side, or a Ph.D. in history and widespread recognition as a learned person. Presidents must have tremendous political skills. They must care about individuals as well as community. The president of the future must also have an eye for opportunity, as well architecture. It is, in many ways, one of the most exciting and challenging opportunities available to an intelligent, committed, highly energetic person in our society. The job is a great privilege, a good opportunity, but it can grind you down and kill you if you're not careful.

Future Survival for Struggling Institutions

I believe that we're not as effective in running institutions as we could be. It's very hard to generalize about all the campuses, but it's clear that institutions are not using all their powers and resources to drive themselves for a number of reasons. Some have to do with the leadership they have, and some with the reluctance of constituents to recognize the state they're in.

I remember when Silvermine College of Art closed in Connecticut. It was a liberal arts school. There was a quote in *The Hartford Current* by a faculty member who was astonished that this school was closing. He said that he noticed the enrollment in his classes getting smaller and smaller. He thought that was terrific, because it gave him a chance to be a more hands-on, intimate teacher. It never occurred to him that there was a relationship between enrollment and the ability of the school to survive. I always thought that was a wonderfully classic faculty comment. The institutions must become more hardheaded and a little less precious about how they run themselves.

I see tremendous opportunity in the sum capital course that we have in our facilities, opportunities that are good for society and for the institutions. For example, the calendar I get every year from the garage has fifty-two weeks in it, whereas the university calendar has less than twenty-eight weeks. We have two fourteen-week semesters of academic work, but if you try to induce the university to run for three fourteen-week semesters, even still with plenty of time for vacations and holidays, there is immense resistance. Universities, like all of us, want progress, but they don't like change. Well, we will have to change. In fact, we will to have to take a hard look at our curriculum. Exactly where in scripture does it say we have to have a four-year experience to get a bachelor's degree? Why do we have to go to school for four years? More and more youngsters are coming to college with advanced placement courses they took in high school. Maybe we can cut an entire year out of the undergraduate experience, make it more economically accessible to greater numbers of middle class and poor families, and move people along into their lives and careers a year earlier. This wouldn't be the worst thing in the world.

Reducing undergraduate time would be particularly useful since a very large percentage of our college graduates are now going on to get master's, doctorates, and law degrees. It is fair to ask what percentage of a person's life should be spent preparing to live that life.

If the time to achieve the Ph.D. in this country averages eight years, and if the productive life of the human being is less than eighty years, does it make sense to have devoted 10 percent of your life to earning the degree for an institutionalized role? Remember, that does not include the years of elementary and secondary school, and college before that. Should society be carrying people for that long a time?

Of a hundred people admitted to doctoral programs, 20 percent will drop out every year or two, a tremendous waste. Many of those who graduate will come away from the experience discouraged and not happy with the outcome. Most are not going to teach at Research I universities where they receive big grants and serve as research professors. Most will teach in small liberal arts colleges throughout the country. Many will be teaching large classes like freshman English 101, and they won't be smoking pipes and writing witty poetry on the side. They have not been socialized for these jobs. They've been prepared for jobs that their professors hoped their graduate students would find. I think a lot of the way we prepare doctoral students has to be rethought, reinvented, as does the way we prepare undergraduates. It is a tremendous opportunity for savings, for better and more efficient administration of universities. That may be the answer for some, but not all, of the institutions.

Advice for Urban Universities and Presidents

In early years at Oxford, one of the reasons they had walls was to protect the students from the town, and the town from the students. They locked those students up at night to keep them out of town. Urban universities have always been like islands in the middle of the city. That is clearly not a sustainable model for the years to come. Urban universities will have to become permeable.

The cities need to see that the universities are at least partial solutions to the problems they have. They have to be the place where their children are liberated. They need to be a source of jobs and an economic engine for the city. Universities have to work with the elementary and the secondary schools, and this has always been difficult to achieve, because the universities always kept themselves at arm's length. That simply won't do in the years to come.

I'd like to see schools of education, for example, based in the middle of the public high schools in big cities. There is no reason for the school of education to be isolated in the university. Just as our medical schools are frequently abutting big city hospitals, and they work with young physicians doing work first in theory in classrooms, but then in clinical programs in the hospitals, schools of education need to be working with the elementary and secondary schools in their cities.

There are areas of expertise in many of our departments that are useful to the city. For example, the school of public health could help the city with problems related to their water supply. We simply have to be partners in dealing with the challenges to our society and, in this way, we will be better at educating our students and will more conspicuously justify the resources and tax exemptions that we are asking the public to give the universities. We need to work with people so they will feel that we are with them and not at arm's length.

However, this is not always easy and the cities are not always reasonable. They have expectations of universities that universities cannot always provide. We don't have magic bullets. There is a role for theory, for scholarship, which doesn't have a practical and applied utility, and people don't always understand that. Universities are frequently misunderstood. When they want to build a building, and it involves interaction with the neighborhood, inevitably there is some resulting bad feeling. Interestingly, the neighbors of various universities will have a variety of reactions to the same initiative. So in the George Washington University neighborhood, residents want nothing more than for the university to build student housing, to have students live in university facilities and not be residents in the local neighborhood apartment houses and family dwellings. By contrast, at Boston College there has been a proposal to build student housing on campus and the neighbors are unhappy because they are fearful that the students will pour out of those buildings and be a source of provocation for them.

If different neighbors in different cities come up with different things to worry about and different conclusions about how to fix them, future college presidents will have to be flexible enough to work with them all to find the best solution. The institution needs to be aware of both their environment and the sociology of their community. People who live next door to universities are all apprehensive. They look at all the young people who are up all hours, who consume alcoholic beverages, who sing at the top of their voices, and they want the university to do something about it. It is difficult. Students, after all, are citizens, and you can't imprison them. Most of the time, of course, the universities have been in place a long time, and the neighbors bought their houses knowing they were next door to the university, but they did that with a wishful view rather than a realistic view of the future.

CONCLUSION

Universities have prided themselves on being changeless from generation to generation, decade to decade, and century to century. They've been consistent and have changed only incrementally. I don't know if that's going to work in going forward. I think the events of the future will be more fluid, more rapid than in the past, and universities are going to have to accommodate these changes. We cannot simply wait.

It would be nice if universities could figure how to get ahead of change, be part of it, and be parties to crafting the future so that institutional interests will be served. Most continue to have their mission substantially in place, even if it comes in new bottles. If we want things to be the same, things are going to have to change. My point is, we have to be more dramatic change agents, and we need to look beyond our tradition to the way other people do things.

We need to look at Silicon Valley. I mentioned at the beginning that presidents need to read science fiction. I'm only half kidding. We have to look at urban planners, the national defense industry, and people who conventionally try to find ways to think unconventionally. Silicon Valley is a good example of a place in which nothing sits still. Things are constantly in flux. Universities need to take a little bit of a lesson from that, and be prepared for an environment of a changing population impacted by changing technology. Students can take a course home on a disk these days. It's just not going to be the same and we need to be ready for that.

Our species is not good at change. We are evolutionary in our nature. There have been simple things like moving a person's telephone from the right side of the desk to the left side of the desk, and it takes the person weeks, sometimes months to adapt. I recently moved from one house to another, right down the block, but of course laid out differently, and I am still disconcerted. Change is hard, but it's going to be more and more a part of our life.

The whole point is for presidents to believe in what they are doing, to do it with their heart and soul, and have a good time. It is important to recognize that this is supposed to be fun. Presidents have to love faculty. They're not always loveable, but presidents have to love them, and likewise, students. Presidents must have some sense of the greater good, be somewhat self-sacrificing. They need a support group, whether it's a spouse, friends, or somebody to pick them up, dust them off when they get knocked down, tell them they are terrific, and make them a bundt cake.

University administration is hard, hard work, and you can't expect to be popular all the time, but you have to always have some sense that you're doing this for some grander purpose. I was privileged to serve for thirty years and I had a terrific time. Not every day, and not every year, was as good as the other, but on the whole, I look back over three decades and I say, "What a privilege." I like professors; I like learning. And I like young people. I think scholarship is important. So as I near the end of a career, it has been a life that was worth doing. There are other things I could have done, and maybe I would have felt good about those as well. I've often thought that it would be fun to be a real estate developer. At the end of the day, you see a building going up that people have the opportunity to live in, to work in, and that's got to be very satisfying. But at universities, you get to do some of that, too.

REFERENCES

Trachtenberg, S. J, with T. H. Blumer. (2008). *Big man on campus: A university president speaks out on higher education*. New York: Simon & Schuster.

Chapter 3

Significant Continuing and Emerging Issues Facing Tomorrow's University

with Claire Van Ummersen, Helen Astin, and William Underwood

Chapter 3 contains three sections, each by a different author. In the first section, Claire Van Ummersen takes a general approach, providing an overview to higher education issues, while in the second section, Helen Astin focuses more specifically on equity related issues. The final section by Bill Underwood examines the future issues surrounding university athletics.

ISSUES, CHALLENGES, AND OPPORTUNITIES FACING HIGHER EDUCATION WITH CLAIRE VAN UMMERSEN

Claire Van Ummersen is vice president of the Center for Effective Leadership for the American Council on Education (ACE). Her responsibilities include development of programs and initiatives in leadership for higher education administrators at all levels and throughout their careers. Van Ummersen served as vice president and director of the Office of Women in Higher Education from 2001 to 2005, where she was responsible for leadership programs and career advancement for women.

Van Ummersen is president emerita of Cleveland State University, and served as president from 1993 to 2001. From 1986 to 1992, she was chancellor of the University System of New Hampshire. She was with the Massachusetts Board of Regents of Higher Education from 1981 to 1986. At the University of Massachusetts, Van Ummersen served as associate professor of biology and later served

---

This chapter is based on interviews that I conducted for this book with Claire Van Ummersen on December 19, 2007; Helen Astin on January 8, 2008; and William Underwood on December 21, 2007.

as graduate program director for biology, associate dean for academic affairs, associate vice chancellor for academic affairs, and interim chancellor.

Van Ummersen earned her Ph.D. from Tufts University and holds several honorary doctorates. She is a member of Phi Beta Kappa and Sigma Xi.

Women in Higher Education Past and Present

Women in Higher Education

Five percent of the college presidents in 1975 were women. Today, roughly 23 percent of the presidents are women, but the rate of change was much more dramatic in the early years through 1990 and has now begun to flatten. We are facing a problem as the first wave of women presidents enters retirement. The challenge is to increase the number of women advancing into presidencies to not only replace the retirees, but also provide a number of ready and able women beyond that number.

Part of the reason we are seeing this flattening is that we are not increasing the number of women who not only aspire to, but also will actually move into these jobs. We also have observed that as women presidents retire, there is a tendency of boards to replace them with men. Additionally, when men retire there is a tendency to replace them with men. We don't have enough data right now, only anecdotal information, but it is probably going to be another four or five years before we are able to determine whether this is just a blip or a pattern.

One contributing factor could be that about 80 percent of boards of trustees are still white males. In the public sector, there is a higher percentage of males than in the elite private institutions. In the community colleges or some of the less prestigious institutions in the private sector there are also more women on boards and these boards are more apt to hire women and/or minorities. In the community colleges, about 29 percent of the presidents are women. In the AAU institutions, the percentage is only fourteen.

These patterns are reflected in the faculty and administrative ranks in these types of institutions as well.

The good news is that women make up 58 percent of the undergraduates and they earn many more master's degrees than men. At the doctoral level, U.S. women have outpaced U.S. men in a number of fields. So, we are experiencing an increase of women in higher education at all degree levels, including first professional degrees as well. Most professions are now moving toward a majority of women entrants and that is the pool from which we will recruit our next generation of senior administrators. Universities will be much more diverse, with many more women in the faculty and administration. This will change the character of our institutions considerably.

We tend to equate Title IX with athletics, but it also has been an important law because it applies to all aspects of women's advancement. Even though there will be more women, the question remains, "Will we be able to change our institutions in ways that will retain these women?" Studies that have been conducted on doctoral students who have received their degrees show that half of the women in the studies do not enter the academy. They pursue other opportunities in government, industrial labs, and elsewhere in the corporate sector. Most of them are working as professionals, but not in higher education. We then lose another half from higher education between the time they enter academia and the time they come up for tenure. These women often cannot keep pace with the academic world because they are also trying to raise a family, and most academic schedules do not allow for both.

So structurally changing our institutions and related policies and procedures is a very important part of this equation going forward. The Alfred P. Sloan Foundation has supported research that has shown these issues will be some of the major challenges that higher institutions will face and that the culture within our colleges and universities must change to accommodate work and family balance.

Dual Careers

At the present time, the issue of dual career couples is on every research institution's agenda. We have never dealt with this issue successfully because we ignored it in the past, partly because, of course, there were fewer marriages involving two academics. Interestingly, when the trailing spouse was a woman, it was not seen as an institution's problem, but a lot of the trailing spouses are now men. Many women are demanding to have their husbands placed either in the institution, some neighboring institution, or an appropriate corporate position. This brings a whole new area to higher education, and is an issue that will have to be resolved. Coupled with the work/family issue, solving the dual-career issue remains critical in recruiting and retaining faculty.

Younger male faculty surveyed by the University of California also want more time to spend with family. They don't want to spend eighty hours a week working at the university. They want a life. There is a lot of work to do. If we want to have a high quality faculty, we're going to need these career option policies, whether we call it moral imperative or enlightened self-interest.

Shifting Demographics

Institutions need good women, otherwise they will not have enough faculty to meet both the replacement and growth needs. Our institutions are all talking about growth, which means they need more faculty. Women make up the majority of several professional areas. This is observed at many medical centers where approximately 65 percent of some fields and of the clinical professorships are held by women. At Iowa State University, for example, 90 percent of the veterinary classes are composed of women.

In medicine, many men are moving to private practice areas where salaries are much higher. Women are more concerned about patient care, as long as they have a fair salary and flexibility. Additionally, minority numbers are going to double in these professions, so we will need to recruit more women and minority individuals to fill the positions to meet the population needs. My guess is in twenty years, they will become the majority.

Minority populations in higher education will double, mostly for Hispanics, but there will also be about a 35 percent increase in African Americans. This massive shift in the minority populations will bring incredible breadth, depth, and an entirely different way of looking at research questions. We will need to capture these new cultural insights in our curriculum and change the way we operate. This is going to be a major challenge for colleges and universities.

The demographics are shifting in certain states more rapidly than others. In California, the minority population as a whole is already the majority population. There are similar demographics in Texas, Arizona, and Florida. The minority populations today are not integrated in the same way as in the past. There are issues that go beyond higher education that the country may be facing as well, and these issues or realities will ultimately impact our institutions.

The Issue of Rising Costs and Sustainability

Higher education is also struggling with the need to sustain and advance its position in the global environment. The cost and accountability issues in higher education are enormous. The people who deal with Congress worry a lot about this, but many campuses are having difficulty responding to the challenge to develop a new cost structure for their institutions, because many states cannot afford to support higher education as their revenues decline and health care and prison costs escalate.

Changes in Higher Education over the Next Twenty Years

A group of presidents convened at ACE several months ago to talk about what higher education might look like in 2027. There were several issues that came to the fore. One was the effect of demographic changes. Another issue was globalization. A third was referred to as "epistemic issues," including the concept that higher education has always created, owned, applied, and disseminated knowledge. That is no longer true. The presidential roundtable talked about things like Wikipedia and the whole issue of innovation, and how people work on discoveries today versus the way they did thirty years ago. Knowledge is no longer "institutional," it is "extra-institutional." Everybody owns knowledge now. How should our colleges and universities plan for such a future? ACE plans to mount a whole year of roundtables examining these issues with presidents of colleges and universities and will hold a summit in spring 2009.

I spoke with a reporter from the Education Writers Association. I gave her a number of interesting examples of experiments on how to organize the exploration process at other institutions. One of the questions included, "Where will future faculty come from?" In my vision, they will be recruited from the United States and many other countries; we may be going to Chinese universities, for example, to entice faculty to leave and come here in the same way China comes here to recruit our faculty to assist them in building world-class universities.

An article I read recently indicated that Britain is very concerned about the fact that British faculty are going to China to help the Chinese learn how to create world class institutions, and they fear that these institutions will then compete with the British universities. The question was, "Should the Brits be doing this?" This is just one aspect of the complex issue of globalization, building world-class universities in the Middle East and beyond by taking the best and the brightest from our premier programs.

What ACE focuses upon on a day-to-day basis is what keeps our presidents up at night. Their issues become our issues.

Primary Presidential Concerns

Recruitment and retention of faculty and students are real issues in higher education right now. Making certain that institutions continue to provide access to new populations and can recruit and retain a diverse faculty is essential to maintaining a civil society.

The cost structure and accountability issues are going to inundate institutions. These are on every president's mind. Tuition is rising so rapidly that Congress is starting to weigh in; this often leads to regulation and increased scrutiny of institutional foundations and endowments. There has been a committee of the Senate in Congress studying whether large institutions with huge endowments are spending enough of those endowments each year. Some of these institutions, like Harvard, Princeton, and

Stanford, provide full tuition for their students from families making less than around $40,000 to $60,000. They are waiving tuition costs to prevent possible new laws that will force them to spend more than they currently spend from their endowments. The whole cost structure issue is a very real concern. Yet costs for health care, technology, and energy continue to rise as fast as or faster than tuition and those costs must be met.

Thinking ahead, globalization also looms large as an issue. If we're going to compete with China, India, and others, we cannot do it as the "United States." We will need partners, perhaps the whole Western Hemisphere or North America and Europe. We currently don't talk seriously to people in Europe about collaborating so we can compete with the rest of the globe. We need to start thinking broadly about partners. When thinking about survival twenty years out, there will need to be a massive workforce in China. There is already a large, educated workforce in India. China, India, and the Middle East are developing world-class universities and will educate many of their people. What are we going to do to assist Africa? These changes are going to have an effect not only on our education system but also on our way of life. We haven't even begun to address them.

Presidents Experimenting with New Methods, Consortia, Partnerships, and International Teams

Some presidents are forming consortia for everything from purchasing to areas of academic research. In the Boston area there are thirteen to fourteen smaller institutions, like Babson and Bentley, which have formed a consortium to purchase all kinds of products to save costs. I'll give you an example from Ohio. The public universities started buying insurance together. Even the small institutions probably saved close to a $100,000 a year and a place like Ohio State saved much more because the buying power of combined universities was so much greater. Now the Midwest Higher Education Consortium is buying energy for all institutions. Other kinds of consortia include those that are doing joint academic programming. One of the oldest consortia includes the five colleges in the Amherst, Massachusetts, area: UMass, Mount Holyoke, Smith, Amherst, and Hampshire College. It's probably forty years old now, and they have a number of joint faculty appointments. For example, one institution may house the dance program for all five of the colleges, and, until very recently, all of the engineering was being done at UMass. Smith now has developed some engineering because they want to try to move more women into those fields. The four universities and the medical school in Northeast Ohio came together to develop the master of public health, which is offered over a distance education system and serves all of Northeast Ohio with a much better program than any one of the universities could have offered singly because it draws the best faculty from all five institutions. All of these programs are highly cost effective.

Research consortia make similar arrangements to carry out cutting-edge research. Instead of everybody having a structural biology lab, for example, the lab is in one place and a whole group of institutions use the facility. This usually leads to joint programming and joint appointments for faculty.

Partnerships with industry are another important development. Cleveland State University (CSU) is two miles away from the Cleveland Clinic, a world-class medical center. Cleveland State had several partnership programs, bioengineering, structural biology, and neurobiology, with the Cleveland Clinic. The clinic has a large research institute, and CSU faculty and graduate students were able to use those facilities at no cost. What we offered in return was the ability for the researchers to become faculty at Cleveland State, have graduate students in their labs, and move toward tenure, so if they ever left Cleveland they would leave as tenured faculty. The university was able to hire much better faculty researchers, which enriched its graduate programs.

Some of the very elite institutions have had good research cooperatives funded by the federal government for many years. When you look at the Los Alamos Labs, Lawrence Livermore Labs at Berkeley, the Draper Lab at MIT, the researchers who work in them come from across the country and, now, from across the world. It is not unusual to have a research team that will have researchers from various American universities as well as universities in China, India, or elsewhere. The Indian scholars, particularly in the areas of math and physics, are really quite extraordinary, and they are often members of these groups. Now industry is also carrying out its research and development (R & D) using international research teams and American companies are opening R & D facilities in both China and India as well as in other European countries.

ACE is playing more of an international role including participation in the United Nations University. ACE works extensively to build stronger institutions in South Africa. A number of leaders from these institutions have been sponsored by the Mellon Foundation to come to the ACE fellows program, a program for senior leaders, ready for rectorships. ACE's former president is also a member of the Quality Assurance Board for the Irish universities. Additionally, ACE routinely hosts delegations from foreign countries to talk with ACE and U.S. presidents about higher education issues. For example, when the government stopped increasing funding to the major universities in the United Kingdom, these universities had to begin fund-raising, and students were concerned because they had to begin to pay tuition. They began recruiting U.S. university advancement people to assist them in developing a capacity to carry out, and are regularly advertising for, these activities.

There is a furor in the United States and Congress related to the Spellings Commission Report about assessment of outcomes and what institutions are doing about this issue. At the present time, the regional accrediting agencies are responsible for monitoring outcomes. The message to these agencies is that assessing institutional outcomes had better improve to maintain their accreditation. That is difficult because accrediting agencies are the creatures of the institutions they accredit. Congress argues that there is a direct conflict of interest and is seeking to regulate the outcomes assessment. Meanwhile, colleges and universities are beginning to track student progress and are using this data to improve areas where students are having difficulty.

Institutions Adapting for the Future

If we start speculating about institutions as they might be, I am not sure we would recognize some of our universities. The ones that have huge endowments perhaps will remain much the same as they are now. Unless something draconian happens, they have the money to survive. The ones that may change the most are the ones that are already at the edge. They will either go out of business or reinvent themselves.

Congress and the Spellings Commission are right in that we do not really build a firm base of quality. There is no cookie cutter way of having a "one size fits all" sort of program. However, I do think there is a way to provide some quality minimum standard. We certainly do that around finance. Why don't we set the same type of parameters for the academic program? The institutions that figure out how to make changes and improve what they do in graduating well-prepared students are the ones that will survive and thrive. I think some of these institutions will have to become niche institutions. They won't try to be all things to all people. They will define their missions more narrowly, and do what they do very well, and that will continue to attract people to that institution. The institutions that continue to try to do what's really beyond their means to accomplish will not be successful.

Continuing Education and the Future University

A population that higher education has not served well is the retiring baby boomer generation. People over fifty-five are looking for enrichment. Many institutions have elder hostels programs, which serve senior citizens who want to travel and learn. They stay at university campuses as they travel. The campuses make money by hosting elder hostels when students are on summer break. It's a way of keeping housing and cafeteria staff employed throughout the year.

Colby College is a good example of expanding summer educational programming. With around 2,000 students, and no summer schools, they host 22 medical continuing education programs that come into Colby in the summer. The college keeps all its facilities open all summer. The doctors live in the residence halls and eat in the dining halls. There is a charge for these programs and the money earned is dedicated to things like academic programming or maintenance of the Colby campus. Every campus looks at revenue needs differently, and it does what it needs to do to stay healthy. Colby is one of the elite liberal arts colleges without graduate programs. The college has to find other ways to balance its budget. There are many models for ways that campuses have kept themselves viable and reinvented themselves.

I think you are going to see a lot more creativity from institutions that are thinking through their approach to the next ten to fifteen years. Continuing education programs may not be the solution for everyone. It turned out to be the solution for some. Emanuel College took a different approach and rented out some of its facilities to the Beth Israel Hospital; and they were turned into research labs for hospital researchers.

In short, these creative solutions are growing and may save a number of smaller institutions from extinction.

Advice for Presidents and Administrators on Preparing for the University Beyond 2020

Institutions need to be entrepreneurial. However, entrepreneurial ventures ought to achieve, or be consonant with, the mission of the institution. Mission should be the driver that determines action on "opportunity one" and a pass on "opportunity two" because it may move the campus in a different direction. Some institutions simply willy-nilly chase every opportunity. Take, for example, opening institutions or developing partnerships in China. The Chinese minister of education is difficult to work with. The minister looks at which partnerships will be beneficial to them and the long-term health of Chinese universities. Our campuses are now looking more carefully at what is going to be beneficial to them. Some are even withdrawing from partnerships or closing campuses in China.

It is advantageous to take the opportunities that make sense, sometimes even taking a little risk in that process, but it is important to be open to these opportunities. It is also essential to create a set of criteria to assess opportunities, so that you are supporting the mission of the institution and achieving the goals that have been set through a strategic planning process. I believe that approach will be even more critical in the future.

Second, I would suggest maintaining as much flexibility as possible to respond to the rapid changes within the environment. Arizona State University is looking at eliminating tenure. That will not be popular with faculty. What would replace this "solution" that is intended to increase flexibility? Medical schools, for example, have developed parallel tracks so that people who do the core teaching, and basic research, are still on a tenured track as full-time faculty in the medical school, although at some institutions they must earn a portion of their salaries from research grants. Clinical faculty do a modicum of research, clinical teaching, and they also have responsibility for patient care. Clinical researchers carry on research full time.

Third, keep an open mind, be creative, and be entrepreneurial. But equally important is to evaluate the risk against the reward. That means keeping flexibility. The reason that community colleges are so successful is that they have managed incredible flexibility that universities do not enjoy. Universities can learn from them.

Fourth is that institutions have to understand how to deploy both human and physical capital. A priority of the institution must be to move from budgeting, fund-raising, and hiring and firing faculty, to thinking about resource development and resource alignment. Resources aren't just money. Resources include facilities and people. People are going to be the strategic advantage of institutions. How do the people align with the mission? How do they align with the kinds of programming that you are offering? Then you have to get a bit draconian and say that nobody owns the positions of an institution. Right now, if you have twenty-five people in the English department, the department believes that until the end of time there will be twenty-five people in the English department. Maybe the department needs thirty or maybe it only needs fifteen. Those positions, as people retire and leave, ought to be captured and realigned within the institution to focus on mission direction and new areas of need.

If the positions are "owned" by departments, you have very little flexibility in growing new programs. You have to think in terms of available resources. There are not going to be a lot of new outside resources coming in to most institutions and at some point tuition will not be able to be raised further. Some states and federal agencies are already bankrupt. Higher education institutions must find more efficient ways to offer programming. Instructional excellence must be the top priority with extracurricular activities a distant second. Somehow we are going to have to think in terms of providing education rather than entertaining the whims of all our students and parents because they are part of the cost escalation problem. If you don't have the highest climbing wall and best residence halls, students don't come. They are looking for all kinds of creature comforts. Most of the growth in higher education has not come in the faculty;

it has come in student services. How much more can we provide as an institution in that area? We are already expending money at incredible rates now. At some point, somebody has got to say, "This is why it costs so much."

Finally, the world is developing and changing so quickly that we won't have the luxury of spending five years to make changes critical to our institutions.

WOMEN, EQUITY, AND SPIRITUALITY IN HIGHER EDUCATION WITH HELEN ASTIN

Helen Astin is professor emerita of higher education and senior scholar at the Higher Education Research Institute, UCLA. She served as the associate provost of the College of Letters and Science at UCLA from 1983 to 1987.

Astin has been a trustee of Mt. St. Mary's College since 1985, and served as a trustee of Hampshire College from 1972 to 1979. She has served on the Board of Governors of the Center for Creative Leadership, the Board of the National Council for Research on Women, and the Boards of Policy and Planning and Education and Training for the American Psychological Association.

She is a former member of the Government-University-Industry Research Roundtable of the National Academy of Sciences, and former chair of the Board of the American Association for Higher Education. She is a recipient of three honorary degrees, numerous other awards including the Howard Bowen Distinguished Career Award from the Association for the Study of Higher Education (ASHE).

Astin's major books include: Women of Influence, Women of Vision; Human Resources and Higher Education; The Woman Doctorate in America; Higher Education and the Disadvantaged Student; Some Action on Her Own: The Adult Woman and Higher Education; Sex Discrimination in Career Counseling and Education; *and* The Higher Education of Women: Essays in Honor of Rosemary Park.

Women and equity issues in higher education have been her life's work over the past four and half decades. Astin's current research is on spirituality in higher education.

Historical Highlights of Women and Equity Issues in Higher Education

With respect to some historical events of significant importance, I would like to mention two that I see as critical. One occurred in the scholarly arena, and the other represents the activism that started in the 1960s and continued through the 1970s.

One of the early books that that has had a great impact in the scholarly arena was Jessie Bernard's *Academic Women*. It came out in the mid-1960s. Logan Wilson, who served as president of the University of Texas, Austin, and later became president of the American Council on Education, had earlier written a book solely on academic men, with no mention of women in academe. Jessie Bernard was able to correct for their absence in Wilson's book with her pioneering work *Academic Women*. Her book is a classic. It was a very critical document for those times.

In the 1960s, we also witnessed a great deal of activism—beginning with the Civil Rights Movement. There were many women who were very much involved in the Civil Rights Movement and most of them were the pioneers in the women's movement. It is an interesting historical evolution both from the Civil Rights to the Women's Movement, and in the overlap that existed between the women leaders in each of the two movements.

In the early 1970s, we saw two events that were critical in challenging higher education and making higher education much more aware of women's needs. One was the American Council of Education's conference on women in higher education in the 1970s along with the book that came out of that conference in 1974. It was significant to have that conversation at a national conference and then publish a book that dealt with some of the issues about women students, administrators, and faculty in colleges and universities.

About the same time, Alice Rossi and Ann Calderwood produced a book that is another classic, *Academic Women on the Move*. In those early years of the second wave of the women's movement, there was a lot of related scholarly activity, activism, and discontent that was expressed by academic women challenging the academy. They challenged the professional associations to recognize issues related to women within the professions, particularly women as scholars within psychology, sociology, economics, and the legal profession. I think that that has had an enormous impact in bringing about change. Data collected and made available played an important role in examining practices in academic departments, especially how women were treated within the academy. At the same time, we saw the development of women's studies, and the eventual establishment of centers for the study of women.

There were also the affirmative action guidelines issued in 1972 and Title IX, both representing important legislative actions.

So there was scholarly activity, social activism, and then legislative activity. All three came together to bring much greater awareness within the academy, and to begin to chip away at old practices that were discriminatory toward women. This brief historical overview highlights the dynamics that resulted in bringing women from the margins more into the center.

Subsequently, the existing scholarly journals began to accept articles about issues of gender, which also resulted in a much greater awareness of issues.

Current Equity and Gender Issues in Higher Education

Two things continue to challenge our practices within higher education. First, even though there has been enormous progress, the decision-making power is still primarily in the hands of men. Women have not captured academic posts and positions of decision-making comparable to their numbers in the academy. There is a need for greater vigilance. The representation of women in academe needs to continue to be examined and challenged.

My second concern is that a large number of the younger women are very ahistorical. They take things for granted and do not question inequities. They're not connected to the history that preceded them or to the inequities that still exist. They don't have the spark, the zeal, the passion to continue challenging dysfunctional practices within higher education. This is true not only with what happens to women and other under-represented groups, but also with dysfunctional practices in general. The power of hierarchies and our reward structures are not particularly healthy for anyone. It has been half a century since the Civil Rights Movement and it amazes me how we are still very wedded to many practices that are dysfunctional. We have been very slow in transforming higher education.

And it is unfortunate that many women today are very passive about the whole thing.

What I see is that the system and our practices are so powerful and so ingrained that women are accepting it. I believe that what has happened to many academic women is that they have become more theoretical in their work and have lost some of the activism that characterized academic women during the early years of the women's movement.

We used to speculate that by having more women in the academy we would become more student-centered and more humane. But I have not seen that happening. I have not seen us changing to become the institution that can lead the nation and our society in so many needed ways.

Solutions

In terms of solutions, I don't know. As a psychologist by training, I have kept much more in touch with what is happening in psychology. In many ways, psychology has become "feminized." We say that is what may be happening to higher education as well. My concern for psychology is that, although women are predominant in the discipline, they have not been represented in equal numbers with men in the subfields within psychology that are canonized in terms of frontiers of knowledge and understanding of human behavior. They have chosen, been welcomed to, and are nurtured in what I call the "softer areas," such as child development and clinical psychology.

Unfortunately, the sciences have been structured in such a way that they are less accommodating to women during their childbearing and rearing years. We have not been able to change either the structure of the science fields, or the way we do our work within science. For example, higher education institutions are still hesitant to invest the resources necessary to provide adequate childcare for faculty and staff. Often there are very few placements available, so I wonder how a young assistant professor with children can be able to engage in the long hours of research in the lab that the discipline requires without support from the system. It's very complicated.

It is important to begin to think creatively about ways that can make life easier for everybody in the system. I remember, in the 1960s, how we argued at the national conferences that there was a need for childcare availability. But the spirit was lacking and the sentiment was that we were all responsible for raising our children. It is worrisome that we continue to feel and behave this way today. It remains a dilemma for many academics, especially women, and solutions do not appear to be forthcoming, unless we think seriously about the values within the academy.

The Future of Gender, Equity, and Diversity

The future of equity issues is difficult to envision, because the whole world is in such turmoil. It is so day-to-day, month-to-month, and year-to-year that I cannot even think "What will the world be like twenty years from now?" That's where our work with spirituality comes in. We must begin to recognize, within higher education, that it is not just the mind, but the spirit also that is essential to be cultivated. If we really recognize and validate the need for the development of the spirit, I can foresee an academy of the future that would be more humane and more caring, an academy that would develop a generation of students who—when they graduate—will take leadership roles that will move civilization forward.

We find in our research on spirituality that students are dealing with many spiritual questions, and are willing to work on their spiritual selves and on developing qualities that are essential for the survival of the species. Some examples of spiritual qualities we have identified include the ethic of caring and an ecumenical worldview, qualities that demonstrate their caring about others and the world. If we in higher education become more aware of the importance of examining that aspect of students' lives, and find ways to validate students along those dimensions, then we can forecast a much better effort in attending to students' spiritual needs. We may be able to create a generation of workers and leaders that are caring, collaborative, less self-centered, and more other-oriented. That speaks much better of what the future might be for all of us globally.

This is why I see it as very important to focus on students' spiritual development—in addition to their intellectual and career development. It could be very liberating for students and very good for the society.

And this is why I am focusing so much of my energy on this kind of work. We need to attend more to what we do in terms of a holistic development of our students. If we do so, then I am very optimistic that we will have a higher education that will be a very different one, twenty years from now.

Advice for Higher Education Administrators

The first thing I would like to see happen is to find ways to liberate and validate the faculty. The faculty will be greater if they are given the permission to be real and authentic. So in many ways we have to find mechanisms within higher education to allow for the spirit to come forth. Although faculty may consider themselves to be spiritual, they don't feel that their personal spirituality has a place in the academy. Why shouldn't it? Why shouldn't the spirit, the questions of "Who am I?" "Why am I here?" and "What is my purpose in life?" have a place in the academy? Those are big questions that are central to a liberal arts education. So why not allow, encourage, and validate your faculty's spirituality? Once the faculty is validated, I think that this will play out in the way they deal with students. There is a lot of work to be done, but it can be done.

The conversations we have had around the country have convinced me of the hunger that dwells within the academy for bringing some of these ideas to the surface, for dealing with these questions, and then for finding the mechanisms for students' holistic development. There is a need to open up the conversation and to make discussions on the topic acceptable. It is a little like what happened with women's studies—that it became accepted as a subject matter, and that women did not have to be apologetic about doing research on gender.

Both faculty and administrators have to be convinced. I think administrators and faculty have to come together and agree that it is not only a legitimate topic, but that spiritual development is also an essential aspect of students' educational experience.

Last year there was a conference sponsored by the Association of American Colleges and Universities (AACU) and the California Institute of

Integral Studies on the topic of spirituality. About six hundred people attended. All parts of the academic community—administrators, faculty, student affairs—were there, and those topics were discussed and reflected upon. So I think that this conversation has begun.

If we do not attend to these issues, if we continue business as always, we may see the demise of the university. I can see other institutions and organizations taking over our work of the education of all youth. We see some evidence of this already. Look at the growth in home schooling. We have not taken good care of the business in our schools: elementary, middle, and high schools. So more and more parents are organizing and working in neighborhoods collectively to home school their children.

We have also seen business organizations taking over aspects of higher education. They can invest in it because that is how they can cultivate their own future labor force.

Another thing we have found with our work on spirituality is that students who have opportunities to interact with people from other cultures and races are much more likely to show growth in spirituality, and spirituality-related qualities. And then there is the connection between the discussion on equity issues and the development of the whole person in terms of qualities that are so essential to the survival of the species. They go hand in hand.

I see such overlap with the work that we started to do in the 1960s and 1970s, about equity, about the questions we posed, and about the passion we had then, with some of the issues today. We need to transform higher education to allow people to be open about their search for meaning and purpose.

Being an optimist, I believe that it can be done, that we can transform our institutions. We can make them much better places, and thus be able to serve society and the global community much better. We need to be persistent, passionate about it, and to have faith that it will happen.

What can institutions do to begin this kind of transformation I'm speaking about? How do we go about opening up the conversation within the academy? While I think it is beginning to happen, it is not occurring in a very systematic way, and the questions remain.

Conclusion

In many ways, I have welcomed the era in which I have lived as an academic, because there have been so many issues to work on. These issues started with the women's movement and related concerns that I continue to have about women in the academy, and moved on from there into my work on spirituality. I have done a full circle with issues involving the need to improve the quality of life for all of us in the academy. I feel blessed that I had that opportunity. My life has been worth living, as an academic, as a scholar, and as a passionate activist.

THE FUTURE OF UNIVERSITY ATHLETICS
WITH WILLIAM UNDERWOOD

William Underwood is president of Mercer University and has served as legal counsel and then interim president of the Big 12 Conference member Baylor University, where he led an internal athletic investigation in one of the biggest basketball scandals of the past decade.

Underwood is an elected member of the American Law Institute and the American Bar Foundation and he has published extensively on a range of topics. President Underwood is a summa cum laude graduate of the University of Illinois College of Law, which awarded him the Juris Doctor degree.

Background on University Athletics

Intercollegiate athletics began as one component of the university's commitment to the development of the whole person—body, mind, and spirit. Athletics played an important part in physical development and was perceived to play an important part in character development, as well. It was believed that students developed unique skills and attributes through the competition of intercollegiate athletics that they might not have developed elsewhere. Initially, athletic programs were a function of the teaching mission of the university. Student athletes were true students in every sense of the word.

In examining the trajectory of intercollegiate athletics from the early days to the present, at some point along the way intercollegiate athletics at many institutions became more important as a marketing tool than as a component of the academic mission of the university. That is the case today at many of our universities. Intercollegiate athletics now serves more as a marketing function and does very little to serve the academic function of the institution. For that reason, there is constant friction between intercollegiate athletics and the academic functioning of the university.

This change in focus is evident with the steady stream of recent athletic scandals. Scandals are not only more frequent, but they are increasingly broader in scope. One example is the recent case where Florida State announced a major cheating incident that required the disqualification of twenty-five of their football players. Nearly one-third of their football team was involved.

Many of the student athletes recruited in universities today are not "student" athletes in any sense of the word. They attend a university to play a sport at a school—"school" being a necessary evil—and that often results in tension and conflict. The scandal that Baylor University had a few years ago was primarily brought about by a number of young men at the university who were not there to do the schoolwork. These scandals are a part of that tension. The tension and even scandalous events are tolerated because it is important to the marketing function of institutions as they search for ways to reach and keep their alumni connected with the university. Athletics plays as important a role at many institutions in recruiting students as it does in keeping donors and alumni connected to the university. Athletics also raises the profile of the university.

This trend toward increased emphasis on the marketing component of athletics, as well as the increased divergence between the role of intercollegiate athletics and the core academic function of the university, will continue to grow. The pace and scope of that increasing divergence has continued to expand and I don't see much prospect for that changing.

At some point in the near future, it will become necessary to recognize that the universities who compete in intercollegiate athletics at the highest levels probably need to form their own separate association. Most schools cannot afford to commit the same amount of money to athletics as the higher-level programs. Those high-level programs will probably have to recognize the reality that many of the young men and women who are there to play football, basketball, and baseball are *not* there for an education. These athletes are on their way to professional sports careers, and they probably should be treated as professionals rather than as students. This trend toward professionalism of athletics at the collegiate level involves approximately seventy-five to a hundred universities.

I think that the vast majority of university intercollegiate athletics programs in this country maintain the connection to that original mission of sports in terms of character and leadership development of students. That is the case at Mercer. Last semester, our student athletes accumulated a grade point average higher than the student body as a whole.

I expect a break between the universities with elite athletic teams and the vast majority of the rest of the colleges and universities. The elite athletic institutions will continue more along the professional route, and the rest will return more to that "whole person concept."

Changes in the Next Twenty Plus Years

Legal Issues of the Future

This is a tough topic, because of the schism between the hundred or so schools that really focus on intercollegiate athletics at a high, near-professional level and the rest of us. The kinds of legal issues that universities like Mercer have related to athletics are very different than the legal issues at the University of Texas. Texas is concerned with licensing, payroll, and television revenue. The kinds of issues that we would have in common with the University of Texas would be the contractual relationship of coaches, what terms are included in those contracts, the length of the contracts, the kinds of bonuses and the incentives included in the contracts.

Some of our smaller institution athletic issues include: How to relate appropriately to the young people who are committed to the institution? What should the terms of those commitments be and how do we insure that during the recruiting process those people are not making commitments that either the institution is unwilling to keep, or are in violation of NCAA regulations?

Level of Power Wielded by Top Coaches for Big Teams

Some of the coaches in the elite programs are paid more than anyone else in the university. When push comes to shove, they probably also have more power than anyone else in the institution. If you had to compare the power of the football coach at a top-twenty football program to the authority of the provost/chief academic officer at the institution, there would be no comparison. That is another component of the athletic/academic tension mentioned earlier. A coach's desire is to have the best athletes possible so that he or she can succeed in the sport, and frequently does not include recruiting individuals who will succeed in the classroom.

Recognition as Professionals Rather than as Student Athletes

Some of the tension can be resolved by accepting that athletes are present to help market the university through competition on athletic teams sponsored by the university—and then separate those out from the academic function altogether. Let them perform as minor league athletes. They're preparing for professional athletic careers.

However, although it might relieve the tensions, a risk is that it might also destroy some of the appeal in the marketplace associated with the idea that these competing young men and women are students at "my alma mater." It will be hard to convince universities to accept the new reality and break that connection.

Possibility of Alternative Educational Plans for Athletes

Some people believe we should analogize the student athlete to an instrumentalist in a school of music, who spends a great deal of time in school practicing and playing the clarinet, with a large portion of his or her curriculum being associated with developing skills as a clarinet player. Maybe we should give academic credit for their performance on athletic teams in recognition of the fact that many of these athletes are preparing for careers as professional athletes or coaches. In other words, treat athletics as an academic discipline just as we do music or drama. This is not happening because people have a hard time accepting the notion that athletic performance should be included as a field in the academy.

Advice for Administrators

First and foremost, the obligation as president is to protect the academic integrity of the institution. One important responsibility is to insure that athletics does not in any way detract from the academic integrity of the institution. Presidents must to do everything within their power to insure that coaches are recruiting young people who can succeed academically at the institution. They must be absolutely intolerant of coaches who are willing to violate NCAA rules and ethical standards in pursuit of success. Those are things that absolutely have to be non-negotiable anchors.

At the same time, the reality is that athletes can provide important marketing benefits for the university. So presidents need to look for ways to enable athletes to compete and succeed. At Mercer, we care about athletic success. We think that the kind of excitement generated by athletic success is attractive to young people who are looking for a full college experience. So, we want to equip these young people with the tools they'll need to be as successful as possible. We want to have high quality coaches, coaches who understand that first and foremost this is a university and that the young people they recruit have to be students. We want coaches who can be successful and can help these young men and women develop as a whole person. Any president today has to recognize the potential marketing benefits associated with athletics, and do what can be done, consistent with these anchors, to achieve success.

I am considering bringing back a football program because I know that there are lots of bright young men who would like to attend our university because of the academic programs, but will end up going to schools like Furman, Davidson, Suwannee, or Washington and Lee because they also believe that participation in intercollegiate athletics, particularly football, will help them develop as individuals. Many students believe that participation in intercollegiate athletics will help them continue to develop self-discipline and leadership skills through their participation in team sports. Many simply enjoy participating. Athletic programs are powerful recruiting tools.

The Cost of Athletics

With the exception of thirty-five or forty schools, everyone involved in intercollegiate athletics loses money. This loss may be justified as a marketing outreach expense of the university. Even at a school like Mercer, which is not in a power conference in athletics, we invest enough in athletics that it is a losing proposition financially, if you just look at the direct cost and revenue. But there is enough indirect value that we do it anyway.

Advice for Future Administrators Who Will Have Major
Athletic Responsibilities

There have to be certain values that anchor athletic programs and institutions. It is important to be constantly reminded that the academic mission of the university is why the university exists. There cannot be any compromises on that. Additionally, competing with integrity is ultimately more important than competing successfully. Administrators must set the tone for the entire athletic program and be absolutely intolerant of ethical lapses. Those standards have to be non-negotiable. That also means they are non-negotiable in dealing with alumni, trustees, fans, coaches, and with athletic administrators. The administrator's responsibility is to protect the academic and ethical integrity of the institution.

I doubt that many of these potential changes will happen soon. The reason is because even at the big power conference athletic programs, there is still perceived value in the concept of the amateur student athlete. People believe that much of the market appeal of collegiate athletics is the perceived fact that the young men and women who are competing on the fields and courts are students of that particular institution. I don't believe people will be willing to give up that connection and the related marketplace appeal anytime soon.

Examples of this loss of appeal have been taking place for years in the minor league professional and semi-professional football leagues around the country. They are never seen on TV, yet when the University of Georgia plays on Saturday, there are 90,000 people in the stands and the game is broadcast on TV where millions of others are watching. The whole state of Georgia is paying attention, and I think that a real part of that market appeal is the perception that these are college students competing for their institutions. They're not being paid for it.

Ultimately, it may be inevitable that athletes, who are preparing for careers as professional players or coaches, are treated as such. College athletics of the future may well be treated as would music, drama, or other similar performance-related disciplines.

Chapter 4

Future Legal Issues

with Robert C. Cloud

Robert C. Cloud served for ten years as president of Lee College in Texas and is currently department chair and professor of higher education administration at Baylor University. His specialty is higher education law and policy.

Dr. Cloud is the editor of Legal Issues in the Community College *and coeditor of* Governance in the Community College, *as well as the writer of many dozens of articles on higher education law and related issues.*

Cloud holds a doctorate in educational administration from Baylor University.

BACKGROUND ON HIGHER EDUCATION LAW

For a long time in American history, the courts deferred to college and university administrators in their performance of assigned duties. The courts chose not to become too involved in academic matters on college and university campuses, public or private, for two reasons: (1) respect for academicians and the academy and (2) the complexities of academic administration. To the judiciary, faculty and administrators were best qualified to oversee instructional, administrative, supervisory, and quasi-legal issues on the campus. The courtroom was not the best place to resolve those and other issues unique to higher education.

The judiciary's relationship with higher education began to change during the mid-twentieth century, fostered by civil rights legislation and the move to democratize American college campuses. The Civil Rights

---

This chapter is based on an interview I conducted with Robert C. Cloud on June 8, 2007, for this book.

Act of 1964, the Higher Education Act of 1965, and Section 504 of the Rehabilitation Act of 1973 in particular obligated the courts to adjudicate numerous issues on the campus and ensure the constitutional rights of students, faculty, and staff. After 1964, a series of federal statutes and Supreme Court rulings (e.g., *Tinker v. Des Moines Independent Community School District*) made it clear that students and employees did not shed their constitutional rights at the campus entrance or the classroom door.

In 1990, Congress enacted the Americans with Disabilities Act (ADA) to ensure "the elimination of discrimination against individuals with disabilities." Title II of ADA prohibits public entities, including colleges and universities, from denying qualified individuals with disabilities participation in or benefit from institutional programs, services, or activities or from discriminating against individuals because of their disability (42 U.S.C. Section 12131). Title III of ADA extends its mandates to private agencies that provide public accommodations (42 U.S.C. Section 12182(a)). Therefore, most private colleges and universities are required to comply with Title III (42 U.S.C. Section 12181 (7)(j)). Although public and private postsecondary institutions have demonstrated a good faith and commendable effort to comply with ADA mandates, the accommodation of disabled students and staff will continue to be a legal and policy issue for current and future administrators.

Today, the courts continue to defer to educators in most academic matters. For example, the courts do not wish to become involved in discussions about what grade a given student made in a class, because student assessment remains the purview and responsibility of the teacher. On the other hand, if a student or teacher is injured on campus because of a foreseeable danger or institutional negligence, the issue may very well be litigated in federal court. Additionally, if a faculty member is terminated without appropriate due process, the case is likely to be considered by a judge and jury.

As a general rule, teachers and administrators remain free to make discretionary decisions about academic matters without significant judicial interference. However, the courts will not hesitate to intervene when legitimate questions arise about the constitutional rights of university faculty, staff, or students.

HIGHER EDUCATION LAW TODAY

Like other social organizations, American colleges and universities exist in a highly litigious environment. Consequently, college legal counsels now play a much more significant role in the administration of universities and colleges than they did twenty-five years ago. Attorneys possess "expert power," and the university general counsel often influences the day-to-day administration of the institution as much as the president. This extensive involvement of counsel in management and administration, although necessary in many situations, is expensive for the institution and stressful for administrators, faculty, and staff. Virtually all universities now employ a full-time general counsel and adequate staff to protect the institution's legal interests. Clearly, the litigiousness in the general society has osmocized into the college campus.

IMPACT OF LEGAL CHANGES
ON HIGHER EDUCATION INSTITUTIONS

The "rush to sue" in American society has posed numerous challenges for higher education. First, budgets have increased exponentially. Maintaining a general counsel's office on campus is very expensive, and it is difficult for many institutions to afford. On the other hand, governing boards and administrators cannot afford to be without counsel when dealing with the many legal and policy issues in governing and administering the academy, including but not limited to the following: campus safety, accommodation of disabled students and staff, sexual harassment, liability for injuries to participants in athletics and extracurricular activities, academic freedom and tenure, employment and supervision, compensation and benefits, collective bargaining, conflicts of interest, athletics, and the governance process itself. These and other issues perplex and confound current administrators and board members, and they are likely to try the competence and patience of their counterparts in 2020 and beyond.

The expectations of students and parents can pose a dilemma for administrators. Today's parents are not only concerned about the quality of instruction and student services, facilities, and food services. They also expect the campus and surrounding areas to be reasonably safe places for their sons and daughters. Many feel that they are paying for security services from the institution and that it is legally and ethically obligated to provide a safe environment. As the Supreme Judicial Court of Massachusetts said in *Mullins v. Pine Manor College*, "Reasonable security is an indispensable part of the bundle of services which all colleges, including Pine Manor, [must] provide their students."

Since the destruction of the World Trade Center towers on September 11, 2001, safety has been a priority for many parents, as much as or more so than instructional excellence or facilities. Consider the tragic incident at Virginia Tech University during the spring semester of 2007—proof that no institution is immune to violence and tragedy. To complicate matters for administrators, college campuses must be free and open places if they are to maximize learning opportunities for students.

Indeed, the hallmark of outstanding higher education institutions is *accessibility—access* to outstanding faculty and curricula, *access* to the library and other facilities, *access* to athletics and other extracurricular activities, and *access* to a wide range of leadership opportunities. Colleges and universities provide this access in multiple sites at virtually all hours. Students are entering and exiting the campus on a continuing basis, and it is very difficult to ensure personal safety and protect property in this setting. Ironically, the more accessible an institution is, the greater the threat to the safety of the campus community. Since the university must remain accessible to achieve its mission, administrators cannot normally lock down the campus and restrict the freedom of students, faculty, and staff. So they secure the campus as much as possible—and hope for the best. Without doubt, administrators in 2020 and beyond will have to commit more effort and resources in a continuing effort to secure campuses that may in the end be unsecurable.

Current concerns for safety and security aside, college students expect and demand personal freedom to come and go as they please. For example, many students do not wish to live in campus housing, but many institutions now require freshmen to live on campus. After their freshman year, many students opt to live off-campus for a variety of reasons, personal privacy and freedom being two. So, administrators must seek a balance between parental expectations about safety and students' desire and right for privacy and freedom—not an easy task. Federal courts are aware of the dilemma facing college leaders and have sought to adjudicate a reasonable balance between the two legitimate and conflicting interests. But as the Court of Appeals, Third Circuit ruled in *Bradshaw v. Rawlings*, personal safety is ultimately the responsibility of the individual student and not the institution. Assuming that institutional leaders have made reasonable and good faith efforts to secure the campus, the Third Circuit concluded that "The modern American college is not an insurer of the safety of its students."

CAMPUS LEGAL ISSUES IN 2020 AND BEYOND

Campus Security

Securing campuses will continue to be a challenge. In the future, security budgets will increase significantly, with subsequent increases in student fees. Greater numbers of certified and uniformed police officers will be visible inside campus buildings, at athletic events, and in vehicles patrolling the campus. Security and personal safety will be major considerations in the planning, engineering, and construction of campus buildings. The number and placement of internal and external windows, the number and location of restrooms, and proposed traffic patterns will all be considered in building designs. Internal door locks will be required; dead end corridors will be eliminated; security cameras will scan facilities; and metal detectors will be used when and where necessary. Lighting will be improved. These and other actions will be necessary to protect lives, secure property, combat crime, and reduce the possibility of terrorist acts against persons and the institution.

Campus police departments will partner more closely with local and state law enforcement agencies, such as the Federal Bureau of Investigation (FBI), and the Office of Homeland Security (OHS). Where necessary, security measures comparable to those now used by the airlines may be utilized temporarily in emergencies, particularly on public university campuses where there are 50,000–60,000 students coming and going at all hours of the day and night. Public colleges and universities, in particular, must be open and accessible if they are to fulfill their mission, but accessibility can equate to vulnerability.

For example, public institutions, who must comply with an increased number of public requirements, have less flexibility in determining their own admissions policies and procedures. Consequently, an undetermined number of convicted felons, including registered sex offenders, are now attending public institutions across the nation. In fairness, most if not all of those individuals have served their sentences, paid their debt to society, and are entitled to equal protection under the Fourteenth Amendment, which includes access to postsecondary education. Public institutions generally have no legal reason to deny them admission. And yet, all have records for assault, armed robbery, murder, or other felonious activity. The majority of these student-felons probably go on to become law-abiding and productive citizens after completing their educations. On the other hand, administrators are prudent to use discretion in dealing with this population and implement policies to protect the interests and safety of all, because the presence of convicted felons on campus can pose a legal problem for the institution if a felon reverts to criminal behavior that harms others. Institutional liability based on foreseeability and negligence could be a result.

Personal safety is now and will continue to be a concern on all college and university campuses because the very nature of postsecondary institutions makes them potentially unsafe places. Millions of students congregate on American campuses daily. Some are away from home and without the guidance and supervision of their parents for the first time in their lives. Other students bring psychological and emotional issues with them when they come to campus. Notwithstanding the increasing costs of higher education, many students have money to spend on entertainment, travel, and leisure activities. Individuals selling illegal substances and others with criminal intent frequently try to take advantage of this situation. Consequently, campuses can become magnates for unsavory individuals who may or may not enroll and who prey on the vulnerability or naiveté of students and employees.

This situation is complicated by the fact that colleges and universities have to be free and open places if they are to maximize learning opportunities for their students. Indeed, the hallmark of quality higher education institutions is *accessibility*. Universities provide this essential access in multiple settings at virtually all hours. Students, faculty, and staff are entering and leaving the campus on a continuing basis literally around the clock.

From a practical and management perspective, it is very difficult, if not impossible, to monitor the activity of thousands of people on a given campus. Ensuring personal safety and protecting property is a daunting challenge in this setting, even at colleges with relatively few students. At state universities with thousands of students and employees, the issue can be particularly perplexing.

Ironically, the more accessible and efficient an institution becomes in delivering services to students and staff, the greater the potential threat to the safety and security of the campus community. The potential for criminal activity on the campus—including possession and use of deadly weapons, burglary, robbery, assault, battery, rape, and murder—is obvious. All of this makes personal safety a continuing concern and priority for every college and university administration and governing board in the United States, now and in the future.

As the expansion of campus populations continues to increase, so may the problem of crime on campuses. As populations increase and become more diverse, it can be more difficult to identify needs and concerns within that population. Escalating stress will likely accompany this rapidly changing environment.

Without an adequate comprehensive plan to identify potential problems and intervene to prevent negative outcomes, the twin problems of crime and injury on campus are very likely to escalate in the future.

Athletics and Other Extracurricular Activities

Athletics and other extracurricular activities will cause legal and operational problems for future administrators just as they do for current leaders. Title IX compliance will continue to be an issue in higher education. As women's programs proliferate, athletic directors and presidents will be pressed to balance budgets, particularly in those universities where the football and basketball teams do not win consistently and therefore do not generate enough revenue, which is, of course, the reality in most institutions. Operational costs are increasing rapidly, and deficit budgets are the norm in too many programs. Very few athletic programs actually generate net revenue for the university. Increasingly, parents and students suspect that tuition and fees are escalating rapidly to cover not only instructional costs, but also an ongoing deficit in the athletic department. Whether true or not, this perception flavors attitudes about the institution and may influence subsequent financial contributions from graduates to their alma mater. Seldom do governing boards clarify why tuition and fee increases are necessary or explain the impact of the athletic department budget on other university operations, which exacerbates mistrust and suspicion and increases opposition to what may well be legitimate increases in tuition and fee costs.

Division I athletic competition, in particular, invariably brings policy and legal issues to the university. For example, there is a perception within the academy and the larger society that spending for athletics is out of control on some campuses and that other university services and programs are being neglected accordingly. Few would disagree that athletics has an important, even necessary, place in higher education, but it is valid to ask *what place?* and *to what extent?* To answer these and related questions, there should be an open and national dialogue in the next decade about the future role of intercollegiate athletics in higher education. The National Collegiate Athletic Association (NCAA), Association of Governing Boards (AGB), American Council on Education (ACE), institutional governing boards, and presidents should facilitate the discussion, announce their findings and conclusions, and recommend alternative strategies for the future (*The Chronicle of Higher Education*, 2008).

Student participation in extracurricular activities is another area that poses legal problems for educators. According to the American Council on Education, some 4,301 higher education institutions enrolled approximately 17,760,000 students in the fall semester of 2006 (American Council on Education). About 13.5 million, or 75 percent, of those students participated in a wide range of extracurricular activities, including student government, fraternal organizations, recreational sports, and intramurals. In addition, approximately 350,000 students are involved in intercollegiate athletics each year, increasing the total participation rate by 2 percent. Although the 77 percent total participation figure is duplicative, the sheer number of participants is impressive (National Intramural—Recreational Sports Association). When one considers the range and scope of extracurricular programs, the number of participants, and the possibility of serious injury or accidental death, the potential liability for postsecondary institutions is sobering. Postsecondary enrollment is expected to increase by 2 million to about 20 million students by 2015, and the number of extracurricular programs and participants will increase accordingly (*Waco Tribune-Herald*). Litigation in this area is likely to accelerate unless institutions refine existing preventive law and risk management programs. At a minimum, postsecondary institutions are obligated to warn extracurricular participants and staff of foreseeable dangers, to supervise all activities effectively, and to maintain facilities and equipment properly. Courts will continue to look for evidence of these preventive initiatives when they deliberate personal injury and negligence claims.

Changing Demographics

The state of Texas's *Closing the Gaps by 2015* plan projects that state colleges and universities will need to make room for an additional 600,000 students in the next eight years (Texas Higher Education Coordinating Board). Most of those students are going to be at risk, nontraditional, and many will be minority students whose families have never been involved in any kind of postsecondary education. These additional students will represent approximately a 15 to 20 percent increase in the students served in the state of Texas through the public institutions. Many of those students will be more difficult to teach and serve than traditional students because many will need financial aid, remediation, guidance, counseling, mentoring, and any number of social services. Serving students with so many needs will place an added burden on public higher education in the state of Texas (and other states), which will result in increased exposure and liability, and related potential litigation beyond 2020.

The Expectations of Students with Disabilities

Two generations of students with disabilities have now moved through the public schools since the enactment of Public Law 94-142 in 1975 (EAHCA), now known as the Individuals with Disabilities Education Act (IDEA). Under IDEA provisions, disabled students are entitled to a free and appropriate education. School officials are obligated to assist each disabled student and his or her parents in the development of an individualized education plan (IEP) that sets realistic goals for the student and includes strategies to meet those goals. IDEA provisions do not now apply to postsecondary institutions. However, public school students and their parents have grown accustomed to IDEA services, and those expectations are going to be transferred from the public schools into the community colleges and public universities. The many special accommodations mandated in IDEA will likely be pressed on postsecondary institutions in the years ahead.

General Consequences of Legal Change

The litigious nature of American society will likely continue in the foreseeable future. Since higher education institutions are microcosms of society in general, the "propensity to sue" will escalate in the academy. For example, as public institutions in Texas recruit an additional 600,000 students in the next eight years to "close the gap," those students will bring issues into the academy that will result in mediation or litigation. It is inevitable. More than ever before, colleges and universities will be expected to serve a diverse population with a multitude of needs, including financial aid, remediation, accommodation for disabilities, language training, counseling, mentoring, safety, progressive discipline, and due process. When colleges cannot meet all of those needs to the satisfaction of everyone, they will be sued.

The United States has more than its share of the world's practicing attorneys. Colleges and universities, particularly public institutions, are viewed as having "deep pockets." Between now and 2020, higher education institutions, particularly public community colleges, will be serving an increasingly nontraditional and socioeconomically disadvantaged population, many of whom are at risk of academic and vocational failure. The increase in at-risk populations coupled with expectations for success will likely result in a rise in litigation from disgruntled students and their families in the future.

The Malpractice Issue

Educational malpractice claims generally result from accusations that a college or university has failed to assess or assign a student properly, or neglected to provide the quality instruction necessary to educate the student. To date, courts have been reluctant to consider lawsuits based on educational malpractice claims (Roth 2007, 12). However, allegations of educational malpractice against colleges will likely escalate in the future as increasing numbers of poorly prepared students matriculate. Many of those students will not master the academic skills that are essential to completion of a certificate, an associate degree, or a baccalaureate degree. Some will then file suit against the college or university for incompetence or failure to provide services for which they have been paid.

Historically, claims for educational malpractice have not met acceptable legal standards of cause, care, or injury. Such claims are discouraged because they are perceived by many to be frivolous and without merit. Furthermore, courts continue to defer to the academic decisions of educators whenever and wherever appropriate (Roth 2007, 12). Consequently, I do not believe that most future educational malpractice claims will be successful, but I do think there will be increasing litigation questioning the competence of educators and the quality of instruction and other services in American colleges and universities. Even unsuccessful lawsuits can be costly. Unfortunately, these can result in scarce institutional resources being expended in defending colleges and universities against unmerited malpractice claims.

The Pressure to Increase Revenue and Endowment

Colleges and universities will be pressed to both raise more money for current operations and increase long-term endowment. Institutions will continue to generate extra revenue through traditional methods such as summer camps, campus-based academic conferences, and lease of facilities. In addition, many other funding options will be considered in the future, some of them now viewed as inappropriate, unethical, or illegal. For example, I think we will see colleges and universities tailoring academic programs to the specific needs of the private sector corporations in return for exclusive long-term partnerships. Corporate leaders will pay for the instruction but then (understandably) expect to participate in curriculum development and selection of faculty. Program effectiveness will be assessed jointly by the institution and corporation on a regular basis with adjustments made to the program as appropriate. Public community colleges have been facilitating these "contracted services" partnerships with private sector businesses and industries for decades, reflecting the two-year colleges' commitment to technical-vocational instruction and workforce development. Four-year institutions will partner with private sector organizations in the future primarily to increase revenue. These contractual relationships will pose new and challenging legal, policy, and public relations issues for future university administrators, board members, and their counsels.

A Changing of the Leadership Guard

An increasing number of university presidents and chancellors will come to the academy from the corporate world. The competition for external funding and endowment dollars will intensify, and corporate executives with successful finance and fund-raising backgrounds will be recruited to lead universities by governing boards that view higher education as "big business." In addition, more and more leaders with law degrees will be appointed to presidencies and vice presidencies because of the litigiousness in higher education.

This anticipated "changing of the guard" may prompt spirited discussion and significant resistance on the campus. The traditional and permanent constituency on university and college campuses is composed of scholars who have committed their careers to teaching, research, writing, publishing, and service. Many of these academicians are not going to support corporate executives and attorneys imposing a corporate financial model on the university. This reality could be problematic for governing boards in the selection of future presidents because American Association of University Professors (AAUP) guidelines specify that the selection of the president "should follow upon a cooperative search by the governing board and the faculty, taking into consideration the opinions of others who are appropriately interested" (AAUP). In reputable universities, faculty leaders have the right and responsibility to participate in the search for and selection of a new president. Governing boards that ignore this guideline in hiring their president do so at their own and the institution's peril. Lacking experience in the university setting and an understanding of the academic culture, these newcomers to the academy will be viewed with suspicion and mistrust unless and until they earn the trust and support of the faculty and staff. Finding the proper balance between financial stability and campus trust and harmony will not be easy. Faculty votes of *no confidence* in presidents and governing boards could increase accordingly with attendant legal and political ramifications. It should be an interesting time for all concerned as higher education continues to struggle both outside and inside the courtroom to resolve conflict.

Intellectual Property

Whether intellectual property is an issue at a particular institution will depend upon the expertise of the counsel and the administration at that particular institution. Ownership of intellectual property will continue to be an issue, but if the matter is handled properly, through clearly written policies, proper contractual relationships, proper orientation, and equitable treatment of faculty, the issue does not have to become litigious and divisive. Intellectual property and related policies and practices will likely be more pronounced in the research-based institutions where there are continuing research agendas that undergird the university mission and influence instruction and services.

Risk Management and Preventive Law

Risk management is essential in today's colleges and universities, and it will become increasingly vital in the future. Postsecondary institutions, public and private, exist in a highly litigious society, and many have been viewed by plaintiffs' attorneys as easy targets. College and university administrators manage multimillion-dollar budgets. Colleges and universities own buildings and land, operate housing and food services, manage summer camps and recreational facilities for thousands of minor "business invitees," own and operate vehicle fleets, instruct and supervise students, and manage human resource services for employees from recruitment to retirement (Sokolow 2004, 85–86). Institutional personnel regularly make discretionary decisions that affect the lives of students, faculty, and staff. Failure to assess the attendant legal risks can cost the institution dearly when it has to pay damages to an injured party.

As institutional budgets have increased and administration has become more complex, the need for risk management has increased commensurately. The qualifications, skills, and competencies of risk managers have become more sophisticated. Students can now complete an academic major in risk management and earn certification to practice the profession. Risk management is no longer an addendum to institutional administration; it is an integral part of the institution's preventive law initiatives and a consideration in virtually every administrative decision. Risk management is now absolutely essential in higher education because of issues like the following. Increasing numbers of students are enrolling with complex psychological and behavioral problems and/or criminal backgrounds. This is particularly true in public institutions. Insurance coverage is becoming prohibitively expensive because of the risk factors documented previously. Insurance assessment instruments are more sophisticated; higher deductibles are common; and insurance coverage for some high-risk activities is impossible to find—at any cost.

Risk management is imperative if the college or university is to protect institutional resources. Risks to the institution must be classified as either low, moderate, or high and then prioritized according to type—strategic, operational, financial, reputational, or compliance-related. Each type of risk has a corresponding threat or danger level. After prioritizing and assessing the risks, college leaders must decide whether to *avoid* the risk entirely by discontinuing the risky activity, *transfer* the risk to an external insurance carrier, or *accept* the risk associated with a necessary activity, take all possible precautionary measures, and hope for the best (Sokolow 2004, 88–91).

Academic Freedom

Any discussion of academic freedom must include comparable attention to tenure, since the two concepts are closely linked. Academic freedom is defined as the right of faculty members to research, write, teach, and publish without fear of retribution based on the unpopularity of their ideas.

Tenure is defined as the right of a faculty member to continuous employment after the completion of a satisfactory probationary period. Tenured faculty cannot be dismissed without adequate cause or due process.

Both academic freedom and tenure are designed to enable scholars to pursue their academic work without fear of arbitrary dismissal or retribution.

Without tenure, there is no assurance of academic freedom.

There are three pivotal cases related to the evolution of academic freedom:

The 1957 landmark case *Sweezy v. New Hampshire* identified "the four essential freedoms of a university to determine for itself on academic grounds: who may teach, what may be taught, how it shall be taught, and who may be admitted to study."

In *Keyishian v. The Board of Regents*, the Supreme Court defined academic freedom as "a special concern of the First Amendment which does not tolerate laws that cast a pall of orthodoxy over the classroom." It describes the classroom as a "marketplace of ideas." This description of academic freedom is the most frequently cited decision in academic freedom juris prudence.

Finally, in *Urofsky v. Gilmore*, the Court of Appeals, Fourth Circuit, decided that academic freedom belongs to the university and not to the individual faculty member.

There is a lot of discussion of the concept of tenure because the general population, legislators, and policy makers often do not understand the concept and some believe that this is a privilege that allows the protection of incompetence and radicalism by providing "a guaranteed job for life."

The concept of the continuance and protection of employment is vital to the free investigation and dissemination of new knowledge and ideas. Without the safety net of tenure, many faculty may have no option but to operate in an environment of fear with the looming possibility of censorship or job loss.

As long as there are fair-minded leaders on governing boards and in administration who share the values of academic freedom, there is less cause for concern. However, those conditions may change, and subsequently, the climate of free exploration, discovery, and discussion may be at risk.

The benefits of tenure outweigh the liabilities. There cannot be a marketplace of ideas with freedom of thought without some type of protection. Faculty are highly educated professionals charged with the duty to advance knowledge and should be entitled to freedom and security in advancing their disciplines.

I am optimistic about the future of academic freedom because of the large number of fair-minded people who understand that freedom in the academy must be protected through 2020 and beyond. It is why American higher education is believed by many to be the best in the world.

PARTNERSHIPS FOR THE FUTURE

College and university administrators improve services on their campuses through a number of common sense strategies like communicating regularly with all constituencies, appointing advisory committees and then listening to them, and facilitating an ongoing dialogue with public school representatives, legislators, alumni, and corporate contributors. More and more, it will be necessary for higher education leaders to bridge the traditional gap between secondary and postsecondary worlds if nontraditional and at-risk students are to be served effectively in the future. Networking between public school and postsecondary professionals will be essential. For example, subject matter specialists from the public schools, community colleges, and four-year institutions must collaborate in the development of sequential curricula that facilitate students' seamless transition from elementary school through a baccalaureate degree. To date, there are too few such partnerships in place, to the chagrin of students everywhere. As colleges and universities serve increasing numbers of nontraditional students in the future, collaborative partnerships will be essential to conserve resources and maximize efficiency and effectiveness.

One other example is germane here. Public postsecondary institutions, particularly community colleges, serve many of the same clientele as public health agencies. For example, community colleges in Arizona, California, and Texas are serving increasing numbers of undocumented individuals who are often poorly educated, unemployed or underemployed, and unable to speak English. Many are without health insurance and health care and dependant on public health departments for the most basic of medical and dental treatment. For the majority, preventive health care is out of the question. Serving this population is expensive and legally risky for public colleges and health departments with limited resources. Higher education administrators and governing boards and public health professionals should collaborate where possible and share limited resources in serving this and other nontraditional populations. The legal, policy, and political ramifications of such collaborations are obvious.

THE IMPORTANCE OF FUTURE BRAINSTORMING

Current and future higher education leaders must find the courage to brainstorm unconventional and unorthodox ideas about their institutions in 2020 and beyond. Too many educators and board members are reluctant to entertain unusual ideas for fear of appearing foolish or naïve. Brainstorming can be discomforting to experienced leaders who are pressured seemingly to do more and more with less and less. Consequently, when new and different concepts and strategies are broached, the understandable and inevitable response from many of these leaders is, "We do not have adequate resources to meet current responsibilities, much less accept additional burdens. The answer is no."

Future higher education leaders must be willing to consider new and different approaches to serving an increasingly diverse student population with an unprecedented array of needs. For example, partnerships with public health agencies, public schools, and private sector corporations will be necessary and commonplace in the future as colleges respond to the needs of traditional and nontraditional students.

There will be brand new emerging areas that will carry their own liabilities, particularly in the electronic arena where copyright laws, privacy, information-sharing, and even potential new forms of cybercrime may continuously test institutions.

The challenges and opportunities facing American colleges and universities between now and 2020 are unparalleled in history. Addressing them satisfactorily will require courageous, open-minded leaders who are willing to take risks in solving new, unprecedented, and seemingly insoluble problems.

CONCLUSION

One of the most distressing realities of educational governance, administration, and leadership is that legal and policy issues are cumulative. Unfortunately, legal issues tend to accumulate and they defy resolution. Stated differently, litigious campuses tend to remain litigious. For example, the safety and security issues now so critically important in higher education did not replace the various previously existing issues as concerns for administrators. Safety and security were simply added to a lengthy list of legal and policy concerns confronting academic leaders before September 11, 2001. Consequently, many legal problems confounding today's administrators are likely to perplex future leaders as well. Without doubt, there will also be significant additional, as yet unknown, legal and policy issues to challenge educational leaders in the future. Clearly, college and university administration in 2020 and beyond will not be a place for the timid or faint-hearted. A thick hide and sense of humor will be indispensable qualities for higher educational leaders then just as they are today.

REFERENCES

American Association of University Professors (AAUP). (April 1967). *Statement on government of colleges and universities.* Amended April 1990. Statement jointly formulated by the AAUP, the American Council on Education (ACE), 1966, and the Association of Governing Boards (AGB), 1966.
American Council on Education, Center for Policy Analysis. Bryan Cook, associate director, personal communication on January 18, 2008.
Americans with Disabilities Act (ADA). 42 U.S.C. Section 12101 (b)(2).
Bradshaw v. Rawlings, 612 F. 2d 135 (1979).
Buckeye's leader believes college presidents should help contain sports spending. *The Chronicle of Higher Education,* January 4, 2008.
The Civil Rights Act of 1964.
Education for All Handicapped Children Act of 1975 (EAHCA). Pub. Law 94-142, November 29, 1975.
The Higher Education Act of 1965. Pub. Law No. 89-329.
Individuals with Disabilities Education Act (IDEA). Pub. Law 101-476, October 30, 1990.
Mullins v. Pine Manor College, 449 N.E. 2d 331 (Mass. 1983).
National Intramural—Recreational Sports Association. Mary Calendar, director of publications and educational resources, personal communication on December 5, 2007.
Roth, J. A., McEllistrem, S., D'Agostino, T., and Brown, C. J. (Eds.) (2007). *Higher education law in America.* Malvern, PA: Center for Education and Employment Law (Educational Malpractice).
Section 504 of the Rehabilitation Act of 1973. Pub. Law 93-112, 29 U.S.C. § 794(a).
Sokolow, B. A. (2004). Risk management in the community college setting. In Robert C. Cloud (Ed.), *Legal issues in the community college.* New Directions for Community Colleges 125. San Francisco: Jossey-Bass.
Texas Higher Education Coordinating Board. (2007). *Closing the gaps by 2015.* Austin: Texas Higher Education Coordinating Board.
Tinker v. Des Moines Independent Community School District, 393 U.S. 503 (1969).
With 400 in a class, who's learning? *Waco Tribune-Herald,* November 25, 2007, 1A and 9A.

Chapter 5

Students of Tomorrow

with Alexander W. Astin

Alexander Astin is the Allan M. Cartter Professor of Higher Education Emeritus at the University of California, Los Angeles, and founding director of the Higher Education Research Institute at UCLA. He served as director of research for both the American Council on Education and the National Merit Scholarship Corporation. He is also the founding director of the Cooperative Institutional Research Program, an ongoing national study of some 12 million students, 250,000 faculty and staff, and 1,800 higher education institutions.

Astin has authored twenty books and more than three hundred other publications in the field of higher education. Many of his books focus on the college student, including: Four Critical Years *and* What Matters in College: Four Critical Years Revisited.

Astin is the recipient of awards for outstanding research from more than a dozen national associations and professional societies. He was elected to membership in the National Academy of Education, was made a fellow at the Center for Advanced Study in the Behavioral Sciences at Stanford University, and is a recipient of eleven honorary degrees.

A 1990 study in the Journal of Higher Education *identified Astin as the most frequently cited author in the field of higher education.*

This chapter is based on an interview I conducted with Alexander W. Astin on January 10, 2008, for this book.

HISTORICAL HIGHLIGHTS AND TRENDS RELATED
TO THE COLLEGE STUDENT

In trying to imagine how we can shape higher education's future, it is important to understand past changes, for they provide us with an understanding of the change process itself: how it is that we have been able to effect major changes in our higher education system in the past.

The student population in American higher education has been changing rather dramatically in the last half a decade, primarily because the segment of the population that attends college has been changing.

Higher education was an elite system in America for many years, primarily serving children of the upper classes. The democratization process began in earnest following the end of the Second World War and continued during most of the latter half of the twentieth century. During this period of expansion, higher education in the United States became known around the world as the most democratic system, given that it enrolled the largest proportion of its citizens in postsecondary education. However, in the past two decades a few other countries have equaled, or even exceeded, the level of college attendance seen in the United States.

The United States was a pioneer in the notion of expanding opportunity in higher education, first with the Land Grant Acts of the late 1800s, then with the G.I. Bill, making higher education available to segments of the population that were not previously able to go to college. The Civil Rights Movement of the 1950s and 1960s helped to expand access to African Americans and, subsequently, to members of other underrepresented minority groups. Still another major factor was the Women's Movement of the 1960s and 1970s, which helped convert a majority male population to a majority female population, which is our situation today.

The lesson to be learned from these past changes is that the student population of higher education can demographically be changed by two kinds of forces: governmental policy—the pioneering laws that established the Land Grant Acts, the Truman Commission's G.I. Bill, and the National Defense Education Act and other forms of governmental financial aid—and social change, such as the Women's and Civil Rights movements.

At the state level we also witnessed during the 1960s and 1970s the rapid expansion of public higher education, particularly the big teachers' colleges and community college systems. California pioneered this type of expansion, particularly in the community college area with a master plan that basically committed the state to admitting anybody who wanted to attend higher education. Government policy and social changes thus altered the demographic composition of the student body, as well as the level of preparation of matriculating students.

One consequence of these expansions of enrollment was that we admitted many more students who were less prepared academically from their secondary school. That created a new set of pedagogical challenges—educating under-prepared students—which the states handled primarily through institutional tracking arrangements where the under-prepared students were supposed to be educated primarily in community colleges.

The women's movement not only encouraged more women to attend college, but also radically changed the interests and aspirations of young women attending college. Compared to earlier generations, many more women began pursing careers in the major professions: medicine, law, business, and, to a lesser extent, engineering. Except for engineering, the gender imbalance in these professions has basically been eradicated or greatly reduced. Eventually, dramatic changes will no doubt occur both in the professions and in the larger society. The fact that just a few decades ago these professions were largely closed to women is something that young women today, even young women faculty, tend to forget.

These profound changes prove that society is capable of dramatic social change in a relatively short period of time, and that such changes can have a profound effect on higher education and on society at large. They remind us of the importance of social change, and of social movements in general.

Another factor that impacted college students relates to changes in the concept of *in loco parentis*. In the 1950s and 1960s, most colleges and universities played the role of *in loco parentis* with rules and regulations governing student conduct, including curfews and restrictive visitation rules in residence halls. The notion of a coeducational dormitory did not exist in the 1950s. With the exception of a few Christian colleges that continue the *in loco parentis* tradition, students today are free to come and go and do as they please. This was another dramatic change that was initiated by colleges, with some pressure from student groups.

Single sex education was largely abandoned. A handful of women's colleges have held on, but men's colleges are virtually a thing of the past. Among the holdouts were a few military academies, but the United States Supreme Court eventually ruled in favor of coeducation. About ten years ago, I was an expert witness for the Department of Justice in a Civil Rights case that was brought by women seeking admissions to the Citadel and the Virginia Military Institute. Eventually the courts forced the two institutions to admit women. The National Military Academies—West Point, Annapolis, the Air Force, and the Coast Guard—had been integrated quite a few years earlier, but these two southern, all-male military institutions held out until the courts forced them to admit women. The women's movement was thus resisted by only a small sector of the higher education system, but eventually even they capitulated to the pressure of that social movement.

Some women's colleges, on the other hand, are apparently still quite viable. Many are able to recruit lots of students and maintain very high academic standards. It's hard to say what will happen to women's colleges. At this time they still appear to be thriving.

THE COLLEGE STUDENT TODAY:
WHAT MATTERS?

In looking toward the future, all institutional heads need to keep in mind that the lifeblood of institutions is the students, and that the ability of the institution to attract new students is what keeps it viable. In the public institutions, resources come in the form of public funding, which is usually based on enrollment. Additionally, for most higher education institutions, support comes in the form of tuition and alumni support. The students and their parents, with financial aid support from federal and state governments, pay all or a large part of the costs of college. The question then becomes how to keep students coming in. I believe that word-of-mouth is a major means: People have the opportunity to speak well of their college experience to others. Former high school teachers, siblings, friends, and so forth hear these testimonials, and that particular college becomes an option for prospective students to consider. People have heard of an institution and know somebody who had a really good experience there.

My theory about institutional viability is based on the idea that the most important thing is to provide students with a meaningful, life-changing experience. This is the best insurance for the future. To ensure that the students have a meaningful experience, are challenged, and leave with something they didn't bring is the best guarantee of institutional viability.

The implications of this for the future are that policies should always be evaluated, judged, and embraced or discarded on the basis of a serious consideration of their implications for the overall student experience. It may be that other considerations also come into play when policy decisions are made, but, at a minimum, implications for students should always be factored into the consideration of policy alternatives. Too many institutions don't do this today.

If you want to strengthen higher education over the next twenty years, institutional leaders would be well advised to embrace this as a standard operating procedure. The implications of even parking regulations, financial aid services, fund-raising activities, whatever it might be, should be judged in part, if not primarily, in terms of what impact it's going to have on the student experience. As an operating principle for controlling an institution's own future, this should be the number one consideration as far as institutional leaders are concerned.

Although the student experience is most important, I think viewing the student as a customer is the wrong metaphor. In the world of corporate business, the customer is someone to be manipulated. The idea is to convince the customer that a given product or service is valuable to them, which gives advertising a major role. The goal is to manipulate the customer into consuming that product or service. Higher education, by contrast, should provide the student with an intense, challenging, meaningful experience, in which case the student will then become a recruiter of future students. The impactful experience is provided because it's the right thing to do. The fact that these same students ultimately facilitate the recruitment process for future generations is a byproduct of that experience.

I suggest a consideration of the student experience as the key to long-range viability because it's a win/win game. A positive experience contributes to the student and the student's life, by definition, but it also contributes to the long-range viability of the institution and its survival. This isn't manipulating students; this is providing for students.

Student satisfaction has to be a major consideration, but it is not the only consideration when it comes to what kind of learning experience should be provided for them. For example, students may not particularly like to be challenged at the time, challenged to put out the effort and the energy needed to overcome certain cognitive obstacles or to engage in certain activities that might seem too difficult or demanding to master. Consequently, some student experiences in the moment might not be judged as positive by the students initially, but in retrospect, they realize that it was something valuable.

COLLEGE STUDENT TRENDS AND EXPECTED CHANGES IN TWENTY-PLUS YEARS

There are some obvious current trends that can be projected at least into the immediate future. One is technology. Younger people today have mastery over gadgets that their professors don't understand. I would worry about the consequences of this for the whole learning and student development process. I don't think we have the foggiest idea what impact technology is having on students, so this needs to be something to be watched and monitored very carefully. It's important that colleges begin to respond to technology in ways that will hopefully minimize its downside, and therefore maximize the potential of technology to enhance the student experience. Much of this is out of our control right now.

Strategically Shaping the Future

There are basically two kinds of futurists: passive and active. First are the people who want to passively forecast with a crystal ball, imagining what the future is going to be like and deciding how to adapt. For higher education, I think that's absolutely the wrong model for institutional leaders to use. Obviously we have to be attending to certain changes, economic, demographic, and what they imply to the future. But the fact is that we have great autonomy in our institutions in terms of what we teach, how we teach it, whom we hire to teach; how we reward these people; how we judge, evaluate, and assess our students; what yardsticks of excellence we provide for students; what criteria we use for student admissions; and so on. We still control these things. Institutional leaders need to recognize that, since they still retain a great deal of autonomy, in collaboration with their faculty and staff, they themselves have a lot to say about how all these critical activities are carried out.

That being the case, the second active way to project into the future is to say, "What kind of future do we want to create, and how do we shape our institutional policies and practices to try and realize that future?" Being constrained by crystal ball projections about the fate of the world, nation, and state seems to me to be a huge mistake, because we're giving up our power. We're disempowering ourselves through "adaptation" as opposed to shaping our own future. Higher education is one of the few organizational structures in our society that maintains this kind of autonomy at the grassroots level. Institutional leaders and faculty tend to forget about this. This autonomy is precious, and needs to be honored and valued, but also used actively to shape our institutional futures.

I've been involved in quite a bit of research on strategies for shaping and changing institutions. A few of the highlights of this exciting work in the area of institutional transformation, most of which we unfortunately did not publish, include some findings regarding "strategic planning"—a powerful means of institutional change and transformation. One of the issues, for those who are trying to go through a change process, is the question of: What are we trying to change, and what do we foresee as the ideal shape of our institution down the road? In some of our case studies we found that every institution that had managed to bring about significant positive change on behalf of their students used the process of strategic planning, but the way they did it was much more important than the fact that it was called strategic planning.

Many people think that strategic planning involves merely projecting enrollments and revenues, working on purely fiscal matters. But we found that the most successful institutions had gathered together leaders from the various segments of the community, including academic, fiscal, student affairs, as well as the students, and engaged them in a long-term brainstorming session about what the institution was about. Who are we? What are we trying to accomplish? Given our resources, how can we best go about accomplishing our goals?

Well-designed strategic planning turns out to be a learning process for key members of the academic community. Basically, the participants became the students of this learning process, and ultimately were able to forge a consensus about most of the major questions. Once this happens, members of the academic community have embraced a shared belief system. The culture has been transformed, because the "culture" of an institution really has to do with shared beliefs about such things as identity, purpose, and what is and is not okay. These shared beliefs become transformed through the process of strategic or long-range planning. From that point on, decisions about resources and how to allocate them are much easier to make because there is a shared consensus about the purpose of the institution. In this way you don't confound means with ends. The means become a way simply of realizing the ends that are implied in the shared belief system that has been forged through the strategic planning process. That was a revelation for us.

At several of these strategic planning institutions, members of the brainstorming groups would share what had transpired with their colleagues, obtain feedback from them, and then bring that feedback to the next meeting of the strategic planning group. In that way, the larger community outside of the strategic planning group was also brought along.

The students have a different role to play with strategic planning because, although it's politically correct to include students in activities like this, the fact is that their interest in the institution tends not to be long-term. That creates a potential problem because they're thinking mainly of things that can be done right now. There is rarely much history that students can fall back on for perspective. Participants from other constituent groups obviously have longer-term interests in the institution and find it easier to think in such terms.

The key element in strategic planning is cultural change—change in the institution's "interior." Most leaders, by contrast, tend to think in terms of what sociologists call "structural change," changes in the curriculum, requirements, teaching methods, reward system, or the grading system— the external things. What supports these external things, however, is a shared belief system, primarily of the faculty but to a certain extent of the whole institution. Cultural changes are critical, as are structural changes, obviously. But changing policies and practices (structures) without appropriate cultural change leads to a dubious future for any structural change.

Another important element is decentralization of the ownership of change, so that change is not just something that is imposed or instituted by leaders so that other people have to like it or lump it. Rather, it should be something that other members of the academic community own and are active participants in. This is a long-term process; it involves giving ownership and responsibility to people down the line who are going to have the responsibility for actually operating the change. It is an educational process and it takes time.

We often think about the change process as something for which the president or the provost or some other change agent is the champion, and while they may recruit other people to buy into their idea, they continue to act in a catalytic leadership role in order to sustain the change. However, if that initial leader should change positions or institutions, whatever innovation has been adopted very often dies, because their continuing presence has been necessary to sustain it. The way to avoid this problem is to institutionalize change by giving people further down the line a sense of ownership. To do that, others need to understand the rationale behind the change, why it's beneficial, and how it furthers the interests of the institutions. That is the educational process: to decentralize ownership of change to the point where it's no longer necessary to have the initial change agent. Too often we don't go to the trouble of putting the people down the line through the same educational process that the strategic planning team might have gone through.

One large public institution we studied transformed itself in miraculous ways. We found that people down the line could articulate what the change was all about, how it fit into the institution's mission, how their particular domain fit into the larger picture. In other words, they were able to articulate the rationale and the purpose of the change as well as their role in it very well. That's quite different thing from the president merely wanting to do something differently, so people just have to go along with it.

Changes That Will Impact the Future

The trend away from public financing to private financing in both public and private institutions is troubling, particularly in the public institutions, because public financing is a statement by the people that we support and value this enterprise in our society. There is a trend even for K–12, as well as postsecondary education, to become more and more dependent on private funding. I would rather see higher tuition than reliance on private funding. One of the troubles with privatization is that there is a tendency to become heavily involved in marketing and competition, which I think is the wrong model for education. This gets us into politics. The trend toward increased reliance on private support by public institutions is a dangerous trend because the shaping of the institution becomes the province of the fat cats. It's very much like what's happened to politics, where people in organizations with large amounts of money increasingly control the political process. It would be a shame if that turned out to be the case with education. There have already been many instances of large donors trying to manipulate the institution toward their particular ends, and some institutions are going along with it.

The move to try to privatize K–12 education is generating the same kind of stresses. I don't know how institutions can respond, except by ganging up on our governmental agencies and pressuring them to give the proper priority to higher education in the public sector. That probably is the most troubling trend that I've seen. I don't know how far it's going to go, but education ought to be a right, supported by the public. The polls indicate the public does support education, but there is a terrible crunch on both the national and state budgets in recent years. Many states have had to cut their higher education funding. California is contemplating $3 billion of cuts from K–14 education, so that's something that ought to be fought by the higher education leadership. It's a very dangerous trend.

In our forty years of surveying students, we are surprised almost every year by what we find, and when we try to project trends into even the near future, very often they don't sustain themselves. A few have managed to sustain themselves, but many other trends are seesawing. Take computer science, for example. Some institutions built up huge computer science departments in the seventies, only to find that nobody wanted to take it as a major. Another example is business. During the late 1960s and most of the 1970s, business was on a meteoric ascendance path, and students' materialistic values were also climbing at a dramatic rate during that time. We tend to think of this period as a time of "leftist activity," but the fact remains that one of the major trends during the fifteen-year period, from the mid-1960s to the end of the 1970s, was a dramatic decline in student interest in teaching careers and a massive increase both in students' materialistic values and in their interest in business as a career. Consequently, many institutions built up their business faculty in response, anticipating that the trend would continue. Then all of a sudden student interest in business started dropping off. The corporate scandals in the 1980s might have discouraged many students from such a career. Whatever the reason, business just fell off the table in terms of student interest. Colleges were stuck with big business faculties and they did not know what to do with them. Business has seesawed in popularity since that time, but the materialistic values formed during that period have basically been sustained. Education has never really recovered as a major.

These are just some examples of how difficult it is to make even short-term projections. Institutions ought to be very watchful, and to look each year at what the new student generation is bringing to the campus in terms of interests, values, and aspirations. This is one reason why we initiated the freshman survey and why it has continued for four decades. From an institutional perspective, what more valuable information could we ask for every year than an in-depth snapshot of our new students, what they aspire to, what their values are, what they want to study, and what kind of career or postgraduate studies they want to pursue?

Future Trend of Various Nationalities of Students in American Higher Education

There is a projected continuing decline in the Caucasian student as a proportion of the student body, and an increase in both Hispanic students and Asian students. I think the diversity issue has become so complex now that we are not dealing with it adequately when we talk about the so-called students of color, or nonwhite students, or minority students, or whatever label you want to give it. That verbal labeling distorts reality considerably by simply dividing our students into minority and white students. We have more and more students of mixed heritage and I think young people today are much less likely to relate to each other primarily on the basis of ethnic identification. This isn't to say that ethnicity is not an important issue for some students, but to just assume that people are primarily identified ethnically rather than in some other way is naive. It is also unrealistic to lump all members of these groups together. There are so many groups now that the politics have become very complex. I think we need to develop a much more flexible approach and more open-mindedness about the whole issue of race and ethnicity than has been true in the past where we have tended to make sharp distinctions.

Additionally, we need to educate our students about the differences among the many types of groups. There are still large groups in our society who are severely disadvantaged regarding education. That does not include merely students of color. It does include many members of certain Latino subgroups and many African Americans, but there are other smaller groups whose members are also severely disadvantaged. By disadvantaged, I mean that the quality of their pre-collegiate preparation is not comparable to other groups, and that they tend to be segregated in higher education by being concentrated in public community colleges and the less prestigious, less well-funded four-year institutions.

Our system appears to be very open and equitable to the outside observer, but on the inside it's still very highly structured in an elitist fashion. There are a small number of very elite, famous, powerful institutions with lots of money, and lots of prestige. On the other end of the continuum, there is a much larger number of institutions with limited resources. The least advantaged students in society tend to be concentrated in these institutions at the bottom of this pecking order. This is not equitable. I've written volumes about this issue. It's an attribute of our system which perpetuates inequality.

Funding and Socioeconomic Representation of Students of the Future

There is not a lot that colleges and universities can do about the inequitable distribution of pre-collegiate opportunities, something that is supported by our state, local, and national governments. Merely by not implementing major reforms, these governments are implicitly supporting these inequities. But there are some things that colleges and universities can do on their own initiative to counteract some of these inequities at the collegiate level. Of course, there are things like need-based aid and remedial programs, but a much more critical issue is how we deal with the institutional inequities. For example, the ideal American system would be one where every community college that educates transfer students has one or more senior colleges with whom they have partnerships. They could work together to facilitate the transition process from two year to four year, and that should involve exchanging the faculty, staff, and students so that it begins to break down these arbitrary barriers between institutions at the bottom of the pecking order and the institutions higher up the food chain. The fact remains that large numbers of students who start out in community colleges with the intention of eventually getting a four-year degree never make the transition to a four-year institution. Those numbers are staggering. Again, a disproportionate number of these students are Latino.

When looking in depth at this problem, it becomes much more complex. For example, community colleges allow a new student to attend part-time, take one or two courses, and hold a job. For an under-prepared student coming directly out of high school to attend college, that's the worst possible scenario educationally because it allows him or her to not become fully engaged in the educational process. Engagement is a necessary part of successful education.

Transfer students coming into community colleges ought to attend full time, and they should be provided with all the support services they need. If they need financial support, it should be provided. If they need a job, a job on the campus should be available. Ideally they should have an opportunity to live on campus. We know these things. We know we can do better with community college students. It's a matter of the will to do it. There is much more we could be doing within the higher education system to counteract some of these inequities and to make the community college experience more equitable in relation to the four-year college experience.

Advice for University Presidents in Preparation for the Students of the Future

The number one piece of advice would be to support by "cheerleading," and providing financial support, for the kinds of educational practices that we know are effective for students in developing their cognitive and other personal qualities. For example, there should be more service learning, courses that include community service. There is a tremendous amount of evidence supporting service learning as one of the most powerful experiences a student can have. It enriches the life of the student and faculty member. It contributes to their learning and personal development in all kinds of subtle ways. The evidence is overwhelming that if you provide students with an opportunity to engage in community service, particularly if it is part of an academic course, it has all kinds of benefits. Campus leadership should support and encourage faculty to incorporate service experiences into their courses. The service experience is much like a lab experience, except that it's with people in the community rather than with test tubes or electronic devices.

The second piece of advice I would give is to support interdisciplinary studies, to provide incentives for faculty to create interdisciplinary courses, and to do team-teaching. This too has been shown to be a very powerful experience for students: to actually integrate the knowledge of various disciplines, rather than to artificially break it down as is the standard practice currently.

I would recommend that presidents support the use of freshman 101 courses, where students are given an opportunity to examine their whole college experience in the light of their own personal needs, goals, aspirations, hopes, and values, and begin to develop a plan for their college experience that rationalizes their course-taking choices as well as their engagement in extracurricular activities, and anything else that relates to their hopes and dreams and helps to make meaning out of their college experience. Such courses are referred to by several different names, such as "freshman seminar" or "freshman 101," but these courses are powerful and useful.

I recommend that leaders encourage much more use of reflective writing and discussion. Students benefit from journaling and other kinds of reflective writing not only to reflect on their life as a student and what meaning it has for them, but also to formulate a kind of life plan. Reflective writing can be used in almost any type of a course to raise self-awareness, and allow time for reflection on what a course has meant and how it has influenced or changed the student. The idea behind reflective writing is to help students personalize their college experience, to become more insightful about themselves, to better understand why they do what they do, and how they make their choices and why. There is a single message that you find in almost all the great books of Western civilization, and that is: "know thyself." And yet if you look at the typical college curriculum, there is generally little emphasis on "know thyself."

Self-knowledge is the key to understanding other people. To understand how your own mind works, and why you do what you do, makes it much easier to develop some passion and understanding for other people. Of course, if civilization is going to survive the next century, people will have to have a better understanding of each other. The key is to have a better understanding of one's self.

Study abroad can be another powerful experience, and there are less expensive alternatives to study abroad that we could provide to students and institutions who don't have many resources. For example, students who cannot afford to go abroad for a year might go for a shorter time, or we could simulate such an experience by spending time at an institution that enrolls very different kinds of students in contrast to the student's own institution. The point is to design experiences that provide some real contrast with what students are used to in their undergraduate institution. Again, the evidence of the educational and social value of the experience of study abroad is quite impressive.

A parallel experience to study abroad would be foreign language mastery, to have an immersion experience in a foreign language. That can, of course, be combined with study abroad. The idea is to find a way to add an immersion experience with a foreign language, perhaps in the language houses that used to be common in liberal arts colleges. We could revive that idea, and maybe do it a little more creatively where students live and speak in a foreign language for a period of time. It's a great experience, and it's very liberating to learn a foreign language. One of the things students can do when they master a language is to begin to think in that language, and to develop empathy for and understanding of other people. One of the big differences between Europeans and Americans is that almost all Europeans are bilingual. That is a tremendous advantage that they have, to be able to talk and think in another tongue. Even most English-speaking Europeans like the British are bilingual.

Another recommendation for presidents would be to provide major support for the arts, and insist that every student have some kind of immersion experience in the arts. Whether it's painting, drawing, sculpture, music, or theater, the idea is to require participation to the point where students actually have an opportunity to perform in the art. Art has been deemphasized at the K–12 level in most areas other than marching bands. Of course, marching band can be a positive experience for students, even if it is quite narrow. Art immersion might be done through the cocurricular process, but it could also be done in combination with a curricular experience. Some kind of an art immersion experience is also very liberating for students. Ideally, it should be something that they haven't done before, but that would depend on the individual student. Learning to play a musical instrument is a wonderful, liberating kind of experience, as is learning to draw a figure, do an abstract sculpture, or perform a part in a play. I was a music major as an undergraduate. I wanted to be a conductor. So now I conduct surveys!

CONCLUSION

My current work involves spirituality. I am increasingly convinced that we need to pay much more attention to the inner life of students, not necessarily to dig into it ourselves, but to encourage the students to explore for themselves that inner life as it may relate to their beliefs, values, hopes, dreams, aspirations, and the meaning they make of their college experience. Additionally, we should encourage students to cultivate that inner life both individually and collectively with other students. We need to encourage discussions of these inner issues among students, and between students and faculty, so that this self-exploration becomes part of the subject matter of higher education, rather than something that you privately carry around inside of you and never share with others, or don't explore yourself.

It's not an easy thing to describe, but it's fairly easy to identify strategies for accessing that inner life. Writing, conversation, and reflection are all ways to do this. But certainly we need to make such activities a regular part of the college experience, where students have opportunities to explore and cultivate their inner lives.

The reason I emphasize this is because I see our culture evolving in the other direction, with much more focus on the external and the material: possessing things, acquiring money, status, on what you "do" rather than what you "believe." Even the colleges have fallen into the same trap of emphasizing the external almost to the exclusion of the internal life. By encouraging our students to begin to look at their inner lives, and examine them critically, we provide a service not only to them but to ourselves.

Chapter 6

The Evolution of International Higher Education

with H. Stephen Gardner and Vivian Bull

Chapter 6 contains two sections. The first section by H. Stephen Gardner explores international issues, including those related to Russia and China, while the second section with Vivian Bull focuses mostly on Africa and South America.

INTERNATIONAL HIGHER EDUCATION OF THE FUTURE: RUSSIA AND CHINA WITH H. STEPHEN GARDNER

H. Stephen Gardner is the Herman Brown Professor of Economics and director of the McBride Center for International Business at Baylor University. He holds a B.A. in economics and Russian studies from the University of Texas at Austin and a Ph.D. in economics from the University of California at Berkeley. He is the author of three books, the editor of one conference volume, and has published numerous articles in academic and professional publications.

Gardner was a recipient of Baylor University's "Outstanding Tenured Professor" award in 1994 and "Outstanding Professor for University Service" award in 2005. Under his leadership, Baylor has developed relationships with universities and research institutes throughout the world, and has offered business education programs in Russia and China.

Gardner is a member of the American Economic Association, the Association for Comparative Economic Studies, the Academy of International Business, and the American Association for Advancement of Slavic Studies, and is a fellow of

This chapter is based on interviews I conducted with H. Stephen Gardner on October 5, 2007, and with Vivian Bull on February 28, 2008, for this book.

the Salzburg Seminar and senior research Fellow of the IC² Institute. He has been quoted in USA Today *and* U.S. News and World Report, *and in numerous other regional, national, and international news media.*

The International Background and Current Role of U.S. Higher Education

Globalization has affected every aspect of our lives, and its influence is particularly evident in the history of higher education. During their form-ative years, American universities embraced the liberal arts tradition that originated in European ecclesiastical colleges and in the British Oxford-Cambridge system. We inherited traditions of academic freedom and sci-entific research from the Humboldt model in Germany. From the very be-ginning, our universities were enriched by the employment of scholars from many countries. Thomas Jefferson, for example, recruited most of the initial faculty of the University of Virginia from British and European universities. So, in a very real sense, our current institutions and tradi-tions descend from a rich international heritage.

At the same time, U.S. higher education is unique in the world. We have blended some of the best international practices with homegrown inno-vations, making us a large net exporter of educational services and ideas. During the past century, American educational leaders have developed new sources of public and private funding, new institutions of decentral-ized accreditation and governance (in the absence of a Ministry of Higher Education), new programs of professional and vocational education that have served the practical needs of society, and new educational institu-tions at the community and junior college levels that have democratized higher education and made it available to a much larger segment of the population. The breadth and depth of U.S. higher education and research have made a major contribution to the nation's competitive position in the world.

In many countries outside the United States, higher education is domi-nated by state-supported institutions that have been less reliant on stu-dent tuition and private philanthropy. During recent years, state funding has eroded in many countries, and educational expenditures per student have fallen far behind U.S. levels. So, in order to defend their competitive positions, some foreign universities have begun to emulate the American financial model. In Europe, some of these reforms have been introduced by institutions of the European Union, calling for greater cooperation among regional universities. As one would expect, reforms based on the market-driven American model have encountered resistance in many countries.

Changing Patterns of Student Mobility

While American higher education has a long history of international co-operation, our interactions have grown exponentially during the new era of globalization. By a wide margin, the United States hosts a larger number of international students than any other country, and that number has grown by about 70 percent during the last twenty years (see tables 6.1 and 6.2). Expansion of international enrollment was interrupted for a few years following the September 2001 terrorist attacks, but growth resumed during the 2006–2007 academic session. On the "push" side, rapid growth of foreign enrollment is explained by the opening of borders, by rapid growth of the college-age population in many developing countries, by the continuing diffusion of English language fluency, and by booming economies in Asia and the oil-exporting countries. On the "pull" side, American universities are recruiting more heavily in international markets to attract high-ability students who can contribute to campus diversity and (in some cases) afford to pay full tuition.

Through the years, the mixture of international students in the United States has changed continuously. In 1950, Canada, China, and Venezuela (in that order) were the leading countries of origin, accounting for more than one-third of the foreign-student population. By the late 1970s, China had fallen off the list, and Canada and Venezuela fell to the fourth and eighth ranks, respectively. Iran and Nigeria were now the major countries of origin, accounting for one-quarter of all foreign students. By 2007, Iran had fallen to the forty-first rank and Nigeria had fallen to the twenty-first. The largest suppliers of international students were now India, mainland China, and South Korea, contributing 37 percent of foreign enrollment in

Table 6.1. Student Mobility: Top Receiving and Sending Countries, 2005

Rank	Receiving Countries	Number of Hosted Foreign Students	Sending Countries	Number of Students Abroad
1st	United States	590,128	China	394,669
2nd	United Kingdom	318,399	India	139,356
3rd	Germany	259,797	Rep. of Korea	97,395
4th	France	236,518	Japan	65,229
5th	Australia	207,264	Germany	63,280
6th	Canada	132,982	France	52,156
7th	Japan	125,917	Morocco	50,637
8th	Russian Fed.	90,450	Turkey	50,416
9th	South Africa	50,449	United States	46,289
10th	Spain	45,603	Malaysia	45,055

Source: UNESCO, *Global Education Digest 2007*

Table 6.2.   Foreign Students in the United States, 1970–2006

	1970	1985	2000	2006
Total number	144,708	343,777	547,867	582,984
Region of Origin (% distribution):				
Africa	6.0	9.9	5.9	6.1
Asia	37.5	45.6	55.1	59.1
Europe	12.7	10.0	14.7	14.2
Latin America	20.2	13.2	11.6	11.1
Middle East	11.8	15.3	6.7	3.8
North America	8.9	4.7	4.7	4.9
Oceania	1.4	1.2	0.8	0.7
Other/Multiple	1.5	0.1	0.5	0.1
Field of Study (% distribution):				
Agriculture	2.6	2.1	1.3	1.3
Arts, Humanities, and Languages	17.5	11.7	13.3	11.7
Business and Social Sciences	13.2	26.1	27.1	26.2
Education	5.5	3.4	2.6	2.9
Natural Sciences and Engineering	40.2	33.5	26.3	29.1
Math and Computer Science	3.1	10.4	12.4	7.9
Optional Practical Training	n.a.	n.a.	n.a.	7.5
Other/Undeclared	17.9	12.8	17.0	13.4

Source: Institute of International Educations, Open Doors.

the U.S. (or 43 percent if Hong Kong and Taiwan are included in China), and accounting for more than 90 percent of that year's *growth* in foreign enrollment.

The number of American students studying abroad has quadrupled during the last twenty years, supported by a broad diversification of the client base and improved access to formerly closed societies (see table 6.3). In the past, U.S. study-abroad programs primarily served the needs of foreign-language majors and other students in the arts and humanities. Today, those traditional majors are outnumbered by students in business and the social sciences. Business students now realize that they must be prepared for careers that will involve competition and opportunity on a global scale. Students in engineering, the natural sciences, and other fields that have been underrepresented in the past seem to be gaining a similar realization. European countries continue to be the most attractive destinations for American study-abroad students, but the traditional programs in the United Kingdom and France are losing ground to programs in China, Italy, Spain, Argentina, Greece, Mexico, and Costa Rica. These are growing much more rapidly, not only in percentage terms, but also in absolute numbers of new students. India has been lagging as a study-abroad destination, but it seems to be joining the league of rapidly growing locations.

Table 6.3.　U.S. Study-Abroad Students, 1970–2005

	1970	1985	2000	2005
Total number	*32,209*	*48,483*	*154,168*	*223,534*
Destination (% distribution):				
Africa	0.8	1.1	2.9	3.8
Asia	6.7	5.4	6.0	9.3
Europe	54.8	79.6	63.1	58.3
Latin America	15.1	7.0	14.5	15.2
Middle East	5.5	4.0	1.1	1.2
North America	16.3	0.9	0.7	0.5
Oceania	0.8	0.9	6.0	6.3
Other/Multiple	0.0	1.1	5.7	5.4
Field of Study (% distribution):				
Arts, Humanities, and Languages	38.6	49.6	30.7	29.5
Business and Social Sciences	13.6	24.6	38.4	39.4
Education	1.7	4.1	4.4	4.1
Natural Sciences and Engineering	17.2	7.1	13.0	13.6
Math and Computer Science	n.a.	1.3	2.0	1.5
Other/Undeclared	28.9	13.3	13.5	11.9

Source: Institute of International Educations, Open Doors.

In Europe, the ERASMUS (European Region Action Scheme for the Mobility of University Students) Program has made an enormous contribution to student mobility since its creation in 1987. Under the program, reciprocal exchanges have been organized among 2,200 participating institutions in 31 countries, and participating students can apply for grants to cover the additional expenses of living abroad. More than 1.5 million students have benefited from ERASMUS grants, and the European Commission hopes to double that number by 2012. To facilitate these exchanges, the European Credit Transfer System (ECTS) was established in 1989, establishing guidelines for assignment of grades and credit hours. Although the ECTS was adopted to meet the needs of European universities and their students, it has also facilitated the study-abroad and exchange programs of American universities in Europe because the ECTS created a standardized system that is quite similar to the American system of grading and semester hours.

Another step toward European standardization was taken in 1999, when the Education Ministers of twenty-nine nations signed the "Bologna Declaration," calling for the creation of a European Higher Education Area. According to the so-called Bologna Process, which now covers forty-six countries, the disparate European systems of academic degrees and quality assurance standards are being made more comparable and compatible. To this end, the European ministers agreed in 2005 to move toward a three-level system of bachelor's, master's, and doctoral education. Once again, this standardization is designed to promote mobility of students and employees within Europe, but it has been accomplished by adopting a system that is quite similar to the American model of higher education.

Global standardization of higher education is also spreading into developing countries. China developed a European-style system of higher education in the early 1900s and a Soviet-style system in the early 1950s, but it shifted to an American-style three-level system in 1981, and now it is developing a diversified system of public and private institutions, comprehensive universities and junior colleges, national laboratories, and science parks. With opening borders and rapid assimilation of the English language, China converted itself from a closed society to a major force in the global education market with breathtaking speed.

All of this suggests that the global mobility of students and professors should continue to increase, and the global education market will grow far more competitive in the future than it has in the past. In the past, the United States has benefited from this competition, because our universities have been strong, flexible, well endowed, and well managed. According to the 2007 rankings published by Shanghai Jiaotong University, eight of the top ten universities in the world are located in the United States, and thirty-seven of the top fifty. But we should not assume that the United States will maintain this advantage in the future. Universities in Europe, Japan, and some developing countries are addressing their problems and making important progress. Many of these will present an ever-stronger competitive challenge for U.S. higher education.

Strategic Alliances

During recent years, an increasing number of universities have been extending their international relationships beyond simple student exchanges to deeper strategic alliances with foreign universities, companies, and other organizations, facilitating the creation of joint-degree and double-degree programs, collaborative research, distance education programs, and a wide range of other activities. Increasingly, universities are judged by the company that they keep, and by the breadth, depth, and quality of their international partnerships. A few examples:

- The new King Abdullah University of Science and Technology in Saudi Arabia (KAUST) has rapidly gained world prominence from its high-profile Academic Excellence Alliance (AEA) program and its huge initial endowment (more than $10 billion). Under a collection of generous agreements, KAUST will collaborate with Stanford University, the University of California at Berkeley, and the University of

Texas at Austin to select and hire the initial KAUST faculty, to prepare the academic curriculum, and to perform joint research.

* Established in 2001, U21Global is a joint venture of twenty-one universities in thirteen countries—four in North America (including the University of Virginia), six in Europe, seven in Asia, and four in Australia and New Zealand. The group offers several online degree programs in business management and information technology. They report that they have enrolled students from more than sixty countries in Asia, Australia, Africa, Europe, and the Americas.

* The European Commission sponsors several programs to encourage the creation of strategic partnerships within the region and beyond. For example, under the Erasmus Mundus program, the commission supports the creation of cooperative master's programs, jointly conducted by European (and sometimes external) universities, and provides EU-funded scholarships for third-country nationals participating in these programs. By the end of 2006, 80 master's programs had been created, involving 323 universities in Europe and beyond, and grants had been awarded to 4,129 incoming third-country students (with strongest participation of India, China, Brazil, and Russia) and to about 1,000 Europeans studying outside of Europe. During 2009–2013, the new edition of the program calls for broader inclusion of non-European universities—more than €950 million has been pledged for European and third-country universities to create joint program or collaborative partnerships, and to grant scholarships to European and third-country students for an international study experience.

Issues for the Next Twenty Years and Beyond

Global Demographics

Earlier, we noted that the Asian countries have accounted for a rising share of international students in the United States, and the world's four largest sources of international students—China, India, the Republic of Korea, and Japan—are all in Asia (see tables 6.1 and 6.2). The strength of the Asian applicant pool is illustrated by the data in table 6.4, which provides results on the Graduate Management Admission Test (GMAT) in 2006–2007 in countries where the examination was given to more than 1,000 people. After the United States, five of the top six countries to take the exam (India, China, South Korea, Taiwan, and Japan) were in Asia, and, with the exception of Taiwan, the average scores were higher in all of those countries than in the United States.

According to United Nations projections (see figure 6.1), the Asian college-age populations will continue to be the world's largest during the

Table 6.4.   GMAT Examinations, 2006–2007

Citizenship	Number	Mean Total Score
United States	117,321	529
India	21,481	578
China	13,048	602
S. Korea	6,811	564
Canada	6,400	562
Taiwan	5,218	525
Japan	3,417	536
France	2,420	559
Thailand	2,091	488
Germany	2,071	549
United Kingdom	1,730	583
Mexico	1,703	489
Turkey	1,633	542
Greece	1,543	518
Brazil	1,356	542
Italy	1,294	571
Russia	1,273	534
Nigeria	1,259	467
Singapore	1,154	581
Pakistan	1,084	497

Source: Graduate Management Admission Council

next forty years, but (1) East Asian population is expected to peak sometime around 2025; (2) South Asian population should bypass East Asian
population during the 2030s; and (3) the rapidly growing African population will grow near to the East Asian population during the 2050s. So, the
adult populations are expected to grow more rapidly in Africa and South
Asia than in any other region, and these are the very regions that currently have much lower school enrollment rates, particularly at the tertiary level, than in East Asia or any other region of the world (see table 6.5).
The higher education institutions of the world will face a massive challenge during the coming decades to address the escalating needs of the
growing populations in Africa and South Asia.

Teaching Staff

In the future, we should expect that the global competition for academic talent will grow progressively more intense. In the United States,
more than 30 percent of academic staff are aged fifty-five or over, and
fewer than 10 percent are under thirty-five years old. With an aging population and relatively high academic wages (compared to those in other
countries), we should expect a continuing flow of academic talent from
other countries into the United States. This trend will exacerbate the diffi-

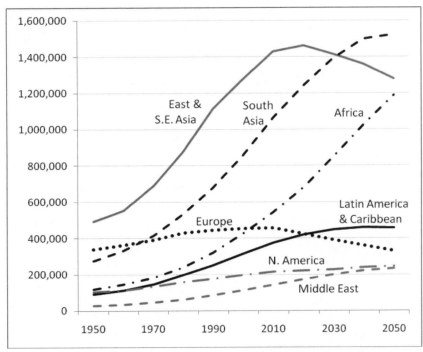

Figure 6.1. Population, Age Sixteen to Fifty-nine, by World Regions, 1950–2050 (in thousands, actual and projected) United Nations Population, Resources, Environment and Development Databank, 2005 Revision

culty that already exists in other countries that have experienced a "brain drain" of professors into the nonacademic sectors and into higher-income countries.

The growing shortage of qualified staff was drawn to my attention during a recent visit to Kazakhstan. I met with Dr. G. S. Seitkassimov, the rector of the University of Economics, Finance, and International Trade. I

Table 6.5. School Enrollment Rates, 2005 (percent)

	Primary	Secondary	Tertiary
High-Income Countries	95	91	66
Developing Countries	85	54	19
East Asia and Pacific	93	68	20
Europe and Central Asia	91	81	51
Latin America and Caribbean	94	69	30
Middle East and N. Africa	91	67	24
South Asia	85	49	9
Sub-Saharan Africa	68	25	5
World	86	58	24

Source: World Bank, World Development Indicators

asked him to list the most difficult challenges his young university is facing. He immediately responded that his biggest problem is the scarcity of qualified teaching staff. Indeed, this will be a growing problem in all countries, but particularly in the developing world where the shortage is most acute and it will be much more difficult to attract and retain personnel.

Technology and Intellectual Property Rights

The demographic and personnel problems that have just been mentioned will make it particularly important for us to make optimal use of educational technology on a global level. Under the force of necessity, some of the developing countries are playing a pioneering role in the broad-based application of distance education.

For example, according to a recent survey by the World Bank, the largest distance-learning institution in the world is Anadolu University in Turkey. Established in 1982, Anadolu now has more than one million students enrolled in distance education programs through three of its academic units—the faculties of open education, economics, and business administration. Currently, most of their programs are delivered through self-study textbooks, supported by e-mail communication and teleconferencing, and by radio and television broadcasts that are produced at the university's own professional studio. The Anadolu information management program is delivered fully on Internet.

China Central Radio and TV University, which was established by Deng Xiaoping soon after he ascended to power in 1978, is considered the second largest distance education institution in the world. Like Anadolu, it delivers courses through a combination of radio, TV, print, and computer applications. Tutoring and examinations are administered in a network of study centers across the country.

In 2008, the University of Massachusetts concluded an agreement with China's Continuing Education Association (CCEA) and CerEdu Corporation (both of which are affiliated with Tsinghua University) to make the University's distance education program, UMassOnline, available to students throughout China. Plans call for UMassOnline to offer credit and noncredit courses, certificate programs, and degree programs from all five UMass campuses throughout China. Forty UMassOnline courses, four certificate programs, and one master's degree program are currently in production.

Global cooperation in distance education will be facilitated by the growing diffusion of English language fluency and by improvements in communication and pedagogical technology. To be effective, however, curricula that have been developed in high-income countries will need to be adapted to the needs of developing countries. Just as we have learned that "appropriate technologies" in developing countries are frequently quite different from our Western production technologies, the "appropriate curricula" will often be quite different from our existing curricula. Again, to meet this challenge, it will be necessary to develop strategic alliances between educational, social, and technical institutions in the nations of the North and South.

Competition for Resources

It is awfully difficult to predict how the future of global higher education will be influenced by the evolution of national and global priorities. Recently, a member of the Indian Planning Commission who was formerly the vice provost of Mumbai University gave a presentation at my university on the needs of the Indian primary, secondary, and tertiary education. He acknowledged that India lags far behind China on many of its measures of educational development and performance, and he described the ten-year plan that they have formulated to address these problems. In the end, however, he said that the most important contribution to Indian education probably could be made by a successful resolution of the hostilities between India and Pakistan. Both countries are devoting far too many of their resources to military expenditures that are desperately needed for education. More broadly, higher education institutions must compete for funding with a wide range of other important priorities, including primary/secondary education, public health, and environmental protection. The future of higher education will depend, in large part, on the outcome of that struggle for resources, affected by war, peace, climate change, and a wide range of other priorities.

Preparing for the Changes Ahead

One thing every university should be doing right now, and should continue to do, is to evaluate its network of relationships with international universities, research institutes, internship sites, and other organizations. University presidents really need to be involved in this process, because they can send a very important signal to the other institution with their presence. In many places, this is viewed as a necessary form of diplomacy that will make it possible to establish alliances with better organizations and with greater depth. It also sends a strong signal to the home university that "we are serious about internationalizing."

When evaluating its network of international relationships, the university leadership should ask questions such as these:

- Have we been proactive in selecting and establishing our relationships, or have we simply responded to others who have made proposals to us?

- Have we monitored the experiences of our students at exchange universities and determined whether these are the best places for their educational experiences?
- Have we established some relationships that are deeper and more meaningful than simple student exchange partnerships? With these institutions, are we able to undertake joint educational and research programs, exchanges of administrative experience, exchanges of internship placements, and other advanced forms of cooperation?

If the answers to these questions are negative, it is important to rethink and realign the entire structure of international ties. Generally, it's helpful to find international partners that have values and quality standards that are comparable to the values and standards of the home university. For most of us, it's a good idea to find universities in other countries that are in a similar position competitively. Avoid working with foreign institutions that are so "prestigious" that they have little interest in the relationship or so "needy" that there's little room for mutual benefit. If you develop deeper relationships with a few institutions, your students will be better received, and your faculty will be able to find joint teaching and research opportunities. Find the places where your students and faculty can thrive, and proactively develop those relationships.

INTERNATIONAL HIGHER EDUCATION OF THE FUTURE: AFRICA AND SOUTH AMERICA WITH VIVIAN BULL

Vivian Bull is president emerita of Linfield College. She served as president of Linfield for thirteen years. Bull came to Linfield from the Department of Economics at Drew University in Madison, New Jersey, where for more than thirty years she specialized in international economics, focusing on economic problems of the West Bank and Gaza. She is a recognized authority on Middle East affairs.

Bull has served as a consultant to a number of institutions of higher education, corporations, and a variety of governmental and nongovernmental organizations, including the executive committee of the Northwest Association of Schools and Colleges (the regional accrediting organization), the board of directors of the National Association of Independent Colleges and Universities, and the board of the Fred Meyer Inc. and the Fred Meyer Foundation. She helped organize the College of Management and Administration of Africa University in Zimbabwe and is a former trustee of the university, where she continues to serve as a consultant.

Bull is currently working with the Board of Higher Education and Ministry of the United Methodist Church, where she chairs the investment committee, serves on the University Senate and is working with a new international education project.

Bull received her doctorate from New York University. She has studied in Norway, Great Britain, and the Netherlands.

Historical Highlights of International Higher Education

In the larger context of the post–World War II movement, we had a lot of counterpart funds available in countries unable to pay their debt in dollars and consequently made funds available for education. I served on one of those programs with the Fulbright Association, and it helped those of us who went into education see what a remarkable experience a year, a semester, or even a month abroad can be in helping students understand the wider perspective. The movement to support student and faculty travel developed the American Field Service (AFS) and Rotary programs, which brought high school students back and forth for long-term and short-term stays abroad. The momentum quickened after the Second World War, when the need for a better understanding of other cultures and identities arose.

From the African standpoint, going abroad into higher education has been a way out of Africa. The tragedy was that these students frequently did not go back to Africa. The best and the brightest would go and stay abroad, and didn't generally take their educational experience back home. Part of that was due to the postwar period countries not being well developed or even independent. There was a dependency relationship, which still exists in some of the African countries today, because languages were determined according to whoever ruled that particular area, along with some indigenous languages. It is a much more complex system now.

We are working in many countries and the primary languages are English, French, and Portuguese. Teaching at the Africa University is mainly in English, but we support the other languages through about the first two years. By that second year students really have to be able to speak English. In a real sense, that's becoming the language of the continent because of aviation, technology, and business contracts. This means that certain countries are really disadvantaged in opportunities for education outside of the continent because of the language barrier.

International Issues and Events in Higher Education

There is the general problem of the lack of resources. Many countries have been through various stages of war where buildings and libraries have been burned or destroyed. Building up the human resources, which are necessary to sustain long-term educational programs, became a problem as well. In certain countries there would be migrations of large numbers of people. Very often when there is trouble in a country the best educated are the most adaptable, and the most able to leave a country, go someplace else, and make another life. That physical disparity that is created by the instability in several parts of the continent has meant the loss of some of the very people who are needed to run the schools, do research, and help the nation grow and develop. But those people were leaving the country. The situation meant that there were few educational opportunities available; so many people had to leave the continent.

Many of these young people found themselves in different parts of the world, established themselves, went on to higher education, and did not return to their country. There was a brain drain.

The idea of creating a Pan-African institution then meant that there was going to be an alternative to the national colleges and universities, which, as in all countries, are very much subject to the resources and revenue flows of their individual countries. In parts of Africa including Zimbabwe, we have seen where faculties have not been increased, but there are increasing numbers of students who are coming into the institutions. Consequently, the student-faculty ratio is in a bad state with a large number of students in classes and very little opportunity for one-on-one work with the faculty. The *New York Times* has done a series of articles in the last couple of years on this situation. Of course, if you add the cost of technology, scientific research, and library development, the very cost is a burden that the educational support systems have been unable to overcome in a quality way.

Programs Assisting International Higher Education

I primarily work with the Board of Higher Education of the United Methodist Church on a global education project. We've always talked about the churches being global, but we haven't always manifested that in the way in which we operate. So this is a major effort, which is now in the first phase of reaching out in a variety of different ways. In Africa, we're examining the possibilities of bringing distance education via either Africa University or other universities into the particular areas of the country that suffered most during the years of war and have consequently not rebuilt their graduate-level higher education programs. We have visited and completed feasibility studies in countries like Sierra Leone, Liberia, Nigeria, and the Congo. A small team of us meet with a representative of each government and the service providers who are in that country. Then the colleges, universities or church organizations begin to provide access to some of the technology that much of the rest of the world has begun to take for granted.

The first site will be opening in Mozambique, with courses coming from a Methodist university in Brazil via satellite, and with courses from Africa University, focusing on leadership development. We're concerned about both health conditions and the ways in which we can make contact with people through the technology that we might not be able to otherwise.

Electricity is a problem in many of these countries. A stable source of electricity will have to be provided. We are leap-frogging about twenty-five years to develop distance education as a viable educational alternative.

In South America I'm currently working with a fifteen-year-old university that has had the opportunity to enter into an arrangement with a corporate entity that oversees a number of companies working in Argentina in the production of soy oil. Argentina is the world's third largest producer of soy oil. It is a major export for the country, much of it going to the Far East. They are going on to the next stage, looking at using the same type of plants but moving into bio-diesel. They are looking at the energy crisis and asking if there are ways in which we can not only feed, but also help provide energy for the world as well. We're looking to negotiate a relationship where a pilot plant will be established. The university will be able to use the pilot plant in its engineering program, but the corporate entities will use it to train employees and do experimental work. We're looking at this perhaps as a model of corporate higher education opportunities in other parts of the world as well, where a similar kind of synergy can be created with people working together to solve corporate problems, but also tying the process to education and academic institutions.

We have a wonderful program in Western Europe where seminaries are placing a number of theological volumes in both German and English on a closed website and will make those available to the new seminaries developing in East Central Europe and Russia. It would be difficult to replicate libraries at these new sites, so these websites make access available to those who might not have access to these kinds of resources. The process will try to develop networks of Methodist-related institutions as well. There are approximately 740 institutions outside of the United States available for faculty and student exchanges. We would also like to begin to move toward accreditation, whether it's on a national or international basis.

We have big plans, and we're going in lots of different directions as opportunities become available that can fit into the broader scheme. We're trying to bring more educational opportunities to bear where we can establish local partnerships. It is long past the time when western countries can be expected to provide everything that's necessary, and our goal is to always work with the indigenous population to facilitate various beneficial processes.

We're not trying to recreate an American education system for other parts of the world, because that's not going to work. I'm a pro–liberal arts person. We need to explore how to begin to infuse flexibility so that a broad concept of education, including writing and teaching skills, can help create flexible students for a lifetime of learning in cultures that don't thoroughly embrace our liberal arts approach. As more and more of these students are leaving home and taking jobs with multinational corporations, and are learning about the world, language skills become survival skills for being able to move into a different cultural environment.

Methodists are now asking how we can partner together to bring about these needed educational changes. It's somewhat like what happened to education on the frontier of this country. Many of those church-related institutions were established before the state was even founded. Within the larger context, the connectional system in the Methodist tradition allows institutions to work together. We generate interest and concern and create a synergy committed to higher education wherever we are.

Twenty Years and Beyond

First, it will be necessary to develop human resources in order to both continue the tradition of education and to deal internally with some of the issues. One of our real challenges right now in many parts of the world is political instability and how that instability affects everything else—including economic issues, living conditions, and opportunities. As we move toward a more integrated world, the hope is that it will have greater adaptability so that long-term planning can begin. For instance, one of our universities in the Congo was burned to the ground when the rebels retreated, so now it's a university in name only. Faculty are holding classes in various places to assist students until they are able to be located someplace else. As long as there is that kind of instability, the educational system has a difficult time sustaining itself over a long period of time. In Liberia, fourteen years of war prevented many of the schools from functioning. Part of the generation of students who are now in their forties and should be providing leadership to the countries are not able to do so. Education must also bring stability, helping people to understand that there are different ways to solve problems, to work together, and to work through international connections.

The oil in Nigeria, diamond mines in Côte d'Ivoire, and the conditions in the Congo are surrounded with difficulty. Yet, there are still pockets of opportunity. There is a need to not necessarily build buildings, but to jump over that whole phase in order to make higher education accessible. The possibility of a student taking courses thousands of miles away where those courses are offered, and having access to the necessary resources, may in some ways resolve some of the problems where there are disruptions because of economic or political conditions.

Africa is being blessed by the World Bank, which has set up fourteen communication centers that are fully equipped to download from the satellite. They also have video conferencing opportunities. These organizations were saying that their students needed not only technical training, but also "generosity" training.

In Liberia, we are discussing whether private universities can cooperate with international organizations without having to replicate the conditions to do the teaching and learning. We may be able to access something that has been setup by a nongovernmental organization associated with the United Nations (NGO), and work through it. They could then draw from sources we have through the connectional system, like access to multiple language possibilities.

The integration comes about with the opportunities to travel, learn about another people and culture, and learn new perspectives. People have begun to interact, communicate, work and learn together, and then put their human resources together as a model of how you can do things. We certainly see it in the young people with whom we're working in Africa. There is a difference in attitude. They don't want to be given things. They really want to be partners in the project so that there is not only some self-satisfaction, but also some self-identification with the project as well. We all know the more you can get people involved and personally committed to something, the more likely it is to be a success.

We now have 2,900 graduates of Africa University, and they're doing the most amazing things when they go back into their own communities. The whole idea of the university is to train students to go back and work in their home communities. The agricultural program focuses on sustainable agriculture. Nursing programs focus on developing nurses who will be able to function in rural areas, not necessarily going into the city hospitals, but taking health care and nursing out to the rural areas. The goal is to provide a strong background so that each graduate becomes a teacher and takes those skills back to help others learn.

One agricultural center community in the Eastern Congo, not too far from where many of the difficulties are, sent fifteen of their young people to Africa University for an education. Thirteen of them returned to the area. It's a different world there. They've come back with new ideas, including setting up agricultural centers for local farmers. Along with the Methodist Council on Relief, the community is building schools and developing an orphanage for children who are found abandoned in the area. The whole community has learned how working together can make a difference.

There is also a developmental spirit in Nigeria. Two young men came to see us in Logos and asked to be partners. They were in churches and didn't have electricity, telephones, or mail service, but they saw that if they could learn how to use computers and generators, and could operate off of the satellite, they could be in communication with each other. When they were asked what they would do in the partnerships, they said, "We will have a luncheon, and make money on the lunch." They want to be involved. So if we can continue partnering, and be able to provide the support for these projects to go forward, we'll have a new generation of leadership.

Africa in the Future

The hope is that we could live beyond the political tribal economic interruptions some of these countries go through. With the increasing disparity in incomes and political issues that are bringing back tribal relationships, this is not going to be easy. Personal identity is a function of one's tribe and economic environment. I would like to see more leadership from this next generation of young people who have greater tolerance, who are more willing to work through the problems at a round table or a campfire.

One issue is that weapons are so readily accessible now in the world and people often resort to those too quickly. As in our inner cities, this is one of the situations we are dealing with. I believe we're still going to find these problems in twenty years: look how many years we have tried to clean up our cities.

I think that the more that we can learn to understand what the issues and problems are and how we can help assist and respond to the needs, rather than imposing what we think should be done, I would certainly hope that we can see greater cooperation, greater interaction in a positive way both politically and socially.

We have some wonderful examples that have worked. Kenya is one of them. Up until this recent situation, we viewed Kenya as strong, with institutions that were ready to deal with the issues that are plaguing other parts of Africa. That will probably still be true.

I don't think it's going to be perfect in twenty years. That's not the way the world works. But each time we're able to develop some responsible leadership, develop opportunities within an area, our chances of doing that in the next village, or the next town, or the next country increase.

There will be costs associated with all of this, requiring different kinds of resource bases. If everybody wants to use as much oil as we use in this country, the world is in trouble. We must find ways to deal with the energy problems, not to replicate what the West has done. We must find other ways in which to deal with that problem so that we don't burden the world's resources more. It's so multifaceted. I think the problem is that it's very difficult to be specific about twenty years from now. I certainly hope we'll have a lot more educated people who are willing to commit to what's necessary to make the continent work.

Risks or Pitfalls That International Higher Education Will Face in the Next Twenty Years

Certainly one concern is adequate resources. We need qualified individuals to serve the indigenous populations, to serve as faculty and political leaders, because those are closely tied together.

Access to outside interaction and opportunities is going to be important. Again, I think we can use the technology in a very creative way. At the same time that technology can be doing destructive things, it can be used for instructive purposes as well.

I think we can rely upon both the indigenous organizations and the religious groups who are committed to greater equality and are willing to work together across borders and interact with people from other backgrounds. There are a number of Catholic churches with commitments in Africa. The Presbyterian Church and many other churches have large commitments in various areas. Coming together to reward the continent for the work that is being accomplished is going to be important. What is important are the same things that affect higher education throughout the world: adequate resources in terms of both capital and human resources, and support from government.

We're going to have to rethink what our universities are. A Zimbabwe modeled after Oxford or Cambridge University is perhaps not so appropriate for today. There are other models where large buildings and huge resources are not necessary. There are other ways that education is going to be accessible, and that's why we're trying distance education. However, I have concerns about distance education, that the interaction we see as so much a part of higher education might be lost if you're sitting at the computer.

At Africa University we have had both Hutus and Tutsis during the worst of the fighting. They are similar in so many ways—their hopes and desires—that there might be some way to begin to deal with these great tribal problems that have developed if people can meet you at the table face to face and talk, rather than resorting to some other ways. We are asking an awful lot of many of these countries that have only been established as democracies in the last twenty or thirty years. Maybe we need to think of a new kind of democracy that would better fit these situations.

Advice for Higher Education Administrators in America to Prepare for the Future

I think we have to help develop global centers, to go beyond how most of us were trained, step out of some of the norms, and ask probing questions. We need to ask what is wrong with sending more opportunities for gainful employment overseas to people who have not had these opportunities. Anytime there is a dislocation, people will suffer. How can we be proactive before the dislocation takes place to ensure there will be training programs and opportunities? When Japan was beginning to be one of the great car producers, they looked at that as a sunset industry and began to export those jobs to areas where the labor costs were lower.

It's interesting that there is evidence that India is now outsourcing some of its work to the United States. We might ask why we have the illegal immigrant problems. The problems are the same in other countries: if you don't have people to do that work, you bring them in from someplace else. It is important to incorporate that into educational and business plans. Since the very earliest times we have seen how people depended on labor from outside of the area to do jobs. As the economy improves and the standard of living rises, local people are no longer interested in doing many jobs. We've seen it in Europe, Asia, and various parts of the world. The Turks came to Germany to work because Germany needed manpower, but they were initially not allowed to bring their families.

We must begin to think more globally. I think it is important for our students, faculty, and administrators to have the experience of living in another culture to understand the difference in perspective that kind of opportunity presents, and how important that is if we're training leadership for the rest of the twenty-first century. If our students can't travel, how can we find ways to bring international students to our campuses and genuinely make them a part of the community as we learn from them?

Students do not even have to be abroad, but perhaps they could find another culture through service in organizations, like Habitat for Humanity, or working with hurricane recovery programs.

This next generation of students is going to be more internationally interdependent than we can even imagine. How can we use technology in a positive way? What is the next step? Young people can talk to people any place in the world with this technology. Surely that's going to change how we think, act, and hopefully how we relate to each other. We have to imbue the educational organizations that we have with an understanding of the importance of this. It particularly needs to be reflected among the groups working with women, because the leadership of women in many parts of the world is going to be a key factor in helping change the old ways and bring new opportunities to those areas. We're already seeing that now in many parts of the world.

Just as I would expect that every institution needs to begin to think globally, I would think that every organization will need to do that, too. More institutions overseas are seeking accreditation from U.S. regional organizations. What does that really mean? What does it mean when institutions abroad are the same as you have in Tennessee?

It would be better to have this infused in every organization as we think more globally, as we think beyond the confines of our own state, or nation, or continent, because if we don't infuse this right in the very core of our institutions, it's not going to happen. It's too expensive to think that everybody is going to have the time or the resources to go and live someplace else, in another culture, to really appreciate what that culture is about.

One of my favorite stories is about a young woman who had never been out of the rural eastern part of Oregon before and went to Paris for a semester. The great concern was about whether or not she was ready for this and would really appreciate it. She told about one time she was coming back from a trip on a Sunday evening and thinking about how wonderful it was going to be to be going home—and home was Paris. Talk about a shift: a young woman who had never been abroad spends a semester abroad, and now knows that she can live internationally.

How do we get that concept of being a part of the international scene if we only see our own backyard? We have to have the leadership all the way through our educational systems, right down through high school and grade school. Educational programs need to be training the next generation of teachers to think globally.

Of course, sometimes you don't even have to go abroad to do that. You can go to some of the communities where the original traditions are still strong. A group of students who did not know much about a Native American reservation spent a semester working in the schools on reservations to understand what some of the problems and possibilities were there. So, these multicultural experiences are not always just "away," sometimes they are close by and yet they still help students develop a new frame of mind to be thinking about these issues.

There are going to be ups and downs in the future, I'm quite sure. But what matters is how we prepare students and faculty to work with those ups and downs in a positive way in order to create some new paradigms for the future.

There are so many exciting opportunities to bring groups together. We have to break down some barriers. We're all in this together and we must find ways to cooperate and participate. It's true at Africa University. Although it's a Methodist-related institution, there are various types of Christians and non-Christians who are coming together to make this such a rich educational experience. Very often we find parallel experiences where we can reach out.

I have worked in the Middle East for many years, and I learned of the care and consideration that Muslims have within their own communities. We rarely hear about the positive experiences of other faith groups.

Having lived much of my life in Jerusalem living with Arabs, Jews, Muslims, Christians, and being a minority in that community, it's important to see how life can be defined by the religious perspective that you have, sometimes positively and sometimes negatively. Some experiences that were very important to me in my faith journey related to being a minority as a Christian. Many things are more difficult when you are in the minority. But we can all commit ourselves to the common good and work together. It makes such a difference.

Chapter 7

Technology Today and Tomorrow

with Jay Box

Jay Box holds a doctorate in higher education administration and is the vice president for technology solutions for the Kentucky Community and Technical College System (KCTCS). He is former president and CEO of Hazard Community and Technical College, which Washington Monthly *ranked as the number five community college in the nation in 2007.*

Box leads KCTCS in the development of an entirely new virtual learning initiative where online courses will be segmented into modules and delivered in an on-demand format. He has also produced a one-day technology training seminar for college presidents where the latest technology applications are presented in a hands-on workshop.

While at Hazard, Box assisted with the creation of the University Center for the Mountains, a central hub for providing access to four-year educational opportunities in southeast Kentucky.

He is on the cutting edge of international technology developments and the role of high-tech in education and industry for the future.

THE EVOLVING CONCEPT OF TECHNOLOGY

Some words that come to mind when thinking about technology today in education are "organizational," "flexible," "always available," "communicational," "powerful," "transformational," "expensive," and "constantly changing."

This chapter is based on an interview I conducted with Jay Box on October 12, 2007, for this book.

From the administrator's view of technology, all employees are expected to either own or have access to a computer at all times, at work and at home. There are many times when employees have to be able to work from home in their jobs. They are expected to be able to log into computers, track and manage their work, and keep up with assignments. All higher education employees today must be computer savvy.

TECHNOLOGY IN ADMINISTRATION

Administrative staff members use technology for everything from tracking students to managing work. Technology that once was reserved for the highest administrators—such as Blackberries and cell phones—are now commonplace for staff at every level. Everyone needs to be in touch and in tune with what is going on. We're seeing the trend moving away from the typical desktop PC to the more portable models, to laptops or mobile equipment such as iPhones. Technology use in administration has become the expectation instead of the exception.

What allows the availability for technology to communicate, manage, and direct us is the Internet. Through the Internet we are now able to have a convergence of all the different technologies for communication. I can speak over the Internet from my home even when a call comes in to my office. Through our voice-over Internet protocol phone system, we can talk to each other across the state without ever having to dial long distance. I can also view e-mail messages from office e-mail at home and I can get up and walk anywhere around the house with my laptop because of the wireless capabilities in my house. None of this was possible two decades ago, and yet it is the rule today.

TECHNOLOGY AND STUDENTS

For years, the push was to make sure that there were enough computers on campus for students. The trend now is moving away from assembling more computers for students to providing access for students to have their own computer, carry their own laptop or their own handheld devices so they can access the Internet. We're seeing WiFi or wireless needs throughout our colleges and universities. Most higher education institutions have wireless activity on their campuses.

The aspect of teaching and learning using technology has dramatically changed. For example, we have 92,000 students enrolled on 65 campuses in the Kentucky community college systems and 59,000 of them are enrolled in some type of online course. They are connected via Internet somewhere, whether it be on campus or at home. Two years ago, that wouldn't have been happening, and twenty years ago it would have never been heard of.

OUTSOURCING AND DISTANT-SUPPORT

It's no longer practical for large institutions to constantly purchase technology because it is so expensive and, even though it continues to decline in price, the fact that technology changes so rapidly means purchasing is not really the best option. We started leasing hardware and linking our services through our technology. We outsource to help manage our technology. It reduces personnel costs because outsourcing is cheaper than hiring more technicians to manage the technology, and we negotiate the cost of that management service. This is referred to as a "utility model." Similar to the concept of utilities in homes (with gas, phone, and water), the same is true now with technology in education. This service manages our network and provides the Internet, phone, and computer connections. The utility model helps colleges and universities to not have to worry so much about how much money they will have to budget each year to purchase technology and instead to budget for the leased equipment and services.

People are managing the systems from a distance rather than onsite. For example, although we are in Kentucky, our phone system and the network are managed out of Cincinnati, Ohio. Our administrative software is managed out of Atlanta, Georgia. Our online software helpdesk is in Canada. Even the helpdesk for some of the regular networking may be anywhere in the world because they provide 24/7 service. It's not uncommon to call at night and get someone in a different country. As we move to a service environment, our employees and our students expect that we will provide 24/7/365.

That kind of access to services means that we sacrifice a couple of things at times. For instance, we sacrifice being able to call an on-campus technician to assist with our computer network. Now when you call a technician, he or she is in Cincinnati, Ohio, managing what is going on with your network by looking at his computer in Cincinnati. He's pushing a few keys, fixing your computer from a remote location.

PRIVACY ISSUES FOR THE FUTURE

We struggle with privacy issues every day in higher education because we have federal mandates and our employees want to make sure that security is in place. It is actually more of a national issue, so protocols have to be constantly implemented to help protect our business. Everything is encrypted to prevent intrusion on private or secure matters. It is important to be able to prove that a comprehensive security plan is in place. In fact, a major part of accounting reviews involve the ability to show that data is secure.

We are seeing the opposite of those privacy trends in the private lives of students, who are much more open than they were ten years ago. The availability of private information on social pages such as MySpace and Facebook is growing. If colleges or universities were to allow that same kind of information to be released, we would have lawsuits every ten minutes. There is a strong tendency for people to be open with their information, but yet they don't want anyone else to control that information. They want to be able to decide when they want particular information to be available and to whom.

INSTRUCTIONAL TECHNOLOGY TOOLS OF TODAY AND TOMORROW

One cutting-edge classroom technology is 3-D visualization. It is not common throughout colleges and universities, but it is beginning to show up in top research universities, and, in isolated uses, in the community colleges. Within the next five years, it will become much more commonplace. Some colleges have established interactive digital centers using 2-D and 3-D visualization technology that provides holographic type of presentation of everything from curriculum to actually recreating a speaker in the room who may not be physically present. This classroom is more like a cinema for the technology, presenting the figures in a fairly dark environment for better resolution. Everything from a small screen to a full wall is used for projection of the learning material. In one emerging technology, an instructor projects a 3-D format model of a human heart and enlarges that image to where the human heart is the size of a podium. This 3-D format can be moved to the middle of the room. Using keystrokes on a computer keyboard, the instructor is able to manipulate that heart model so that it rotates, and may be dissected to show different parts or heart functions. Labels may be placed on various parts of the heart model and actual demonstrations can be performed. Students can also demonstrate what they have learned by having them manipulate the heart through a computer keyboard.

Some of the more advanced new technology allows the instructor to actually stand in front of the polarized screen that projects the 3-D image, instead of the instructor controlling the model with a keyboard. The instructor can control the movement of the heart or the model with hand movements, so the hands become the keystrokes of the computer. That is the newest classroom technology. The heat from the hands is actually detected by the screen.

These 3-D images can be much larger. On a campus in Florence, South Carolina, a manufacturing center was recently built with an 850-seat auditorium with an interactive digital center displaying a 25-foot screen. They can project presentations to any seat in that auditorium. The 3-D objects come out within a few feet of each person seated in the auditorium.

The demonstration I saw was a marketing piece for an office chair company where a chair was dismantled to show all the different parts and how it was put together. The chair was visually exploded, the labeled virtual chair parts came out into the auditorium and then they came back together as the assembled chair. There was an option of custom building a chair by changing colors, and making alterations. This technology is currently being used more in industry than it is anywhere else, but that will change shortly.

Another currently available advanced technology tool is the "icube," where a student wears a headset and enters a 12 x 12 room that becomes a 3-D environment using three of the four walls, the floor, and the ceiling—one wall is open—similar to what might have been seen on *Star Trek: The Next Generation*. Wearing a visor that actually becomes the computer, scenes change with you as you walk around that room. You can immerse yourself in a location. It is currently being used for such things as taking students to a historic location, letting them walk around Greek ruins, and actually seeing what it must have been like during a particular era. This technology enables an architectural student to walk through a holographic display of a building being built, and see how they built the stairwell or a room. It too is becoming more widely accessible and sophisticated.

Still another piece of an interactive visual center approach that is coming will have a "holo-podium," with a holograph of an instructor talking in the classroom. The professor can see each student, no matter where they were being broadcast from, and the student is interacting with the professor as if he or she were in the room. In this format the instructor would be in a 3-D format instead of a 2-D interactive television screen format. This technology is still cutting edge. We are in the early stages of evaluating curriculum in various areas and finding digital bits that would be good to convert into a 3-D format for the classroom or for the online environment. Five years from now it will be common to present a 3-D animation presentation in front of the classroom.

We expect that this will transfer over to where people could wear glasses and see the 3-D image on their computer screen. My guess is that at least some form of 3-D format will soon be available for students' computer screens. We are already planning on using 3-D technology on a limited basis within our new online program.

THE FUTURE OF HIGHER EDUCATION TECHNOLOGY

I believe that everybody will soon have access to on-demand learning. In other words, from any place and at any time that an individual wants to learn something, it will be possible to do so. People could say, "I want to learn French right now." They can actually pick the parts of French they would like to learn. On-demand learning will be expected in the near future.

How this will be delivered is the issue. Currently, people can access information over hand-held equipment via computers, the Internet, or mobile devices. But what I see is a totally different environment ten or twenty years from now. Just as I mentioned earlier about the instructor who is able to use his hand to manipulate a 3-D projection on a screen—move it around and break it apart—I believe that every student will have the ability to project images and manipulate those images anywhere, not just on a computer screen, but in the air. By simply turning on a battery on their clothes or on their glasses, the projection of a 3-D image will emerge in front of them. They will be able to manipulate that image and extract the information they want via a virtual touch-type screen in midair—a holographic image in front of them.

Microsoft has developed a new tabletop computer that is first being released in restaurants. Basically, it's a tabletop flat screen where patrons place their hand over items on the screen, manipulate them, and select what they want. It will initially be two-dimensional, but before long, it will have 3-D images.

Twenty years from now, I believe that our technology will advance to where individuals will be able to have a type of hearing aid that will allow them several different functions. It will allow them cell phone communications anywhere in the world by simply thinking who they want to communicate with. They will be able to hear the person and talk to him or her. At the same time, I believe the technology will advance enough to where, if you're talking to someone in Japan, they'll be hearing Japanese, and you'll be hearing them in English. This will also happen via the ear instrument.

Imagine a currently available mobile phone and reduce that to a hearing-aid size implant that connects to a mobile phone device, and add the ability to use simple voice commands—which is something that is already available on some cell phones. A phone number may be found by simply raising a hand to search the portable holographic screen, which can also allow the caller to see and hear the person being called.

Changing Curriculum Format and Delivery

Related to the concept of the learning environment, we are currently conducting discussions with our faculty about a virtual learning initiative that we plan to implement sometime in 2009, which will be a model where all of our course work will be developed into modules. Instead of your typical sixteen-week, four-semester credit-hour course, that course will be divided into more flexible small parts or modules, so a student might take one module in a two-week time span, or even in one day, depending on the content of the module. The modules will be delivered online and will be available 24/7/365 so that students may start a class at any time. Students may also take a competency-based pre-test to assess whether they may test out of a particular module and move on to the next. Therefore, students do not have to sit in a classroom studying material they've already mastered. They are constantly progressing at their own pace according to their level and at whatever time is convenient.

The challenge is in finding the ways to prepare faculty to deliver that type of education. The reality is that it cannot be done with a faculty-centric model where faculty determine the delivery format over a certain amount of time, and the student adjusts to that format. We are moving toward a more student-centric model, where the students determine what, when, and how they want to learn, and how they want to access the course work. So the role of faculty in the future must change to that of the facilitator of learning. Most of the time faculty will provide the material at a time and a place where students can access it. We have seen gradual changes in learning with the use of the Internet and online education. It has both advantages and disadvantages, but one advantage is that it allows flexibility for the student to control the learning time. A challenge is that the student still must adjust to variations in when to start and when to stop, rather than necessarily fitting into a traditional academic semester format.

As far as the future changing role of the faculty, there absolutely will be two changes. Faculty will be experts of knowledge, experts in specific areas of curriculum. They will be much more specialized. The instructor of the future will become a specialist or expert in one certain portion of a curriculum. That expert will constantly provide online expertise to any student, anytime he or she needs it. The expert facilitates the learning and will serve as a resource guide to help lead that learner to where he or she needs to go to acquire the necessary knowledge. The instructor would perform the role that a specialized doctor would perform for a patient, although the difference would be that the role of that specialized doctor is to treat the individual, whereas the role of a specialized faculty member would be to educate that student to have competence in that portion of the curriculum.

For example, in an institution with a hundred sections of English 101, there would be a team of English teachers. One may specialize in grammar, and perhaps create streaming video pieces for the English 101 in grammar. Another instructor may prepare a writing piece. There would be one lead instructor to coordinate the team through the process of facilitating thousands of students in the same classroom at the same time.

In an online environment, we currently envision a text version of delivery method where students are on the computer reading course materials and responding through e-mail. We now have new software that allows students to connect small cameras to their computers and allow text or e-mail messaging while those interacting can also see each other. The session may be recorded so that the student can later hear and see the instructor talk about the material. The student can respond in text, voice, and/or video, and can use live-chat with text, voice, and/or video with their instructor or their fellow students. That's all available right now.

If we project ten or twenty years into the future, students will not be sitting down in front of a laptop with wireless Internet; instead, you will be able to do this type of learning anywhere. Students will create a virtual screen with only a thought in the years ahead. They may push a button and a holographic screen will emerge in front of them. A faculty member in Italy may see something that would be great for their students, and they can immediately produce a short video snippet to share with the class, as well as the appropriate audio accompaniment.

The sharing aspect of information is available to us now, but it is not currently being used fully because of the necessary scale to make it profitable for colleges and universities. It is not cost-effective with a college of ten thousand students. But if you had 50,000 students, is would be feasible for a faculty expert to produce and deliver a highly specialized piece of Italian art history. There could be e-tutors and e-proctors to assist with the grading and testing of students.

That concept could be transferred into a national partnership, and ultimately a global partnership, to make some of these courses truly integrated with every piece of state-of-the-art technology.

If an instructor in England wanted to serve as a curriculum provider for a particular new virtual learning model, he or she could choose how many students to facilitate. The options and structure could become highly complex. The big challenge will be how to manage all that. Who will direct that learning process?

TECHNOLOGY ASSESSMENT AND EDUCATION OF ADMINISTRATORS

The Kentucky Community and Technical Colleges System (KCTCS) holds an annual President's Leadership Team Retreat, where the sixteen college presidents and the cabinet of KCTCS plan for the next year. We always bring in nationally recognized experts to talk to us about cutting-edge technologies. This past May we had an education specialist from Cisco Systems, Inc. She travels all over the world, to all the universities and community colleges, listens, discusses, and advises on best practices in the use of technology. The presidents then began to brainstorm about what they believed to be the most central issues facing them for the coming year.

What came out of this most recent discussion was their feeling of ineptness with technology. They were amazed with what's going on in higher education that they didn't have a clue about. Many didn't know about MySpace and other commonly used social networks. They declared their number-one goal for 2008 was to become more technology-savvy, and the responsibility for that charge fell to me. I developed a survey (see appendix 7A) for the presidents to complete and submit. It requested nearly thirty-five different technology aspects, from social and educational technology to business and industry technology, and it asked each participant for his or her knowledge level and willingness to learn about each of these technologies.

Subsequent training sessions were designed to bring the presidents up to speed on these key technologies. This is important because the number-one challenge for higher education administrators, presidents, and senior-level leadership teams is to try to keep up with the technology and related terminology enough to be able to assimilate and communicate that knowledge. They have to learn enough to understand what is and is not useful, so that they can help lead their faculty and staff in using that technology to effectively assist the learning process, and thus become more generally efficient and effective at their institutions.

ADVICE FOR PRESIDENTS

Some advice I have for presidents includes:

1. Presidents need to attend at least one technology-related conference each year. They should particularly attend conferences on education technology where they can see and experience that technology.

2. It is critical for presidents to build relationships with the technology companies of the world so they can talk specifically about ways that technologies can help their colleges better educate students. What we are discovering from the presidential level is that corporate or industry CEOs often say that the graduates they are hiring are still deficient in important skill sets. This occurs across the nation. Companies are then forced to retrain and retool employees after they hire them. We are all missing the boat somewhere and technology can help us get on that boat.

Technology companies spend a lot of money in research and development. The research universities have an advantage in that they already have a relationship with those companies, like the University of Texas has with Motorola, Apple, and Dell. Colleges and universities need to have at least some association with Microsoft, Cisco, Hewlett Packard, Dell, and others to be able to understand where they're going with their technology, and be able to see the potential beneficial relationships between these industries and higher education.

In our survey, we identified the main technology-related tools that colleges and institutions need to be familiar with. Businesses and students may already be aware of these technologies, but college presidents also need to be at least aware of them. It is hard to find the time to keep up, but I have experts who help me with what I need to know.

I think that presidents need to know the big picture of everything related to technology.

The higher education institution of the future, for example, in the year 2030, will be easily distinguishable from our current institutions. We now have lots of buildings that are all very much related to certain curricula. They serve particular functions for the students, everything from administration to science labs to dormitories in a university setting. Those will still be around, although I believe they'll be taking a different direction in the future.

When I envision the institutions of higher education of the future, I see them built in an environment where students can virtually visit the campuses of many different colleges and universities simply by entering specially equipped virtual rooms on a university campus. The experience will be similar to going around to the separate stores of a shopping center or mall. Each virtual room could provide the students of the future with the opportunity to learn whatever they choose to learn, from whatever faculty member (content expert) they select, and from any college or university in the world. The comprehensive university or even the comprehensive community college of the future would then take on a totally different meaning than our current model.

In the future, more than half of the learning will most likely be happening at home, wherever "home" may be. Learning will be delivered virtually to the residences of the students, whether that residence is in a dormitory room or in a home or apartment.

However, the actual facilities of learning for higher education institutions will be completely different. They will be truly engaging facilities that a student could not afford to have at their own residence. The future colleges and universities will be the Disney World of learning—total entertainment and highly interactive. I can see how a student could stroll down the different avenues of the college campus and choose to go into the foreign language building, and inside the foreign language building step into France or Spain. They will be transported by technology.

The student of tomorrow might be able to live in Seattle but study at Oxford or Cambridge without ever leaving home.

The Microsofts and Googles of the world will partner with the Wal-Marts of the world to develop this. The technology companies, along with the other conglomerates, have outstanding market penetration with desirable locations and high visibility. They most likely will partner, for example, with universities like Cambridge and Harvard, thus tying together the best brand names in the corporate world with the most elite universities. There may very well be an educational mall that has outlet stores specializing in the best programs for each of the major universities. Other partners will include all of the communication and media companies.

I think it's inevitable that we will eventually have one huge virtual college where there are partnerships and buy-ins from all the major universities of the world, and that they will share and partner in the entire concept.

The reason this makes sense is because the cost of delivering higher education continues to go up. It will only be possible for institutions of higher education to pay for what students need and want by having enough students enrolled. It's not going to be possible for universities, charging the tuition they are now, to be able to provide everything that the twenty-first-century student is going to expect. That student of the new twenty-first century will want the institution that gives him or her more. The first collaboration, the first major group of universities that can partner to provide those outlets at their own campuses and give access to the other campuses of the world, will be the group of institutions that becomes most profitable and will be most likely to sustain themselves in the twenty-first century.

In the university of the future, everybody will be paid according to their specialty. That's why it will be much more important for a faculty member to have a specialty, rather than be a generalist. Additionally, it is going to be much more important for faculty and staff to be experts in technology. They must understand how all technology works so as to be able to deliver their specialty through technology.

Even the custodians' role will change a lot. They will be true technicians who complete specialized college-level education and training to be able to work as a custodian.

The research that we're doing indicates that a high school education will not lead to good jobs anymore. What employers will want across the nation and the world is for people to have a minimum level of education in math, science, and communication skills, in some cases at least at a community college level, and that will be needed to do technician work. It will be the norm. So the current lower level of labor will disappear. People who build houses now, or who take care of yards, will be using some kind of technology to do their work. The process will be very different from what it is now. That's where the universities will have to play a major role.

In addition, I think there is going to be a huge market in teacher preparation, both for higher education faculty as well as public school teachers. The universities that are training educators will have to totally revamp how they are training these and most other professionals.

APPENDIX: TECHNOLOGY SURVEY FOR KCTCS COLLEGE PRESIDENTS: TECHNOLOGY TODAY AND TOMORROW

In order to help increase your technology proficiency and become more technology savvy, I will be conducting a tailor-made technology session with you. Please complete the following survey of current knowledge and desire to know more for each category. I will then schedule a day for you and I to review the technologies indicated by your survey.

Categories	Current Knowledge of Technology					Desire to Know More!				
	Low 1	2	3	4	High 5	Low 1	2	3	4	High 5
Millennial Trends:										
Classmates.com										
Del.icio.us										
Facebook										
Flickr.com										
Linkedin.com										
MySpace										
Second Life										
YouTube										
Other:										
Main Stream Applications:										
Ask.com										
Blogs										
Ebay										
Google										
iTunes (podcasting)										
RSS (Really Simple Syndication)										
Streaming Media										
Text Messaging										
VoiceOver Internet Protocol (VOIP) Phone System										
VISTA										
Wikipedia										
Wikis										
Windows Office 2007										
Other:										

(continued)

Categories	Current Knowledge of Technology					Desire to Know More!				
	Low				High	Low				High
	1	2	3	4	5	1	2	3	4	5
Educational Applications:										
Authoring Tools										
Blackboard										
Decision Support System (DSS)										
GoTo Meetings (desktop conferencing)										
PeopleSoft										
Sharepoint										
Simulation Based Learning (Interactive Digital Learning)										
Virtual Human Teleportation (2-D to 3-D)										
Other:										
Technology Hardware:										
Assistive Technologies										
Blackberry (or other cell phone tools)										
Data Storage										
iPods										
Laptop: Tablet										
Stereographic Display Systems										
Tele-immersion and Gesture-Based Display Technologies										
Tele-podium: Holographic Virtual Presentor Technology										
Video Conferencing Technology										
Visualization Technology (3-D)										
Other:										
Utility Model Options:										
Call Centers										
Leasing Desktop Computers										
Outsourcing Network Services										
Other:										

Chapter 8

University Libraries
of the Future

with James G. Neal

James G. Neal is the vice president for information services and university librarian for academic computing for twenty-five libraries at Columbia University.

He served as the dean of university libraries at both Indiana University and Johns Hopkins University, and held administrative positions in the libraries at Penn State, Notre Dame, and the City University of New York. He has also held positions on the Council and Executive Board of the American Library Association (ALA), on the board and as president of the Association of Research Libraries, on the board and as chair of the Research Libraries Group (RLG), and as chair of the Online Computer Library Center's Research Library Advisory Council and chair of the RLG Program Committee of the OCLC Board.

Neal currently serves on the Board of the Freedom to Read Foundation, and on the board and as incoming chair of the National Information Standards Organization (NISO).

He has published widely and has worked on numerous scholarly communication committees and editorial boards of journals in the field of academic librarianship. He was selected the 1997 Academic Librarian of the Year by the Association of College and Research Libraries and was the 2007 recipient of ALA's Hugh Atkinson Memorial Award.

This chapter is based on an interview I conducted with James G. Neal on February 19, 2008, for this book.

HISTORICAL HIGHLIGHTS OF HIGHER EDUCATION LIBRARIES IN AMERICA

Academic libraries are diverse. They respect the missions and philosophies of their particular institutions. There are teaching and learning institutions, institutions that have soft research, and there are other universities where research is one of the primary roles and responsibilities.

Historically, libraries operated independently. While they provided a benevolent service, they did not work closely with each other. Academic libraries across the country provided the basic capacity and capability to purchase materials, catalog them, and put them on the shelf for people to locate them as well as the necessary services to assist people in a stable environment.

There has long been a strong national cooperative effort where institutions could progress in areas such as cataloging and historical collections. In time, technologies came into play in the library with automated basic processes, including circulation, the back room operations like acquisitions and cataloguing, and the increasing representation of our traditional core catalog and long catalog systems. Traditional language procedures were moved online. In short, the process was rethought. Although change was made relatively quickly, libraries had not envisioned the even more revolutionary shifts yet to come.

Soon, library content became available in electronic formats. People no longer had to use the physical library as their location, but rather could view, from any location, traditional references, encyclopedias, indexes, and dictionaries via work station–based CD-ROM technologies. Eventually, this all became networked and, by the mid 1990s, the phenomenon of the World Wide Web emerged, which allowed even wider distribution of various media, not just text. This included the ability to deliver them 24/7—electronic journals, electronic books, films, maps, and all the media the library had collected. It was at this time that libraries began to think about producing and distributing access to the content for the purpose of future learning and research. People care about functionality. So libraries began to integrate services for institutional research and learning into the environment, including reference, document delivery, and electronic reserve services. They also began to recognize the tools that people needed in order to apply that content. Libraries became much more sophisticated information and learning systems, where a lot of the power or capabilities were placed in the hands of the user who wanted self-service and a more customized environment for the use of information—information where they wanted it, when they wanted it.

LIBRARIES TODAY

The Space and Function

Reference is the real purpose of the library. There was a period in the 1990s when libraries began to question their roles and impact, but particularly in the last century, there has been a renaissance of the role of the library in an academic community. There is recognition of the need to continue to be a social, intellectual, and collaborative space on campus to facilitate interaction with professional consultants and technology. Libraries have seen a rejuvenation in their purpose as well as the ensuing additional responsibilities. More libraries are overseeing the teaching of technologies, and providing research settings that enable faculty to capture, curate, and archive their research data. Libraries also often provide publishing programs and revised teaching and learning capabilities far beyond traditional bibliographic instruction, including lifelong learning skills.

Libraries are beginning to measure impact and quality. There is more of a commitment to assessment, developing a relationship with our user communities, and understanding what users want, how they behave, and how we can best support their information needs.

Libraries are much more active on national and international platforms, advocating for public policies, particularly information policies that support the interests of faculty and students. This includes the arenas of copyright, privacy, and Internet certifications policies.

Over the last fifty years, there have been all kinds of manifestations of this shift in the future and purpose of library space, the increasing importance of electronic space, the online work spaces provided for users, as well as the building of services and tools into those work spaces.

Additionally, there has been much more of a focus on innovation and entrepreneurial activities, trying to leverage assets to bring new income streams into the library—the leveraging of space, expertise, contracts, and the knowledge of technology. There is more and more focus on research development, grants, experimentation, and fund-raising to provide more money to build collections and increase support for faculty and students. The nature of staff, the expectations that the university has for our participation and our partnerships, the level of cooperation that takes place between the library and the faculty, between libraries and other information organizations, and the culture of the library have shifted dramatically, particularly over the last ten to fifteen years.

The Changing Staff

When we look at the visual implications of the nature and content of library education, information professionals are emerging from a variety of experiential backgrounds as they prepare to work in the academic libraries. We're seeing much more diversification in library staff and their professional credentials in the library environment.

Relationships are really important within the library, particularly in our internal structures. We have much broader and much more flexible organizational structures. Instead of emulating the traditional hierarchy, we are now much more of an academic governance structure. It's really much more of a hybrid structure where there are self-starting, self-creating teams across the library organization, allowing them to develop their own structures in order to get the job done.

LIBRARIES OF THE FUTURE

In the future, there will be even more diversity across the academic library community. We will see certain types of libraries that support teaching and learning institutions, largely without physical collections. There will be much more focus on the licensing or creation of electronic content, and the delivering of that content directly into a classroom or teaching and learning environment.

Libraries will be spaces for people to gather to work on projects together, with the necessary technologies to support that process. This social, intellectual, and collaborative space will be fully implemented and fully developed. There will be a shift in focus from the libraries' perspective into training, education, and information understanding. In that context, people will look to the library professional more for guidance and coaching in what will continue to be a complex information environment. Libraries will be less thought of as the agent on the campus that provides access information because in twenty years information will be shared more aggressively and on a greater scale throughout its entire media. More will be available, not through purchase, but through the ability to connect and use that information effectively.

Research universities will continue to expand at the other end of the spectrum. I don't think the world twenty years from now is going to be totally paperless. There will continue to be significant amounts of information produced in traditional formats, and it will be the role of the hybrid research universities to continue to acquire those materials on a global scale. They will particularly focus on unique collections—materials with rare, unusual, archival, and manuscript features—and will increasingly make that content visually available. Twenty years from now, we may reach the point where a high percentage of all library content will be available electronically.

Libraries will increasingly focus on capturing, organizing, and archiving the visual record, because most of the communication information will be digital twenty years from now. Libraries will have an even more customized environment, customized not just in terms of the type of library that supports a particular type of academic institution, but also one that is a more personalized working environment for individuals, and more responsive to individual needs, to individual learning styles, languages, and personalities. The library will be an important agent within the university to enable those types of individualized approaches to teaching, learning, and research.

The library will have space, but in many settings there will not be the familiar stacks or the usual quiet seating environment. These are becoming more modern today, much more diverse in terms of the types of spaces, and they will be an important asset for the user community, both physically and electronically. That is not very revolutionary in our current thinking about libraries. It is going to be a progression on the path that we've already begun to tread. Some libraries, because of their nature and their missions, will reach those inklings relevant to twenty years from now much more quickly than others, because they have a different societal and institutional goal.

Library spaces may not be dramatically different in the future. However, what is in those spaces and what goes on in those spaces will shift dramatically. Spaces will be much more adaptable. Librarians, or information professionals, will not be tethered to the physical library. There will be information professionals in the classroom, in the laboratory, at the research bench, in the hospital, at the bedside. Therefore, I think the library will be less populated by the librarian and more populated by the users. Each university will shape the space to meet user needs.

The intelligence of the spaces is an important concept. "Intelligent space" means that the intelligence is not at the desktop, in the computer or a device, but rather in the space around us, in the physical objects, in the walls, and in the air. The ability to use visual information and tools without keyboarding, mainly through verbalization and possibly even through thinking will be more and more the case. Systems will be far more intelligent. If we can work through the issues of privacy, we will be able to have more embedded information about our purposes, our needs, our styles, and our requirements. Systems will be much more responsive, based on individual profiles, and prepared specifically for what our information needs are, how we like information organized and presented, how often, in what form, and in what place. The intelligence of the environment will be a very important part of the library setting.

The whole notion of text or data mining begins with not just looking at traditional forms of searching for text, but also really looking for relationships and patterns of information. This will require more sophisticated tools, and higher expectations of what the interface of information can deliver. People will not be limited to working with those on their own campus. We're seeing more and more of that today through students participating in classes on a global scale, and research teams working together on shared research problems. The libraries will be an important part of supporting those types of working and scholarly collaborations. In many cases, the library will look the same, but more importantly they will behave very differently. Those differences will be user-driven and enabled by much more sophisticated technologies, including embedding intelligence spaces into academic library stations.

LIBRARY-RELATED FUTURE CONCERNS

Critical issues that define higher education are quality and peer review. Regarding the traditional methodologies where teaching is evaluated and research output is assessed, whether we can find new tools for this evaluation is an important question. We need to be concerned about the survival of tenure and the academic press. If those traditional assessment methodologies fall by the wayside, are we prepared to develop new ways of evaluating quality and performance in the institution?

Another issue is the long-term archiving of digital information. We have traditionally, in the analog paper-based world, seen the acquisition and duplication of holdings around the country and the world as creating de facto archiving and preservation systems. We know that there are libraries that have materials from centuries ago that are still on the shelves and in beautiful condition. We also know that there is information that was created this afternoon in digital form that is no longer available. So, there is a concern about how we are going to document history, the human experience, the cultural and scientific records over the next twenty years—particularly if we don't have collaborative technology refreshed capabilities to manage digital information. Additional questions include: How we will view past letters, diaries, or laboratory notebooks? How are we dealing with digital research data? There are very important issues that the academy eventually has to grasp. Teaching, learning, and research will suffer if we do not develop a viable plan across the higher education and research communities.

LIBRARY-RELATED RECOMMENDATIONS FOR HIGHER EDUCATION LEADERS OF THE FUTURE

It is critical to build, maintain, and grow a robust technology infrastructure, both within our institutions and across our institutions. We need to be sure that we are not creating barriers. These may be information or technology divides within our institutions and across our institutions that discriminate against disciplines or types of institutions in terms of their ability to access and use technology and visual information well. In the same way that universities have sometimes lost control of the buildings on campus to deferred maintenance, we have the same challenge moving forward in upgrading and refreshing the technology infrastructure at our institutions. Too often, the focus is on administrative computing infrastructures at the expense of the academic computing infrastructures.

Additionally, we need to be sure that state, national, and global information and policies address the needs of the higher education community. We must have sufficient funding in place to support research. Along with financial aid for students, the federal funding agencies, foundations, and global organizations that fund research must continue to see higher education in the United States as the center of research and development in society. That is an issue that is at risk. Universities and college leaders need to advocate for that continuing support, but also to make sure there are policies related to intellectual property and confidentiality in telecommunications and Internet development that are supportive of the needs of the higher education community.

Lastly, in relation to the library, we need to be supportive of the diversity across the disciplines, recognizing that universities are not entirely about funding research, that we have very important disciplines—particularly in matters of the social sciences—that do not receive much external funding, but that represent a very important part of the education, national research, and cultural experience. Universities are impacted by economics, and need to be cautious not to undermine the health and vitality of liberal education and humanities research. Libraries play a part in supporting humanities research, particularly because of the number of collections. Glancing forward, libraries need to consider whether to make their unique and special collections available visually, and revisit their ability to capture and archive the individualistic record as it becomes more electronically accessible, as with visual music and online books. These are some challenges that integrate well with the library's mission to the academy.

It is important that advisors assess aggressively or have some type of input approaches to measure quality, based on either physical or electronic evaluation by people who use the library. There need to be new approaches to looking at the impact of the library. How are libraries supporting successful alumni? How are they enabling productive faculty? How are they supporting efficient administration? What is the rate of user satisfaction, or user penetration? How is success measured? How does the library determine impact, cost effectiveness, and usability? Libraries must step up to the expectations for accountability and assessment and answer the questions clearly.

Academic libraries are part of an "information pool" or "information profession." They are inadequate in terms of building the research and development capacity. To produce new knowledge, to make informed decisions, create laboratories for experimentation, take risks, and better position the university for foundations and corporate and federal investments, libraries have a greater opportunity to partner with the researchers at their institutions than any other entity. They can help shape new understandings of where they are going and how to get there. That means developing skills, new resources, and new relationships with the business, technology, and academic communities.

THE CHANGING FACES OF LIBRARIES

There will be a gradual migration of employees along with the responsibility of the librarians. Librarians will take on much more of a sophisticated service relationship with the faculty and students.

Even more than it has changed in the past, I see a massive shift in the backgrounds of the library professional staff. There is an article in the Association of Research Libraries on higher education this year that documented that nearly 70 percent of the professional staffs in the Association of Research Library institutions were individuals without master's degrees in library science. In some cases, these were individuals in traditional librarian positions who held Ph.D.s or had deep subject knowledge, language capacity, and technology skills that were not recruitable out of the traditional master's degree in the library science community. As the technology programs in libraries expand, there will be more of a focus on people with strong, well-developed skills, including instructional technology, programming, technology support, and teaching and learning skills, as well as participation from postdocs. People using the libraries of the future will have available to them physical facilities, planning capabilities, fund-raisers, resource specialists, and training people necessary to accomplish any task. A whole new array of professional backgrounds will be needed to run and enable the developing academic library.

A new position that will emerge within our research institutions is a science/data/research specialist. There is a need for more individuals in the library who have scientific backgrounds and knowledge, but who also understand the needs of big science and big research: in other words, a person with the ability to measure, curate, organize, and archive the scientific record. Scholars, scientists, and researchers want to create new knowledge. They want to start a research project, get it done, publish the results, and move on to the next project. There is a new profession developing that will partner with the research community to take responsibility for that territorial research role.

An interesting type of digital library specialization is beginning to develop as a result of two important trends. One trend is a massive version of traditional archival information in the library that involves rethinking and reenergizing that information online so that it is much more dynamic, usable, and integratable in terms of the research experience. That means a very different type of experience and expertise in the library. The other trend is capturing the visual record or information, and making that accessible, usable, and preservable. I see both digital library and research data curation expertise as two very important trends over the next several years.

CONCLUSION

What we do, how we do it, and how we can refocus and reallocate resources to meet these new roles and responsibilities of the future university and the library are the challenges of the future. There has already been a reintroduction of vitality, because of the energy needed to rethink what we've done, to do things faster, and to infuse innovation into doing new things. These will be definitional for libraries going forward. Can we develop our library staff to focus more on that sort of mutability or sense of constant change with hybrid approaches and structures? For that to happen, we must overcome the high level of anxiety and the overriding sense of apprehension that accompanies a change of this magnitude. There will also be a lot of disruption that will characterize our world, along with a certain amount of chaos and unpredictability. Complex systems are by nature largely chaotic. But in many ways chaos brings life, and that's very important in thinking about the library of the future. These disruptive and chaotic realities of the future are also very exciting.

Chapter 9

Financing the Future of Higher Education

with Randy Livingston and H. Stephen Gardner

*Chapter 9 includes two sections. The first section by Randy Livingston empha-
sizes endowments, investing, tuition funding, and entrepreneurism in the future
university. The second section by H. Stephen Gardner focuses primarily on budgeting, commercialization, and investing.*

ENDOWMENTS, INVESTING, TUITION FUNDING,
AND ENTREPRENEURISM WITH RANDY LIVINGSTON

*Randy Livingston is vice president for business affairs and chief financial officer
of Stanford University. Livingston oversees the Controller's Office, Human Resources, Administrative Systems, Information Technology Services, Information
Security, Internal Audit and Institutional Compliance, Research Administration, Public Safety, Risk Management, Finance and Bondholder Relations, and
Business Development and Privacy.*

*From 1985 to 2001, Livingston worked with several emerging technology com-
panies in Silicon Valley as chief financial officer, in both corporate development
and marketing roles. He led two companies through IPOs, founded a company,
sold a company, and completed several acquisitions of still other companies. From
1999 to 2001, Livingston was executive vice president, CFO, and a director of*

This chapter is based on interviews I conducted with Randy Livingston on May 29, 2008,
and with H. Stephen Gardner on October 5, 2007, for this book.

OpenTV, an interactive television software company. Earlier in his Silicon Valley career, Livingston was director of corporate development at Apple Computer, and from there helped start a joint venture software company between Apple, IBM, and HP.

From 1979 to 1985, Livingston worked with McKinsey & Company as a management consultant based in their San Francisco office.

Livingston graduated with an MBA from Stanford in 1979. He also received his undergraduate degree from Stanford, in Mechanical Engineering, in 1975.

University Endowments and the Future

There are a number of financial trends that are becoming increasingly significant for top Association of American Universities (AAU) institutions. Chief among those is the reality that endowment investment returns have grown dramatically more important in financing these institutions. I believe that trend will continue over the next twenty-plus years.

State appropriations to top public research institutions have been declining in real terms since the late 1980s. Historically, we have seen steady growth in federal research, averaging about 2.3 percent per year in real terms, roughly proportional to growth in the overall economy. However, federal funding has declined in real terms over the past couple of years. There are so many other pressures on the federal budget that we can no longer depend as much on the government to support research, or to provide financial aid or fellowships and training grants for students. The areas that are taking up the slack are a combination of ongoing gifts coupled with the investment returns from endowments. These resources have already grown dramatically for the top institutions, and I think they will continue to do so over the next fifteen to twenty years.

It is critically important that institutions focus on building their endowment every year. Many institutions tend to focus their fund-raising efforts on periodic major campaigns, but the institutions that have been most successful are focused on adding gifts to their endowment as well as reinvesting returns year-in and year-out. Some institutions, like Princeton, have more than 50 percent of their operating costs funded from their endowment. We are coming into an era where baby boomers are retiring and moving into the part of their lives where people tend to be most generous in giving away their assets. This bodes very well for the potential to bring in new money.

Universities have been blessed with terrific investment returns over the last twenty years. I certainly can't predict that returns will continue at the same levels, but nonetheless, investment returns will be critically important in funding top research universities over the next twenty years.

Investing for the Future University

Strong investment management is absolutely crucial in building and managing an endowment. Very small differences in returns between institutions over fifteen or twenty years have enormous impact, and I can give you one example of that. We examined the investment returns of twenty of our peers from 1980 through 2007. The top institution had average returns of about 17.5 percent and the institution with the lowest returns averaged about 9.5 percent during that period. That's quite a wide difference of average returns over a long period of time. If you had $100 million of endowment at the beginning of that period compounded with the best return in the peer group, it would amount to $8 billion today. That same $100 million endowment compounded at the worst return of the peer group, would be a little more than $1 billion today. That really speaks to the power of compounding small differences. Even the difference of about 1 percent in investment returns over that time period today would represent about a 30 percent difference in the value of the principal twenty-seven years later. So the importance of top-notch investment management cannot be overstated.

Making safe investments takes on a whole new meaning in this context. Being too risk-averse can be costly. Institutions must find the right position on the risk-benefit curve. Some of the institutions that have been very aggressive have done well. Yale has been the exemplar—their returns under David Swenson have been phenomenal for more than twenty years. It can completely transform the institution. The difference in the investment returns that Yale has earned in comparison to their next highest performing peer is several billion dollars in current endowment. For institutions that already have decent endowments, there is no question that investment management is even more important than fund-raising. That would be true for many of the AAU institutions.

Public universities have come fairly late to focus on development and endowment management because they have been able to depend for so long on state financial support. That state support has been like an endowment. It provides a stream of income that the private institutions have not had. For example, the University of Washington received about $370 million last year in state appropriations for operations, which is equivalent to a 5 percent payout on a $7.4 billion endowment. However, state appropriations are declining when adjusted for inflation, while payout from endowments with strong investment returns has been growing. Public universities have to increase their focus on endowment and gift support instead of public funding if they're going to compete long term. Some of them are doing that very well. There are public institutions, such as the University of Wisconsin and UCLA, that have had terrific growth in their development efforts and rank among the top fifteen universities in annual gifts raised.

Advice for State Universities Building New Endowment Investment Accounts

The model that has been very successful for the top university endowments is to set up an independent investment management office, recruit top-notch investment management talent, provide appropriate compensation for the value they deliver to the institution, and emulate the diversified portfolio, fund-of-funds approach of top private institutions. Institutions like Yale, Stanford, Princeton, Duke, and Notre Dame are all good models.

One of the challenges that all of our investment offices have faced is how to retain good people. Once university investment managers are successful, the amount of money they can earn from hedge funds or in the private equity world is just astounding. It is very important to hire people who feel a strong sense of loyalty to the institution and who are willing to forgo maximizing their own compensation because they feel some greater calling in support of the institution. David Swenson is a great example. He has been at Yale for more than twenty years. Clearly he has had opportunities to make far more in the private sector, but really loves what he's doing at Yale. Finding that emotional tie to the institution is essential.

I think every major university except Harvard has adopted a fund-of-funds model where the role of the institutional management company is to allocate assets across different categories and then select managers to pick the individual securities or investments within those asset classes. That model seems to work very well across the board and is the norm today. Harvard still does some individual security selection internally, although I think they are now doing less of that than they used to.

The university's investment management company should have an advisory board or board of directors comprised of alumni and friends of the institution who have deep experience within various investment asset sectors. The board is very important in advising on asset allocation, identifying the best managed funds within the different investment segments, and sometimes in providing entry into hard to access funds. In the world of private equity, venture capital, hedge funds, natural resources, and real estate, there is tremendous need for sound advice; you don't want to be investing blindly in those segments. Being in the top funds is very important in terms of achieving good returns. Sometimes, getting into the top funds requires some kind of connection or contact. Also, being able to assess and evaluate the performance of the top funds over time requires good managers within the universities' investment management companies. Finally, investment portfolios are becoming much more global, and so having the knowledge and skills to look at investments across the world, and not just in the United States, is increasingly important.

Tuition Funding in the Future University

Tuition as a percentage of total revenues for top research institutions is already relatively small, less than 20 percent of consolidated revenues in many cases. However, it's a critical source of unrestricted funding for the university and therefore it is, in some ways, the most valuable revenue because it can be applied to any university expense. Whereas research revenue, endowment payout, and gift support are usually restricted to specific purposes, tuition revenue is much more flexible.

For the past two decades, stated or gross tuition has increased significantly faster than inflation. I think we're nearing the end of that era, if we have not reached it already. The stated tuition at top private institutions is formidable for any family, and I think political pressures will make it difficult for us to raise tuition much faster than inflation in the future. At the same time, top institutions have been dramatically increasing their financial aid to enable any family to send their children to college, irrespective of income. The definition of *need* is going to continue to evolve. Today, for example, with the financial aid programs that Harvard and Yale are offering, only 5 percent of American families are expected to pay full tuition. In other words, 95 percent of American families are eligible for some level of financial aid. This includes families with incomes up to $180,000 to $200,000 per year. The pressure to continue offering more aid to a wider band of students is very much with us. It is terrific from a family affordability standpoint. It will reduce a lot of the pressure that families have felt in deciding whether to send their children to college or in choosing between private and public institutions.

However, it does have other effects. A real challenge all universities face is sufficiency of unrestricted money to fund the internal administration of the institution, buildings for which gifts are not available, and some of the core humanities and academic areas for which it is hard to raise money. We will all feel a lot of pressure to find ways to generate new sources of unrestricted revenue.

Role of Entrepreneurism in the Future University

Stanford has long been a highly entrepreneurial university and I think that has been, and will continue to be, the secret to our success. We know that individual faculty will need to continue to find creative ways to gain financial support for their initiatives in order to maximize the growth of their own research. To me, part of entrepreneurship within an institution means that faculty members proactively take responsibility for their own funding. Historically, this was largely done in the engineering and sciences through proposals for federal research support, but increasingly faculty are raising gifts or creating affiliate programs to support their interests.

We are seeing a proliferation of laboratories, institutes, and centers focused around a group of faculty aiming to advance knowledge and leadership in specific areas. Depending on the situation, that topic or issue can generate financial support from outside donors or government institutions. One example at Stanford includes the Woods Institute for the Environment, which has faculty from a variety of different disciplines working on environmental sustainability. We have a similar institute in the international area, which looks at a variety of different global societal issues and problems. Stanford has a Center for the Study of the Novel that has attracted national interest from faculty who are interested in the novel as a focus of research. We have a Center for Longevity that examines the issues, problems, and opportunities that result from an aging global population.

One particularly successful center is what we call SCPD, the Stanford Center for Professional Development, which is a division within the School of Engineering. It started thirty or forty years ago as a way of providing continuing education to engineers working in Silicon Valley companies. Initially we provided technology for the engineers to sit in on classes via TV so we would essentially broadcast an engineering class. They could participate in it remotely, phone in questions, and get a master's degree through that route. SCPD has now evolved to an enormous enterprise, offering online courses and many more short certificated classes where people might spend several days, weeks, or months to earn credit. It's a variation on executive education, largely based online. It has been very successful and has seen a tremendous amount of growth.

We have dozens of these different institutes and centers. One of the challenges these centers and institutes create for the university is how they will intertwine with the traditional departments and school-based structures for faculty appointments, promotions, and funding. I think we haven't fully come to grips with that yet.

Continuing and workforce education programs can be high income-generating programs and a lot of top business schools have been at the forefront of this market, often running classes from a couple of days to a full year.

At the opposite end of that spectrum, we have what is called The Education Program for Gifted Youth, EPGY, which focuses on online classroom education for children from kindergarten through high school. You might think of this more as pre–higher education rather than continuing education. Johns Hopkins has a similar program, the Center for Talented Youth.

Typically, revenue from continuing education programs stays local, so part of their entrepreneurial nature is that they provide direct financial support to the various schools or departments in which they reside. In the case of the engineering school, the Center for Professional Development provides financial support directly to the School of Engineering. The GSB Executive Education program provides financial support for the Business School. In contrast tuition from regular degree-granting programs at Stanford for the most part still comes to the center. This differs by university. Some universities distribute their tuition out to the schools. Stanford, for the most part, has a centralized budget allocation process for tuition and other unrestricted revenue.

Any one of the centers, institutes, or continuing education ventures generates a relatively small amount of revenue, but together, they are more significant. I think of Stanford as a conglomerate with many $20 million businesses. We are a nearly $4 billion institution, but we have an enormous number of mini-enterprises within the grand enterprise.

Financial Advice for Future University Presidents

I would never cast myself as someone to give advice to university presidents. But, from the standpoint of the institution's financial well-being, I would say that the most important thing to worry about in terms of the future financial well-being of the institution is, by far, investment management. Second is building a very strong development or advancement organization, and working at that continuously. Third is focusing on, to the extent possible, building an efficient institution from an administrative and operational standpoint. That in part runs in the face of entrepreneurship, and this is something we struggle with all the time at Stanford—that to be entrepreneurial you have to be very decentralized. That means you have to have a high tolerance for duplication of administrative functions, and we do. Trying to find that balance between efficiency and affective entrepreneurship, striking the right balance, is going to be an ongoing challenge.

So, one of the challenges for the presidents of these institutions is trying to strike the right balance between encouraging entrepreneurship and building efficiency into the administrative operational structure of the university. They tend to work against each other.

Increasing Financial Efficiency in the Future University

I am always looking for ways to increase efficiency. We have a continuous process of looking for how can we make processes simpler and more efficient. The mission of my organization is to make administration more seamless and efficient so that the academic staff can focus their time on value-added activities.

Although we're going to make a stab at benchmarking against peers, it is incredibly difficult because everybody is organized differently. So looking at one controller's office versus another and saying "How many employees do you have?" is meaningless because in every institution the responsibility of that office is different. The same would be true of research administration, IT, and the core functions; it's very hard to do effective benchmarking. We look within ourselves and ask what we can do to address the *points of pain*. Complicating this issue are the increasing compliance requirements that are imposed on us by federal and state, and even local, authorities. Institutions are being asked to address a steady stream of new issues, report on them, and comply with various requirements. And while we are in favor of transparency, the administrative burden is huge.

Globalization

The other broader perspective impacting university finance is the importance of globalization. We are moving from an era where the American higher education system has viewed their milieu as other top American research universities. For the first time in many decades we are seeing significant investment in and development of new research in universities globally in China, India, Singapore, Korea, and the Middle East. We all need to rethink what our peer group is going to be twenty years from now. At the same time, our students and faculty are becoming dramatically more global. The whole world is becoming more portable, as Tom Friedman says in *The World is Flat*. We have already seen that 60 percent of our postdoctoral population comes from overseas. Globalization is going to flow both ways twenty years from now as more and more Americans build their careers in other countries and we have more people coming here. That is a very important trend that we all have to understand. It's much more than a financial issue.

BUDGETING, COMMERCIALIZATION, AND INVESTING
WITH H. STEPHEN GARDNER

H. Stephen Gardner is the Herman Brown Professor of Economics and director of the McBride Center for International Business at Baylor University. He holds a Ph.D. in economics from the University of California at Berkeley (see his extended biography in chapter 6).

Financial management of a modern university is a broad and complex task that includes budget planning and coordination, investment of endowment and other funds in a growing list of financial instruments, procurement and subcontracting, credit management (which may include interactions with financial intermediaries and direct participation in bond and other credit markets), payroll, cash, risk and foreign exchange management (increasingly important during periods of unstable exchange rates for institutions with large overseas programs), oversight of subsidiary enterprises and commercial operations, financial reporting, and many other activities. Here, I will touch on only a few of these topics.

Budgeting

The budgeting system of a university should be based on several broad principles. First, the system should be *realistic* and *reliable*. This means several things: (1) underlying forecasts should be based on reasonable or slightly pessimistic assumptions; (2) budgets should be prepared on a multiyear and multi-within-year basis to maintain the realism and consistency of long-term and short-term decisions; and (3) communications with all constituencies should be full, accurate, and credible—they should steer between "rosy scenarios" and "doom and gloom."

Second, the system should *reward* academic units that contribute to the broad mission and financial health of the university. This may mean, for example, that there's a direct and reliable link between student enrollment and budget authorizations. It may also mean avoidance of the inefficiencies caused by "use it or lose it" budgeting.

Third, when the budget is based on realistic assumptions and incorporates an effective system of rules and rewards, it should be possible to strengthen the *distributed financial authority* of the academic units. Deans and department chairs should be able to estimate, on their own, the benefits that will accrue from structural and curricular changes. Within their area of responsibility, they should be able to capture those benefits by reallocating expenditures from one budget category to another.

Although the majority of American universities continue to use centralized models of budget administration, at least fifty institutions have adopted distributed systems of budgeting and management that are variously known as "responsibility based" or "responsibility center" or "revenue center" or "value center" or "enrollment based." There are notable differences between these systems, but they usually share two important characteristics: (1) each major academic unit is allowed to retain and utilize the tuition revenue that it generates after payment of an overhead fee (or "tax") to the central administration to finance the general needs of the university, and (2) each major academic unit is responsible, in principle, for the compilation of its internal budget and for covering its own expenses. One of the most extreme versions of this program, with few cross-subsidies between academic units, was developed during the early nineteenth century at Harvard, where it was (and is) said that Every Tub must stand on its Own Bottom (ETOB).

I am a great believer in the decentralized and incentive-based approach, but systems of this kind must be introduced carefully. Generally, it is a good idea to phase in the program on a "no harm" basis—that is, the internal taxes and subsidies are structured to insure that each academic unit receives the same overall budget in year one that it would have received under the old centralized model, but its budget in year two will grow or decline according to enrollment or some other measure(s) of performance. Careful implementation also means that the centralized funds, collected through internal taxation, must be large enough to cover the collective needs of the university, including, for example, support of interdisciplinary programs that may be neglected by the individual units.

Careful implementation also means that the new procedures should be stable and credible (providing a basis for long-term decision-making), transparency, and relatively simple. Some universities have formulated elaborate procedures to allocate tuition revenues, and then have learned that it's better to use a simple formula based on semester hours. Likewise, attempts to allocate all overhead costs between the accounting units have imposed significant costs with little benefit. The University of Minnesota concluded a few years ago that the "budget model has become excessively complicated, which has led us away from the aspirations, goals and objectives of the original concept of Incentives for Managed Growth."

Critics of decentralized budgeting generally raise two objections. First, they claim that departments will have an incentive to offer narrow curricula and to dumb down their courses to attract more students and financial resources. Of course, grade inflation has been a problem under centralized budgeting systems, and maintenance of strong academic standards should be a high priority under any budgeting system. Universities that have introduced decentralized systems have not, to my knowledge, experienced a destructive form of competition for students. In the long run, "dumbing down" the curriculum is not an effective strategy for attracting high-ability students, either at the university or the departmental level.

Second, the critics of decentralized systems are concerned that they will short-change the general needs of the university, such as the library, and will not give the central administration the flexibility it needs to set priorities and solve problems. As noted before, it is important to maintain centralized funds that are sufficient to prevent this problem. In the end, however, a decentralized system should contribute to the financial health of the overall institution, and this should provide stronger support for its collective needs.

Commercialization

Commercialization is a topic that I've spent a fair amount of time thinking about and working on. One good program to study is the University of New Mexico, because they have a really interesting program for commercialization of technology working with the national laboratories. This is an example of the kind of cooperation that can exist across disciplines in a university because of effective commercialization.

The University of Texas (UT) at Austin has the IC^2 Institute, which George Kozmetsky, one of the founders of Teledyne Corporation and later dean of the business school at UT, set up when he retired. The IC^2 Institute focuses on commercialization of technology. Kozmetsky set up the Austin technology incubator, and through that he played a big role in getting Michael Dell started.

If you consider the histories of universities, stretching back to the Humboldt model at the University of Berlin, we have long believed that universities should play a role in both teaching and research. Now I see the development of a new university trinity, with teaching, research that goes on inside the universities, and also research that happens outside of universities in places like the national laboratories. The universities are playing a role in basic research and also in taking that research into practical application.

We have a study abroad program in Shanghai where Greg Leman from the Baylor University business school, who has a background in industry, works with Cynthia Fry from our Engineering School to take a group of business and engineering students to work on projects related to commercialization of technology alongside Chinese business and engineering students, working with companies in Shanghai. Our students are doing study abroad, working across cultures, languages, academic disciplines, and—at the same time—on this issue of commercialization of technology. So if you look at the whole picture of higher education, it is made up of teaching, research, and how you take that research into applications. In business schools, that means applications that are profitable. For universities, this is a vitally important area. It's a very American kind of thing, but again, it's been exported now to China and other countries. American universities, more than European or other universities, have always been a bridge, because they historically have had a closer tie with the business community than universities in other countries.

In our business school, we have a venture assistance program for innovators who want to find out whether their ideas are commercially viable or not. It's a way for our students to have connections directly with the local business community, to work on real problems, to serve the local community, and to generate the creation of brand new business, or the development of new commercial technologies. This also serves the financial needs of the university. It is a service that universities are now expected to perform for local communities, states, and the federal government. And again, we are now performing this role on a global level, because now the largest numbers of engineers are being trained not in the United States, but in China, India, and other places. We need to have the contact with the engineering talent in those other places, combining that with the innovative talent, and the market power of the United States.

Preparing for the Future

Higher education is going to grow ever more competitive than it is right now. Both domestically and internationally, we are facing competitive pressures from "for profit" educational providers, in-house educational providers, and from remote educational providers via distance education techniques. This is not a strictly financial issue. It is the growing competitive environment of higher education.

On the strictly financial side, I think there will be a move away from centralized systems of budgeting to more rational systems of budgeting in universities. In the long run, when you are under more and more competitive pressure, rationality tends to win out.

Investing

In terms of the investment side of the financial system in the United States and the world in this global financial market, there is a growing complexity to that system that means an ever-increasing number of financial instruments to choose between. There will be growing securitization and other wider ranges of assets so there is more diversification and more stability, depending on the investment. If all the eggs are in one basket, all things go the way of that particular basket. Mainly, I see a positive side to these changes. There will be the ability to diversify both across different grades of investment instruments and geographically across countries. If the whole financial system develops the way I think it will, we will end up eventually with the U.S. dollar as a strong currency, the Euro continuing to develop as a reserve instrument, and eventually some Asian currency, possibly the Renminbi in China, developing in the same way.

It will also be possible to diversify across currencies, so when there is movement of exchange rates across the world, there is not as much risk of loss as currently exists. All of that means that there is opportunity, depending on what particular basket one's eggs are in, because you've got some baskets that are going to be unstable. There is an opportunity to diversify in a way that will provide a lot more stability.

At the same time, universities are not only interested in stability. They are also interested in return, and so the value to universities of effective investments and modes of handling those investments increases. To compete with other universities, it will be critical to have people who have a better understanding of that.

Hopefully, board members are able to evaluate all of this and set reasonable goals for those investments, because if you're pushing your investment people into riskier returns, one thing that won't go away is the risk-return tradeoff. There may be higher returns on riskier assets, but many universities are already in riskier assets than universities have traditionally trusted. There is going to be pressure to push that envelope further. It is important to have realistic expectations, an ability to assess the level of risk that the university has taken on in its investments, and to keep that in some reasonable balance.

Chapter 10

Advancement in the Future University

with Ronald D. Vanden Dorpel

Ronald D. Vanden Dorpel is senior vice president for university advancement at Brown University, where he directs a $1.4 billion comprehensive campaign. Previously, he was the vice president for university development and alumni relations at Northwestern University, where he planned and successfully executed a $1.56 billion campaign.

Vanden Dorpel received a B.A. in history from The Ohio State University in 1969 and an A.M. in history from Brown in 1971. He has twenty-nine years of progressively responsible experience in the development/advancement field at three institutions: Brown, Northwestern, and Yale.

OVERVIEW OF UNIVERSITY DEVELOPMENT

Development, resource development, or what is now frequently called institutional advancement, all essentially mean those programs that raise financial support and understanding for a college or university. As an enterprise, it is a post–World War II phenomenon. It started, of course, with the major private colleges and universities.

My experience is entirely with private universities. Before I came to Brown, I was vice president for development and alumni relations at Northwestern University, and spent fifteen years in that position. Prior to that, I was at Yale University, and prior to that, I was back at Brown. Yale was one of the earliest to have something called the "Alumni Fund." That

---

This chapter is based on an interview I conducted with Ronald D. Vanden Dorpel on April 23, 2008, for this book.

dated back to 1891. Yale alumni got together, raised money, and then voted on an annual gift to the university. There was this real sense among alumni that it was part of one's obligation as a graduate of Yale, Brown, or Northwestern to give a gift every year, which then expanded to talking to alumni about their estates.

The tax laws were changed in 1969 to make it more advantageous to make charitable gifts to universities, hospitals, and other not-for-profits. These laws created special types of charitable remainder trusts that helped institutions build their endowments. It is interesting that most of the great endowments in this country were really created by bequests, as opposed to outright gifts. It is a relatively new phenomenon, dating from the 1970s and 1980s, for people to make large outright gifts to endowments. Concurrent with cutbacks of state support, state universities have also created separate foundations to raise and receive gifts and to invest endowments. State universities now continue to raise funds very effectively and are clearly the equal of their private counterparts.

So philanthropy has become a major enterprise for all of higher education, and continues to grow today. It continues to be the institutional revenue that is seen as not quite finite. It is in fact finite, but it's often deemed by administrators to be infinite! There is only so much indirect cost revenue we can recover. The federal government is being more stingy on indirect cost rates. Tuition increases are limited by market forces and our endowment spending rules are prudent. Really, the only source of additional revenue is increased fund-raising. So it is certainly a growth industry for every institution and promises to be so in the future in a big way.

There are some cautionary concerns. The make-up of our alumni bodies is changing in a variety of ways. That will change the mix in the primary prospect constituency, which is the alumni body. Will the alumni have the same commitment to our institutions as previous generations? Will they have the same sense of identity with their class at places like Brown, Yale, or Northwestern? Will they understand the role of philanthropy in the development of American society? All these are interesting questions.

I don't think any institution is trying to address the importance of philanthropy with its undergraduates. There are courses in philanthropy and social philanthropy, but there's not a lot of talk about it with enrolled students by university administrations. At Brown, we start talking to students at the end of their junior year, about forming the senior class committee and creating a senior class gift operation. This has been remarkably successful. We have had close to 70 percent participation since 2002, but that drops off to about 35 to 40 percent, during their first five years out of college. This is still good but our constant effort is to improve our percentage of alumni participation. In the 2007 *U.S. News and World Report*, Brown ranks about as high as one can get in the alumni giving metric. We are seventh in alumni participation in giving. There are just a few places that are better. It is still a challenge and it remains a challenge broadly through all of American higher education. So one caution, as we look to the future, is what will our support group look like? Will our constituencies have the same sense of giving back?

Some believe that we should deemphasize annual giving and instead put our resources into raising major gifts and principal gifts (which have been defined as gifts of $5 million and more). All big campaigns—and we're in one at the moment with a $1.4 billion goal—are largely dependent on raising about 90 percent of the dollars from 3 percent of the donors. So there's a heavy emphasis on bringing in very large gifts. In our current campaign to date, we have solicited and received two $100 million gifts, which are the two largest gifts in Brown's history. We have also had one $60 million gift and seven at $10–25 million. In an effort to raise such large gifts, the question for the future is, "Will people have the wherewithal to make such large gifts?" Thus far in the United States, the economy has created great wealth. Some people may disagree about the way it was created, but nevertheless, a hedge fund manager who can buy a $100 million work of art can also give a $100 million gift. The magnitude of those numbers was hitherto unheard of in higher education philanthropy, but they should continue to exist and be the objective for many institutions.

All told, I think there is a very bright future for the role of advancement in the future university. The tradition of giving and volunteering from the founding days of the university may not continue in exactly the same ways, but it is a concept that has to be guarded and nourished. Higher education and other not-for-profits have to be alert also to what public policy might do to effect philanthropy, making sure that federal and state policy always tries to encourage philanthropy and not discourage it.

CHANGES IN HIGHER EDUCATION ADVANCEMENT/ FUND-RAISING IN TWENTY-PLUS YEARS

My sense is that fund-raising is going to grow, and institutions are going to be increasingly reliant on it for providing not only more money to build endowments, but also money for the basic operating budget. Our challenge is always to raise large amounts every year in pure, unrestricted support that can be spent in any way. This year our goal was $35 million. That takes tremendous effort. To get there, you have to raise a couple of $1 million total expendable gifts within a fiscal year. Such large, expendable gifts are going to continue to be challenges. There is a limit, but we're not sure where it is. Princeton brought in $41 million last year and they were the best in the country in unrestricted annual giving. We raised $34 million and we continue to be optimistic about increasing annual giving by five percent or more each year. But it's like building a sand castle and having the waves wash it away at the end of the year, then having to build it up bigger and higher each subsequent year. It seems to me that there has to be a limit to that.

The question of public policy and endowments is now being raised in Congress. It has had a chilling effect on those of us who are amongst the 135 institutions that Senator Baucus and Senator Grassley "invited" to submit defenses on how we invest and spend our endowments. As ACE past-president David Ward has said, leaders in Congress are getting so much pressure in their states because of rising state university tuitions that they're lashing out; they think that if colleges and universities spend more money from their endowment, such spending will somehow help flatten tuition levels. It's just not true. Higher education, which used to be a labor-intensive enterprise, is now a capital-intensive enterprise, especially for institutions doing research.

We, along with nearly all of the major leading private colleges and universities in the Council on Financing Higher Education (COFHE), voluntarily restrained tuition this year because of the scrutiny of Congress. The average tuition increase was about 4.7 percent last year. This year it is less than 4 percent. There hasn't been much in the way of inflation, yet we have had to raise our cost higher than the rate of inflation, so that presents a real challenge.

In the future, fund-raising is going to be more at the center of what institutions do. We are all going to reach some limits, because the philanthropic marketplace is very competitive and colleges and universities have had a dominant philanthropic position over the years, at least since the end of World War II. That may change. Whether hospitals will continue to be important recipients of philanthropy will depend greatly on how we finance health care. There are similar concerns for cultural institutions like museums and performing arts organizations.

Again, I worry about our donor and prospect constituencies as we move forward. I don't know what's to come. I don't have a crystal ball. The past is prologue and I can look at the past twenty years and see how philanthropy has grown and become a big business with statistics that are the rival of any sales marketing staff that you can find in a mid-size corporation.

There has been a shift in the composition of our staff as well. When I came into this business in 1979, our staff was about 80 percent men. That has completely reversed. Seventy-five percent of my staff are now women. We pay good salaries, but the nature of the business especially attracts women with families, and those who want a career that meshes with their family life. That has been one major and very positive change.

The way money is raised is one thing that does not change. I quoted to one of our trustees recently something that Benjamin Franklin said when he was asked how to raise funds. Franklin said, "In the first place I advise you to apply to all those whom you know will give something; next, to those whom you are uncertain whether they will give anything or not, and show them the list of those who have given; and lastly, do not neglect those whom you are sure will give nothing, for in some of them you may be mistaken." Franklin reported that his questioner took his advice "for he asked everybody, and he obtained a much larger sum that he expected." We have a motto around here, "Ask or all is lost." That's actually a wonderfully productive philosophy of fund-raising.

The other philosophy that is as true now as when it was written are the four phases of securing a gift. The first is *identification*. You identify the prospect. The second is *interest*. You might interest them in the institution. The third is to go beyond interest and get them *involved*, and then finally you get them to make an *investment*. These are the four "I"s: identification, interest, involvement, and investment. These phases and pursuing them effectively are as important today as they ever were.

What is manifestly different today is what we used to call the "dotcom generation" or the "new philanthropists." They see their gifts as more of an investment, so they want solid evidence of outcomes and return on investment. People who have managed development in our institutions are not quite experienced in providing such evidence, at least not in the way that is done in the corporate sector, so we are having to learn. Stewardship, therefore, is a big part of what we do. On the theory that "your best donor is your past donor," being sure that he or she is satisfied with what you have done by way of your annual reporting is vitally important. For example, we have about eight hundred endowed scholarship funds at Brown. We write a detailed report to each of the living donors or descendants of donors about what their scholarship students are doing. We include letters from the students, financial reports on how much the endowment is earning, and what the total payout rate is. These usually amount to six- or seven-page reports. I can only imagine that stewardship of gifts is going to become an even bigger issue in the future.

I cannot emphasize enough that I don't think fund-raising methodology has really changed. We do discuss fund-raising on the Internet, of course. It really has had an effect for certain charities after major disasters, like the American Red Cross after Katrina, and for certain political campaigns, but it is not the rule. There still has to be a personal touch to philanthropy. There still has to be identification, interest, involvement, and investment, and you don't tend to get that online. Philanthropy is fundamentally not a business transaction. It is an emotional and philanthropic transaction. It is something that benefits someone. It is the transaction without a tangible quid pro quo.

I would hope that philanthropy continues in American society to be this uniquely American thing. The Europeans talk to us all the time and say, "We can't quite make it work the way you do." The British remind me that philanthropy started in America in the colonies. I respond that the colonies were diverse and there were other philanthropic traditions including those of the Dutch, the Swedes, and the Jews. There were all sorts of religious entities that didn't thrive in England and brought their philanthropic spirit to America.

There are clearly things that are unique about our system. I think that over the years we have proven that if you want to improve society, one of the ways to do it is to make a gift to a university where people can be taught. There is an old adage that you can buy a hungry man a fish to satisfy his hunger but if you teach him *how* to fish he can feed himself for the rest of his life. I think that's what universities tend to do. They offer unique hope for future generations.

Expected Future Changes in Stewardship

I would say we will see a demand for more and more accountability. It's not that we're not accountable now, but there may be an expectation for more detailed information. We may be bucking up against privacy laws when it comes to information about students and the information that students are willing to provide, because there is no obligation in these scholarships that says you have to tell the donor exactly what you are interested in and what you want to do.

Our president, Ruth Simmons, is a Texan and the daughter of a sharecropper. She was the youngest of fourteen and the only one to go to college. She received a scholarship to Dillard University, which is a historically black college in New Orleans. President Simmons has a very powerful testimony. At a recent scholarship luncheon she said, "You know, the one thing I love about this luncheon is that you Champlain scholars get to meet the philanthropists who gave you the scholarship. I will never know, and I have no idea who gave the scholarship to send me to Dillard University, but I would love to tell them what's become of me. I would love to write their relatives." The most powerful thing about philanthropy to higher education may be the ability of someone to affect the life and career of someone else by providing a way to get an education, to better themselves, and to better society. It's a very powerful concept.

Our current campaign had a goal of $300 million in undergraduate scholarship endowment, and we are at $240 million with thirty-two months left to go in the campaign. Now we are doing something very bold. We are going to add another $100 million to that $300 million and try to raise $400 million in scholarship endowment before the campaign ends on December 31, 2010. That is going to take some doing, but we have simply got to do it because the only way we are going to perpetuate and solidify financial aid for all time is to endow it. Princeton actually gets close to 90 percent of their undergraduate financial aid budget from their scholarship endowment. We get about 40 percent, but at the beginning of our campaign we only got 22 percent from endowment. The rest had to come from the general operating budget. Next year Brown will give away $70 million in undergraduate financial aid. That includes the amount of money we had to add to the budget to eliminate loans.

Another concern for the future is litigation. There is a huge case at Princeton involving the Robertson family, which gave the endowment for the Woodrow Wilson School at Princeton. That endowment has grown to almost a billion dollars. The Robertson family is saying that Princeton has misused the endowment and they want it back. Both sides have spent millions of dollars in legal fees. It's that kind of thing that really has a chilling effect on philanthropy and donor interests.

To be sure, there are certain things that academic freedom demands that we can never compromise on with donors. One is, for instance, selecting the holder of an endowed chair. You don't get the right to name who will hold the chair. Some donors try to put restrictions on the position to control it from the grave. They may want to make sure that no Marxist economist ever holds the endowed economics chair that bears their name.

Again, these are all stewardship issues, and there has been a lot written about how colleges and universities are not living up to the agreements they have with donors. Every once in a while something like the Robertson case comes along and stirs things up, and perhaps rightly so. In my thirty years in advancement, I have seen how, through necessity, institutions have stretched the terms of gifts to endowments. There will be more scrutiny on such issues.

On balance, I think it's a good thing for donors to be involved and to scrutinize our institutions. That is one way that donors build confidence in us. The worst thing is for colleges and universities, and especially university presidents, to say, "Now, we know better than you do. We know how to do this." That's absolutely the worst thing to say to a donor, to Congress, or to any interested party. It's much better to engage them, and to explain how you're using their gift, and how you think it complies and comports with what they believe.

ADVICE FOR ADMINISTRATORS OF THE FUTURE

The first thing I would tell future administrators is that philanthropy is *not* a necessary evil. It is something that they should learn to enjoy doing. Indeed, the first thing they ought to do is become philanthropic themselves. When I first got into this business, I believed that the senior administrators I worked with, whether they were deans, or provosts, or presidents, didn't solicit well, because they themselves were not philanthropic. They found it distasteful. They did not like to be asked to make a gift, and, therefore they didn't want to ask someone else to make a gift. Administrators have to eschew that attitude completely.

I cannot imagine either a public or a private university appointing someone to the position of president or chancellor these days who is not comfortable with fund-raising. That should be an automatic disqualifier for any of these positions. This is not to say that all of a leader's time must be devoted to fund-raising, but it is essential to develop a conviction that one is not asking for himself, but rather is sincerely seeking the betterment of the institution. And if one believes in that institution, there is really no higher calling.

One could argue that the greatest living American philanthropist was John D. Rockefeller Jr., the son of the founder of Standard Oil, who graduated from Brown in the class of 1897. He was a good Baptist, and he tithed. He was an extraordinary philanthropist. He did most of it anonymously. When you think of his giving, he started Colonial Williamsburg, the United Way, Rockefeller University, the United Negro College Fund, and he gave massive support to the University of Chicago and Brown. He was an excellent fund-raiser and had a wonderful philosophy of asking for a gift. He really "got it." He gave of himself, and he did not mind asking others.

My fundamental point is that presidents have to take Rockefeller's attitude. Some presidents can do it and some cannot. Probably the ones who cannot are just shy, and they just cannot quite come to grips with the personal nature of a one-on-one solicitation. The presidents I have worked for have said, either boldly, or through their actions, that, "I'm really the chief development officer for the institution; I have to pick up that mantle; that has got to be one of my primary duties if I want to advance the institution." Presidents that do it well always tend to get along with the faculty, because they can look at their faculty and say, "I'm out there fund-raising for you. I'm raising chairs. I'm establishing centers. I'm building buildings."

Lastly, presidents need to support the development staff in whatever ways they can. It is important that, once an institution has reached a new plateau in fund-raising, they use that as a springboard to the next level.

The way to do that is *not* to cut back on staff and resources following a campaign. Some places are obviously under lots of pressure to do that. It's an easy thing for presidents to do, to say to the faculty that they have reduced a third of the people in the development office campus because it is more important that we invest in the faculty.

CHALLENGES FOR FUTURE PHILANTHROPY

Looking to the future, there will be certain principles and paradigms for fund-raising that are not likely to change just because of the nature of it. Both institutions and philanthropy have endured all sorts of threats and challenges over the years.

One of our challenges now is to become more international. We have international alumni. We have pockets of wealth in South Asia, East Asia, Hong Kong, and in Western Europe. They all tend to be prosperous. I think the challenge for us will be international fund-raising, as we become a more international university. But raising funds outside the United States is decidedly different. There is not the same understanding of philanthropy everywhere. In some places, it is more of a quid pro quo transaction. I learned this years ago when I was at Northwestern. The dean of the Kellogg School of Management and I met with two ranking executives (one Japanese, one American) from a large bank in Japan. The bank had decided to establish endowed chairs in finance at the leading American graduate schools of business. They identified Harvard, Stanford, Northwestern, MIT, and Penn to give $2.5 million each. The Japanese gentleman looked at us and said that there was one more thing they wanted: two guaranteed admission places for their best junior executives in the Kellogg MBA class each year. The dean immediately said, "Never." The American banker turned to his Japanese colleague and said, "See, I told you they wouldn't do it. That's not the way philanthropy works in the United States."

CONCLUSION

Every time we slip into a recession, we get the same prediction that a lot of colleges and universities are going to go under. But when we come out of the recession, we see that not many places have actually closed. Institutions of higher education are remarkably resilient. In fact, they are among the oldest institutions in the western world. Financial distress is almost a requirement. If you are in financial stress as an institution, you've really got to think creatively about fund-raising. But you clearly need to do other things, too. You have to think about marketing and enrollment management, but philanthropy has to be a major piece of it. The best way is to view it is as a comprehensive strategy to raise the institution: part philanthropy, part enrollment management, part curricular development. You have to move forward on all fronts.

So, that's what I would say to future leaders. Don't give up. Keep swinging. Take a multifaceted approach to what you want to do and keep hoping that it is going to work—because it almost certainly will.

Chapter 11

Continuing Education, Workforce Training, and Lifelong Learning

with Andrew L. Meyer

Andrew L. Meyer is vice president for learning at Anne Arundel Community College in Maryland. He is a past president of the National Council for Continuing Education and Training (NCCET), an affiliated council of the American Association of Community Colleges (AACC). He currently serves as the Corporate Liaison for NCCET.

Meyer was a contributing author for Developing the World's Best Workforce: An Agenda for America's Community Colleges *(1997) and has coauthored "Community Colleges and Workforce Training: Past Performance and Future Directions" in* The Maryland Association for Higher Education Journal *(Vol. 18, October 1995).*

Meyer was the 1999 recipient of the NCCET national leadership award for exemplary service and the 2001 recipient of the NCCET national leadership award/inside the field. He currently is vice chairman of the Board of Directors of Anne Arundel Workforce Development Corporation. In July of 2007, Meyer was elected chairman of the board of directors of the Global Corporate College.

OVERVIEW OF CONTINUING EDUCATION, WORKFORCE DEVELOPMENT, AND LIFELONG LEARNING

Continuing education and workforce development have continued to grow significantly over the past several decades. These are the pieces that make complete the comprehensive nature of the community college.

This chapter is based on an interview I conducted with Andrew L. Meyer on April 22, 2008, for this book.

Traditional transfer programs, credit occupational programs, and related learning activities are put in place for our community via open enrollment continuing education classes. Workforce development often focuses on contract training and working directly with business and industry.

What is happening at many institutions, including Anne Arundel, is that there has been an emphasis on blurring the lines between credit and noncredit, as well as on learning in general. The focus is no longer centered on whether a student is enrolled in credit courses or noncredit courses. There is a simultaneous emphasis on credit and noncredit courses for both lifelong learning and workforce development.

The University

All community colleges are involved in continuing education and workforce development. However, that is much less frequently the case for baccalaureate colleges and universities. Some universities have taken a proactive role in setting up colleges or schools of continuing studies, where others have not explored the continuing education world. In Anne Arundel County, along with Anne Arundel Community College, we have the Naval Academy and St. John's College, two institutions that play a minimal role in continuing education and workforce development, which, for the most part, makes us the only game in town. However, in other cities like Boston, there are other community colleges, such as Bunker Hill Community College, as well as baccalaureate colleges and universities, some of which do a lot in continuing education. I think that the community colleges have solidified their role as the provider of contract training. I am unaware of any universities that are doing much contract training.

Why universities are not more involved is a question that I cannot answer. I often think that if I had a role to play after my community college life, I would seek out a university that was interested in developing a more aggressive continuing education program, generating new revenue, and serving the community at the same time. I think the level of involvement for any institution is often mission driven. Most universities only see themselves as being institutions that prepare people for baccalaureate or graduate degrees.

There are potential opportunities for university partnerships with various entities; for example, the university and the community college could partner with a company that wants to provide a baccalaureate degree beyond the associate degree that a community college may provide.

The focus on Continuing Education and Workforce Development at Anne Arundel is so large that it includes nearly one-third of the college's full-time enrollments (FTEs)—this is one-third of the total instructional contact hours—and employs more than 140 administrators and professional staff including deans, executive directors, directors, assistant directors, and coordinators. So, Anne Arundel has made an incredible commitment to continuing education.

Current Trends

One of the growing areas for Anne Arundel is continuing professional education, which includes mandatory continuing education for the professions. We monitor professional requirements very closely and begin programs when the state legislature in Maryland changes CPE requirements. English as a second language is also rapidly growing, as is instruction in adult basic skills. Increasing emphasis is being placed on online instruction in Continuing Education where demand is rising steadily.

Another ever-growing demand is from the senior population. More and more students who come to Anne Arundel are sixty and older.

In 1989, there were approximately 1,700 FTEs here in continuing education compared with 4,000 in 2008. In our area, this translates to about 35,000 students a year, and approximately 100,000 individual enrollments a year.

Lifelong learning is perhaps the most dramatically changing aspect of continuing education. Many of us who were in the field very early foresaw the potential growth in lifelong learning, but now we are seeing people returning to the community colleges. This has also resulted in the biggest change in overall community college enrollment patterns. We use the term "access" to talk about making higher education accessible to high school students or returning adults for degree programs or certificates. I think we now have a broadened definition of accessibility; it has been expanded to relate to responding to the needs of all learners at all ages. The comprehensive community college continues to respond very quickly to the needs of the community.

CONTINUING EDUCATION, WORKFORCE, AND LIFELONG LEARNING IN THE FUTURE

Continuing Education, Workforce Development, and Lifelong Learning will all have more of a global focus in the future. This expanded focus will challenge both the traditional recruitment boundaries of the university and the service delivery boundaries of the community college. Most people perceive the community college as serving a county or multicounty region. There is evidence already that the boundaries for delivering services will be far more expansive, which will require the governance structures, including the trustees of these organizations, to understand and embrace a broader mission.

There will be an expansion of partnerships, certainly among community colleges but also among universities. I'm involved in a very exciting project called the Global Corporate College where we're putting together a network of community colleges to deliver workforce development contract training for companies who have a national and international presence. This initiative will generate more revenue and leverage existing resources for the partnering colleges. It will build the capacity of a college to be involved nationally or internationally and, in some cases, use those same resources on the local level. We will be working with institutions who want to build capacity to do more across the spectrum of continuing education and workforce development.

We have eleven founding members who created the Global Corporate College in April of 2006, and our mission is to close the talent gap both in America and around the world by working with national and international companies. For example, a company in Anne Arundel County that we have worked with for many years also has locations throughout the United States and around the world. We can refer them to the Global Corporate College, which has a mechanism to deliver that same high-quality, standardized training to all of their incumbent workers throughout their various global locations. We have had tremendous interest from manufacturing, banking, retail, and companies who recognize that the community colleges can best deliver the contract training. Thus far, we are the best entity to deliver contract training for incumbent workers and corporations are recognizing that the Global Corporate College could be a one-stop shop for them for virtually all of their training. With commitments from colleges in nearly forty states, the network is already in a good position to deliver most national locations.

Credentialing and Certifications

We have increasingly become a credentialing society and I think that growth will continue. We have placed a lot of value on college degrees. We will see expansions in industry standards with subsequent increases in required certifications. We saw this in information technology (IT), and I believe we will see it in emerging new fields such as the production of green and renewable energy. Although some renewable energy programs exist, the field has not yet fully developed. The field will include many areas, such as wind, solar, and wave energy, which will all require technician training that we can provide to prepare people to manufacture, assemble, repair, and maintain products and equipment related to the industry. Additional preparation courses will be required in the sciences, mathematics, and basic engineering. I think there will be a whole new interdisciplinary opportunity for the training of these technicians to make them more adaptable. There are some jobs that aren't on the horizon yet, but they will be related to this bigger initiative that many people are calling renewable energies.

New technology-related fields are emerging constantly. When everything was becoming computerized in automobiles, colleges and proprietary schools dramatically changed how they trained automotive mechanics. Now they're called technicians. Who knows what the automobile is even going to look like as we progress with hybrids, which would obviously require different types of skills from what we're currently teaching.

For the future, I am most focused on renewable energy and information system security. Cyber-crime is a significant emerging area. There will be innovations that will take cyber-crime to new levels, requiring new programs and vigilance with the new technology needed to ward off cyber-crime.

Homeland security will remain another viable programming area. It will include the current basic programs, but also in higher levels such as intelligence analytics, as one example. We're sensitive to these programs at Anne Arundel because the National Security Agency is in our backyard.

There will be a heavy emphasis on career changers. We have left behind the paradigm of working for the same company for thirty-five years. More and more people are moving from one company to another and, even more importantly for higher education, many are moving from one career to another. In some cases, they may already have the baccalaureate degree, master's degree, or even a Ph.D., but they will need to be retooled and re-skilled. This is likely to increase.

Additionally, I think we will see more emphasis on cross-cultural and world language competencies. There is enormous interest in world languages, especially in languages that are less commonly taught, like Arabic, Russian, and Chinese. These are all classes at our college where we now offer multiple sections each semester. There will be a greater emphasis on surviving in a more global environment, and that will necessitate Americans, in particular, becoming more multicultural in their own areas of expertise or awareness.

The final emerging areas would relate to health and human services. This would include advances in technology and how we're going to be training at higher levels in the health professions. What is that going to mean for the updating of the curriculum and the acquisition of more advanced technology in order to train to the standards we will find in doctors' offices, hospitals, and clinics? This area will intersect with general innovations in technology.

The enrollments in the continuing education programs are going to equal or exceed the traditional credit enrollment.

The Role of the Government

Government will become involved in higher education in more and more ways. We will need to have a proactive U.S. Department of Labor, which we have seen to some degree, particularly as it relates to the community colleges. The U.S. Department of Labor sees community colleges as the primary provider of workforce development. We will need more support for our colleges on the state level. States must recognize them as economic development engines. In bad economic times, we should be receiving support to return people into the workforce and for retraining people for new and emerging technologies.

The Role of Business

Business needs to become more involved in the K–12 systems, the feeder systems for community colleges and universities. They can participate in a curriculum advisory capacity, taking some of their best people who are career changers and working with school systems and local teacher preparation programs to move people into second careers in teaching, particularly in math, science, and engineering. Fortunately, we're beginning to see that happen, but it needs to happen more consistently.

Business has a role to play in helping the higher education institutions maintain a certain level of currency with technology, particularly given the cost and ever-changing landscape of technology. This is not happening consistently or in a broad geographic way. Many colleges and universities could do a better job in expressing to business and industry their specific technological needs and how they could help support curriculum.

The Role of Distance Learning

I think we will see a proliferation in the number of products that colleges and universities put online for learners. If we don't, we are going to run into competition with other organizations and associations who will be doing that, competition that could actually take the community college or the university out of the market. One example would be within the professional associations: I would much prefer to collaborate with the Maryland paralegal group on their continuing education and training needs rather than turn to the professional association to fill those educational needs alone.

When "Education to Go" first came to the National Council for Continuing Education and Training (NCCET), to begin working with the community colleges, I helped to broker that initial relationship. I told them that the idea was wonderful, but they needed to make a commitment to work through the community colleges and not compete with them. The community college could broker the Education to Go programs and both would profit.

What Will Disappear?

At the risk of sounding negative, I do wonder how some colleges and small universities are going to survive given the encroachment of other institutions and other organizations on their primary markets. We just interviewed a candidate for a VP position who told us that a school in Cleveland closed because it was no longer financially viable. I'm wondering how the higher education landscape of the future is going to look when a number of existing colleges may not be around.

ADVICE FOR UNIVERSITIES AND COLLEGES

I recommend that colleges and universities look for nontraditional revenue streams, and by that I mean what's nontraditional in the university's history. Continuing education would be a traditional revenue stream for most community colleges, but it could be a nontraditional revenue stream for a university or college that hasn't fully developed continuing education, workforce development, or lifelong learning.

Particular areas that might be a natural opportunity for smaller colleges and universities would be continuing professional education. Why say goodbye to your graduates just because they get a baccalaureate or a master's degree? Why not look for programs that would be of interest to them, and would bring them back? For example, looking at professional schools like law or social work or pharmacy, a college could carve a niche for itself in terms of the graduates who need to come back and be recertified, relicensed, or who just need CEUs. At the same time, it could strengthen alumni relationships.

Campus satelliting could bring to the table more resources that could expand the role of the colleges, if efficiently managed. I think colleges have been more successful when they have amplified their mission rather than retracted it, but it is a very fine balance. You can't be all things to all people, but you can build instructional programs that attract populations, and that can be done very efficiently. It doesn't all have to be done with full-time faculty and cadres of administrators. I've said for years that the most efficient FTE in the community college is the continuing education FTE.

For the future, there must be full engagement in environmental scanning. There needs to be more than just an institutional research office that is determining what the future is going to look like, or what is happening out in the environment that's going to have an impact on our future. We have created an Institute for the Future at Anne Arundel. We have faculty, staff, and individuals from the community who meet regularly to look at future trends and issues.

We are connected with the World Future Society, the organization based in Washington, D.C., that, in more formal ways, looks at future trends. This is one way to be proactive. We did it because we're very involved in strategic planning and interested in factoring in, from as many people as possible, all of the trends that we need to pay attention to. The decision to participate was faculty-driven. Core faculty are the champions and executors of where the Institute for the Future is going. Among the faculty involved are sociologists and business and technology faculty members. We have people in the community who might be associated with certain agencies that have an interest in this. There is a lot of interest among other community colleges in what we are doing in the Institute for the Future. Our people regularly speak at national conferences or do consulting with colleges throughout the country.

ADVICE FOR HIGHER EDUCATION LEADERS

Higher education leaders need to make sure they have individuals who are very open to entrepreneurial ways of doing business. I think you're going to see more continuing education and workforce development administrators become college presidents because of the track record they have established in meeting the needs of the communities they serve by being entrepreneurial. It is a very important aspect of leadership in this day and age to be able to be responsive, proactive, and to look at generating resources differently. Everybody thinks we're "not for profit." I use the word "profit" all the time. There needs to be a new skill set with leaders. There has been totally different focus on entrepreneurship and translating that into other programs throughout the institution.

CONCLUSION

I do believe that, with the change of leadership due to shifting demographics and with the aging of college administrators, we are going to see a new type of college or university leader who is going to be very entrepreneurial and who looks for opportunities for collaboration, partnering, and cooperation. These leaders will move their institutions to be more cutting-edge and more concerned about what's going on in their environment and in the world, rather than being insular to their particular campuses. We are entering a new era in higher education.

Chapter 12

Higher Education Marketing

with Karen Fox

Karen Fox is an internationally recognized expert on marketing for educational institutions. She is the coauthor, with Philip Kotler, of the leading guide in the field, Strategic Marketing for Educational Institutions *(1985 and 1995), which has been translated and published in Japan and Brazil. A third book on "marketing for the new world of higher education" is scheduled to be released in 2010. She has advised higher education institutions in Mexico, Russia, and Singapore, as well as in the United States.*

Her marketing-related articles have appeared in Journal of Marketing, Journal of Marketing Research, Marketing Theory, European Business Review, Planning for Higher Education, Journal of Marketing Education, *and others.*

Fox received her Ph.D. from Stanford University. Before joining the Santa Clara University faculty in 1980, she was a professor at Teachers College, Columbia University, and at Northwestern University. Fox has worked extensively overseas as a consultant on health-related social marketing programs and marketing for nonprofit organizations. She is the coauthor of the first book on social marketing in the Russian language. She is the recipient of four Fulbright grants, and taught at the École Supérieure de Commerce, Rouen, France; the Faculty of Management of St. Petersburg State University, Russia; and the Plekhanov Russian Academy of Economics in Moscow.

Fox is an associate professor in the Department of Marketing at Santa Clara University.

This chapter is based on interviews I conducted with Karen Fox on April 8 and 16, 2008, for this book.

HISTORICAL HIGHLIGHTS
OF HIGHER EDUCATION MARKETING

Marketing higher education is not a recent innovation. Promotion, one component of marketing, has been around for millennia. Two thousand years ago the Greek sophists strolled in the marketplace, displaying their eloquence and skills of argumentation to attract students to them. In the late 1860s, Iowa Agricultural College and Model Farm, the precursor of Iowa State University, sent out recruiters to explain the value of formal education in farming techniques to rural young people. In 1869, Harvard College placed an ad on the back cover of *Harper's Magazine*, producing amazement because such promotion had never been heard of before.

Higher education marketing is about more than attracting students: American colleges and universities have also sought financial resources, and students' tuition payments have rarely covered institutional needs. Colonial American colleges, including Harvard College, were usually church-supported institutions to prepare young men for the ministry. The Morrill Act of 1862 provided grants of federal government land to the states to be sold to create state colleges. State and other public colleges and universities had to appeal to legislatures for funding. Building relationships with the wealthy yielded major donations that continue to bear fruit. The Cooper Union in New York City has never charged tuition because the revenue from Peter Cooper's donation of land continues to generate adequate funds. Named buildings on college campuses attest to the largesse of donors past and present.

The distinction between promotion and marketing is that marketing is the broader term that encompasses segmenting the market and making choices about which students and others to serve, and then developing a marketing mix of programs, delivery systems, locations, promotional activities, and prices—in time, effort, and money—that will attract and meet their needs.

REACTIONS TO HIGHER EDUCATION MARKETING

Public reactions to higher education marketing focus almost entirely on enrollment marketing, the application of marketing tools to attract and enroll students. These tools include promotion (advertising and other communications, events, and other activities), pricing (usually in the form of financial aid packages), and the offer of attractive programs at convenient locations or through alternative delivery channels.

Some critics argue that the value of higher education is obvious and that marketing should be unnecessary. Yet there are very good colleges that would not attract the number and diversity of students they can serve without an investment in marketing activities. Other colleges are criticized for being unselective, admitting anyone who can pay, and then pandering to under-prepared, lazy students to retain them and their tuition payments, providing no real value in return. Alternatively, some critics complain that enrollment marketing is too sophisticated, seducing the naïve, unwary prospect with expensive viewbooks and hype. Some higher education promotion has been criticized as excessive and intrusive, with some good students receiving thousands of college mailings.

But as higher education enrollment marketing efforts have intensified, prospective students and their parents have become more sophisticated consumers of education. Prospects have greater choice of institutions, and can gather information more easily, and compare college communications with the opinions of others online with a mouse click. Prospects are getting professional help to craft applications, applying to more institutions, weighing more offers, and negotiating more forcefully for financial aid.

In contrast to enrollment marketing, successful donor marketing is lauded and donors are rightly admired for contributing to education. Recently, however, donor marketing has come under some criticism when it is too successful. The value of endowment funds at the most prestigious universities has risen to levels that attracted Congressional hearings in 2008, with institutions being pressured to spend more of their endowment income for student scholarships and other educational uses.

Critics may believe that marketing is unnecessary, and that the right types and number of students will naturally find their way to one of the United States' more than 4,000 institutions of higher education. Marketing is the process of creating mutually satisfying exchanges with selected groups and individuals. Direct mail, websites, advertising, and other promotional tools are components of marketing, but they are not marketing itself.

The best and most successful higher education marketing begins with a deep understanding of the college itself, its history and unique character, and the mission that it has pursued. A marketing approach will direct the college's representatives to consider the resources they want to attract—students, faculty, staff, donations, positive image, and favorable public opinion—and to examine what they can offer that will attract these resources. Which students would want to attend our college—and why? What do we offer them? Which professors are the best match with our college and its academic program? Where do we find them and what can we offer to attract and retain them? The college asks the same question about other resources, human and financial.

NEW DEVELOPMENTS IN
HIGHER EDUCATION MARKETING

Enrollment Management

During the 1970s leading admissions professionals considered how to go beyond typical student recruitment and financial aid practices. At Boston College, Jack Maguire and Frank Campanella examined time-tested recruiting activities and admissions policies. They conceived an approach that linked identification of the best prospects, coordinated communications and other recruitment activities, and financial aid awards to yield not only the desired number of entering students, but also the best entering class for the college. This approach they named *enrollment management*, a term that has become the dominant concept for modern enrollment marketing. At Northwestern University, William Ihlanfeldt described the admissions challenge as attracting optimal enrollment numbers in various programs and levels (including undergraduate and graduate), and achieving optimal tuition revenues. Ihlanfeldt viewed this as a marketing challenge that involved institutional analysis, planning, and decision-making, as well as the correct mix of marketing tools and tactics.

Data-Driven Marketing Decision-Making

Student recruitment had been viewed primarily as public relations and outreach. Admissions staff visited high schools year after year, promoted the college to prospects, parents, and high school counselors, mailed out brochures and application forms, and then waited for the applications to arrive in the mail and selected the best applications for admission. Fortunate colleges had natural constituencies that traditionally favored them—with Catholic high school graduates going on to Catholic colleges, for example, and high school graduates going to state colleges and universities in their own states. Demographic and geographic shifts disrupted traditional patterns, and colleges needed to look more widely for new students. Colleges that had achieved or aspired to greater stature wanted to attract better students, and this meant larger prospect and applicant pools.

Affordable computing, the diffusion of social science research methods, and greater knowledge of marketing research techniques attracted the attention of admissions professionals. Colleges traditionally tracked recruiting numbers—numbers of inquiries, applications, accepted, and enrolled—on a year-by-year basis. By the early 1980s some colleges were carrying out surveys and focus groups of current students, prospects, admitted students, and those who enrolled, to better understand what they were seeking in a college education and how the college stacked up against competing institutions. Admissions publications were put to the test. Messages were pretested, direct mail campaigns were tracked to measure their effectiveness in reaching the right prospects and getting their attention.

Higher education development professionals carried out in-depth prospect research, drawing on multiple databases to create profiles of current and prospective donors, including demographics, giving potential, and much more. Research on institutional reputation gained impetus from publication of college ratings in *U.S. News and World Report* and other magazines.

New Technologies

Technological advances have opened new paths to reach prospective students. In the early 1970s the College Board, developer and administrator of the Scholastic Aptitude and Achievement Tests, began a new service called Student Search. The premise was that colleges wanted current, accurate contact information for young people applying to college, and that students would benefit from learning about colleges that would be interested in them and which matched their interests. Student Search drew on the College Board's huge database of test takers and sold to colleges the names and addresses of prospects matching the college's preferred characteristics. Student participation was voluntary, and colleges used the purchased contact information to send postcards, letters, catalogs, and other print materials to elicit interest and possible applications. By the late 1980s students could use software from the College Board to search a database of colleges and universities using their own criteria, including state, type of community, majors offered, student body size, and others. Some colleges began providing videotaped "tours" for high schools to make available to students.

By the mid-1990s the Internet had revolutionized how colleges provided information to prospects and how prospects interacted with colleges. Campus tours went online, and websites became central features of enrollment marketing. Over the next decade, a prospective student could do an Internet-based search for college information, and find not only official information from institutions, but also blogs and other comments by current students. Communications between prospective students and colleges took the form of emails and even instant messaging. By 2008 some universities, including Notre Dame and Stanford, required that all applications be filed online. Notre Dame calculates that eliminating paper-based applications saves $20,000 annually that can be better spent on constant updates to their website, which in turn encourages potential students to return to the Notre Dame site more often.

Tuition Pricing and Financial Aid

Most higher education institutions have limited funds for financial aid, which should be applied to enable the right number of the best prospects to attend. Sound pricing decisions are essential for the long-term survival and success of the college, since every scholarship grant is, in effect, a discount off the tuition price. Sophisticated quantitative models are now widely employed to set individualized financial aid packages for each student. Applying these models has enabled colleges to allocate their limited aid money efficiently while attracting the best applicants.

Wealthy institutions with immense endowments, including Harvard and Stanford, have recently taken a bold approach to tuition discounting, reducing to zero the cost of attending for students with family incomes under a stated threshold.

Longer-Term Perspective on Development Opportunities

Longer lifespans, the maturing of the Baby Boom generation, and the financial success of many of them have reinforced the importance of alumni connections. No longer do colleges rely solely on the fortuitous super-rich alumnus. Instead they aim to develop and deepen connections over the lifetime, starting with the youngest alumni, and continuing with alumni events, travel programs, and reunions. Magazines, newsletters, websites, and alumni databases strengthen the ties that encourage alumni to recommend the college to prospects, to volunteer, and to donate.

To encourage donors to include bequests in their wills, colleges and universities have begun to organize special events that recognize the generosity of these donors while showcasing the college's programs, faculty, and students. Stanford University started the Founding Grant Society for this purpose and hosts an annual spring luncheon that includes two talks by outstanding faculty, and a performance by one of the many student musical groups.

Image-Enhancing Efforts

American higher education is a big, complex enterprise. Most students can pick only one institution to attend for each degree level, and sorting through the vast offerings is difficult. Educational institutions realize that they need to differentiate themselves from other potential competitions by being distinctive in a relevant and meaningful way. In marketing parlance, each college aims to *position* itself in the minds of those whose opinions matter—prospects, the media, and the general public. The most memorable positioning strategy requires a lot of self-examination to identify the root values of the institution that historically set it apart, to see if these values are still important and also relevant to today's students and donors.

Everything about a college communicates about its *image*—its buildings and landscaping, the on-campus atmosphere, student dress and behavior, the performance of athletic teams, and more. But the foundation for a solid and attractive image consists of the academic and other programs offered, and the faculty who offer them. Clever communications have never replaced sound performance of the core academic mission. Institutions aim to present themselves not only through their communications, offerings, and faculty, but also through the success of their students and alumni—grants received, career success, community involvement as volunteers, and other evidence that graduates carry out the values of the institution. Santa Clara University aims to encourage "the three C's"—competence, conscience, and compassion.

The goal is to make the institution's name a well-known and highly regarded *brand*, one that represents something of substance in the mind of the viewer, listener, prospect, or potential donor. Trying to convey a unified identity that benefits each constituent of the institution is a real challenge. Some departments want to develop their own image and do not want to participate in the larger university branding effort.

THE NEXT BIG CHALLENGE

The United States has been a strong importer of students from abroad—over half a million international students were enrolled in U.S. higher education institutions in 2004. Now the competition for students and donations is global, with U.S. enrollments growing very slowly while in the United Kingdom, Germany, France, Japan, and Australia foreign-student enrollments have grown much faster. Australian universities are attracting English-language learners from Southeast Asia, and American undergraduates are looking to more affordable Canadian universities. Foreign universities are creating American-style campuses and programs to appeal to students who want to study closer to home. Monterrey Institute of Technology, founded in 1943, now has over thirty campuses in Mexico, and over two dozen business incubators, and offers state-of-the-art facilities and programs to learners in Mexico and Central America.

American institutions are already expanding overseas. Education City in Doha, Qatar, has attracted programs provided by five U.S. universities to Qatari and other students, with luxurious facilities and all costs paid by the multimillion-dollar contracts with the Qatari government. American MBA programs now offer degree programs around the world. American colleges and universities export their own students to study centers abroad.

CONCLUSION: WHAT PRESIDENTS SHOULD KNOW ABOUT HIGHER EDUCATION MARKETING

American college and university presidents are the de facto chief marketers for their institutions. Acquaintance with a marketing perspective can add another dimension to their decision-making, and an appreciation for its fundamentals can be invaluable. Books, articles, and workshops for presidents can provide the knowledge foundation.

Presidents should seek out and hire the best applied marketing talent, experts who also understand academic culture and are in tune with the values of the college.

Where are the higher education marketers of the future going to come from? Some of the best are alumni of the institutions, which gives them a sense of connection and insight into why other people would care. But alumni status and institutional knowledge are not enough. Often the best candidates have experience at other institutions along with formal backgrounds in modern marketing tools and concepts.

Having hired the best, presidents should listen to them and give credence to their insights and judgments. The experts—in enrollment marketing, donor marketing, and marketing communications—can educate others in the institution and help keep the "big picture" in view.

Student and donor satisfaction are created in all the points of contact with the institution, with staff, faculty, and other students. David Packard, the cofounder of Hewlett Packard, stated: "Marketing is too important to be left to the marketing department." The best institutions understand that marketing will be most effective when it is augmented by the efforts of all the members of the college community.

Is all this easy? Daniel Saracino, admissions director at Notre Dame University, compares the challenge of higher education marketing with a stomach-jolting amusement park ride with his son. After some sharp turns and sudden drops, their car emerged from a tunnel long enough for his son to exclaim, "Dad, this is scary." Dan replied, "No, son, it's exciting."

Chapter 13

The Future Physical Plant

with John Carmody

John Carmody is the director of the Center for Sustainable Building Research at the University of Minnesota.

Carmody holds bachelor's and master's degrees in architecture from the University of Minnesota and teaches in the new master of science in architecture program focusing on sustainable design. He has worked in building-related research for thirty years and is the author of several books on building design and construction, including Window Systems for High Performance Buildings, *with Lawrence Berkeley National Laboratory. He is coauthor of* Residential Windows: A Guide to New Technologies and Energy Performance.

Carmody was one of the leaders of a team that developed the State of Minnesota Sustainable Building Guidelines, *which are now requirements on state-funded buildings. His work includes research on window and façade design, affordable housing, life-cycle assessment of materials, post occupancy evaluations, and development of decision-making tools for designers.*

Recently, the Center for Sustainable Building Research received funding to lead the State of Minnesota in its transformation to zero net energy and carbon emissions by the year 2030.

SUSTAINABILITY CHANGES IN UNIVERSITIES AND COLLEGES

My expertise is in the area of sustainability: the huge transformation going on in the building sector across the board, at this university, and

This chapter is based on an interview I conducted with John Carmody on April 18, 2008, for this chapter.

everywhere, and how building is going to change in the next twenty years. The university has some special issues and some special opportunities. It has the responsibility to be the leader in the transformation.

In response to things like climate change, awareness of environmental and energy issues—especially the last five years—architecture and the whole building industry have been undergoing a revolution. And it will continue to escalate. People are trying to adapt to green building guidelines and principles for campus planning, which are definitely steps in the right direction.

Architecture 2030 is a major initiative led by Ed Mazria, an architect from New Mexico. This initiative essentially says that if we're going to solve the climate problem, the fact that almost half of all energy is associated with buildings will have to be addressed. Therefore, we need to set a target that we have zero carbon emission buildings by the year 2030, and we need to work toward that with significant steps. We need to be 60 percent on the way there by 2010, and 70 percent by 2015, and 80 percent by 2020. So it's really laying down the gauntlet and stating that we have to go to a whole different level of how we look at buildings and their performance. The concept of sustainability has really captured the imagination of government and the architecture profession. In fact, our state has adopted it as policy, as has California.

So you're seeing things happening now that weren't happening five years ago. What this means is that buildings will be designed in ways that are much more resource conscious in terms of energy, materials, and water. These will also be buildings that are powered more by renewable fuel.

Some people envision a future where buildings become net producers of energy. I know this all sounds a little far off, but I think climate change is going to continue to worsen, and come down on us to the point where fairly radical ideas are going to seem pretty commonplace five or ten years from now. That is the biggest single trend I see out there.

The whole business of "building" is going to change. Any campus that has a lot of older existing buildings and infrastructure has a problem on their hands. Those buildings need to be radically upgraded to avoid enormous costs. Last year, the University of Minnesota's energy bill was around $95 million. And they had actually negotiated good prices on gas and electricity. So as costs move up in the future, it is difficult to imagine all of the change.

Achieving zero carbon emission buildings is approached in two ways. First and foremost, buildings must be designed so they don't use much energy. This means using much better insulation and windows, and using daylight as much as possible to avoid electric lighting. We know how to do this, yet few are demanding it.

After reducing building use where possible, then the fuel supply can be moved toward renewable sources. In Minnesota, that is already happening. By the year 2025, a quarter of all our utility energy will be wind-generated. In fact, in Minnesota there are three small liberal arts colleges that have their own huge wind turbines. In one case, Carleton College is generating half the electricity for the campus. Carleton College is a leading liberal arts college in Minnesota, and I understand that their students pressured the administration to take some of their investment funds and put it into renewable energy for the campus. So we are actually seeing pressure coming from students who believe the colleges should do more. I think I've seen that on our campus, too. It kind of reminds me of the 1960s, actually.

As I said, on the supply side of a campus there are two scales. There is an individual building, and then there is the whole campus or district. Some changes would apply to a campus as a whole, like the wind energy at Carleton, which has a wind turbine that supplies power to the whole campus. That is more of a district energy system. Additionally, campuses may add site waste treatment, move toward organic locally produced food, composting, collecting rainwater, and waste management. Waste water treatment may begin to occur more on campuses. These are things that help create a more natural system, closing the loop at the campus scale. Consequently, there is less reliance on infrastructure.

You don't want hard surfaces that allow water to run off and create pollution and ecological problems downstream. So, it is important to consider land use, water, energy, materials, and then healthy buildings. Those tend to be the categories under sustainable design that people consider. The district system changes are made at the campus scale, and then conservation and onsite renewables can occur at the building scale. Buildings will require increasingly cheaper, better solar collectors and better windows. Daylight and natural ventilation will be more commonly used. We must go back to basics, using smarter equipment so there is less waste. For example, timers or sensors should be used to turn lights on and off according to actual need. Energy and water will be valuable resources. We are experiencing radical changes that affect the way we must think about our whole environment, resources, building, and landscaping. At some point, lack of water may be even more of a limiting factor than energy.

THE UNIVERSITY IN TWENTY-PLUS YEARS

Universities, unlike any other built environment, have a powerful role in educating or reeducating everybody about how the world really works. I think the campus of the future should look very much like a closed natural system. To use a model from biology, it would consume all of its own waste, it would generate all of its own energy, and it would purify all of its own water. It might even grow its own food as a demonstration of how self-sufficient systems will need to work in the future. Perhaps you have heard about how the average portion of food travels 2,000 miles to get to your plate. In America there is so much embodied energy and so much waste because of the very inefficient way we do everything based on cheap energy. I think that campuses will be a place not only where people come to learn about the subjects they're being taught, but also where the campus itself will be a teaching tool. It will show them how the world can work effectively. If the "biosphere" concept could work at a campus scale as a completely closed system, it could be a model for how communities should work everywhere.

ADVICE ON THE FUTURE FOR UNIVERSITY PRESIDENTS AND ADMINISTRATORS

Campus leaders should clearly be signing on to climate change declarations. The last two or three years, there has been a wave of university presidents doing just that. That's the first step. I remember there was a debate at our university about it, but we finally signed.

There are tools out there that campuses can use. There are rating systems for campus sustainability. It is important to set some clear performance metrics, like reaching a certain level of carbon emissions, energy and water use, waste production, and stick to those as major goals. This generation of students is often more knowledgeable about sustainability than are faculty and administrators. We have students in the architecture program that literally want to save the world. They push the administration to respond. If specific environmental goals were articulated to these students and the support provided, these students would provide the energy and creativity to reach many of those goals. Administrative "top-down" approaches are generally not as effective.

Sustainability must be factored into the construction costs for future campus buildings. The classic problem with public buildings is that they're always on tight budgets. If our campus goes to the legislature and says we need a new building, and the budget for it is $25 million, the legislature might allocate only $20 million. It is difficult to go back and tell them that if they spend an extra $2 million, we could cut the energy and carbon emission in half on this building over the next fifty years, which would save lots of money in the long run. At this point, legislators would not provide the additional 10 percent needed for sustainability. Consequently, there is often a real disconnect between capital and operating budgets. With our political system, there is a disincentive to do long-term thinking and planning for publicly funded buildings. It would be helpful to set up some kind of financing mechanism that would allow universities to finance the longer-term options that make the most sense. Our university has actually made some progress in that direction. They have a loan fund where they can spend more money on a building if it's going to save more money in the long run. Overcoming these kinds of institutional barriers is absolutely essential.

THE TURNING POINT

I think we're seeing the turning point. Consider the increased awareness of climate change, resulting in part from Al Gore's movie. Every couple of months we receive additional bad news on the state of the environment. The trends are direr than people think. That is going to accelerate, and eventually, people will respond. The energy crisis will drive the rise in awareness. I think we may be approaching the end of the industrial era and that the next twenty years is going to be an incredible time to be alive. I believe we will see a transformation in virtually every area in society.

There is another interesting side to all of this. Everything I've talked about so far addresses these questions: "How do we design the building of the future?" and "How do we make them super energy-efficient, put solar collectors on them, and use a technology-based approach to fixing things?" This is assuming that we're going to keep building buildings, expanding, and that universities will remain the way they are. Another way to achieve a sustainable future is to have fewer buildings and do more telecommuting, utilizing what we have much more intensively. Additionally, there are buildings on many campuses that aren't utilized all the time or in the most efficient manner. Figuring out how to do more with less is going to be a big part of our future as well.

At universities with high-end research, the facilities are expensive, and energy intensive. The research facilities are often the glamour buildings, because they attract the big research dollars and big name faculty. I often wonder about the obsolescence of facilities like that. You make these enormous investments in very specialized buildings and then I wonder what that is going to look like twenty years from now when the technology has changed. While some buildings must be built in a specialized way, we should also attempt to build them in an adaptable way. Build them so you are creating building shells and basic infrastructure that can be converted into other uses later without having to tear them down entirely, and start over again.

WHERE TO FIND INFORMATION AND BEGIN

There are tremendous resources in this field of sustainable design. One obvious place to look is on the U.S. Green Building Council website for particular projects and campus scale issues. There are many other guidelines, rating systems, case studies, design strategies, and other information (listed below). This trend toward green buildings and campuses is accelerating. It is important to remember that the guidelines and rating systems are only tools and are rapidly evolving. The focus needs to be on setting goals and measuring progress toward real performance outcomes such as energy, carbon emissions, water use, and waste.

Any time there is a chance to build a new building, it should be as innovative and high performance as possible. It not only saves money and improves the environment, but it also educates the public and the students about these issues. It is important to go as far as possible with making sustainable and educational buildings. There is no question about that.

Additionally, universities need to embrace rehabbing buildings, energy conservation, and upgrading their existing facilities, along with more effective utilization of those facilities.

The third thing would be to think outside the box, and realize that we are facing more of a holistic problem. It is not just about energy, it is also about what we are doing with our grounds: watering, landscaping, and storm water runoff. Runoff is a huge pollution problem in any urban area. These go together with the issues on food and waste, in a holistic way.

David Orr, a professor at Oberlin, has written some well-known books, including *Ecological Literacy*. He was one of the early thinkers in the green-building movement. He gave a keynote speech about how we needed to educate all students in ecological literacy. He built a "zero energy building" at Oberlin. I had lunch with him about three years ago and the conversation was striking because he said that he would redo all university curricula, and require every freshman student to take courses on how natural systems work. We have become so disconnected with where things come from, and how things work, that we need to start from scratch and give everybody the basic literacy of ecology or we're not going to survive. We are not going to know how to take care of ourselves. He was saying that new forms of education, the way people now are getting information off the Internet, will be more responsive than the traditional academic model, which can be slow to respond and change. He said that the form of education as it exists today could be obsolete twenty years from now.

There need to be radical revisions to curriculum. Universities are not that quick to change curriculum. I can see that in our own architecture school. With the issue of environmental sustainability, there are a lot of professors who have been here for thirty years, and who are resistant to change. The students and some of the younger faculty are really geared up for major change. They demand changes in the curriculum that address what they view as important societal issues. It gives me hope. It is the only hope we have.

CONCLUSION

According to *Architecture 2030*, the most important environmental priority is to place a moratorium on coal-fired generating plants.

I think the future will be very interesting. People need to realize that there are some very big changes coming.

Ultimately, I think the technology and the materials are coming. I think they can come really fast if we make the right kind of investments. There is no question we can create zero energy buildings. It's going to take some research and development investment for the country as a whole to do it, but it's very achievable. I think the most interesting thing is this shift in consciousness where people actually realize that we're not stuck, that transformation is possible, and that you can make a change and walk away from the previous inefficient and destructive ways of doing things.

One of my favorite books is *Promise Ahead* by Duane Elgin. Elgin looks at the ongoing evolution of the human species. He asks the question, "As a species, are we in our childhood, adolescence, mature adulthood, or old age?" His answer is "adolescence." We are a species that has hit an evolutionary wall essentially because we have so many adverse trends right now. We have expanded all over the world, consumed enormous resources, and we have climate change, water and food shortages, poverty, and war. All of these trends are converging at once. Elgin says that normally when a species hits that evolutionary wall, it either goes into decline or it makes an adaptation, takes an evolutionary bounce, and continues to survive. In his book *Promise Ahead*, he outlines the things he is hopeful about that will cause us to potentially make that evolutionary bounce. Most of the things he talks about have nothing to do with technology. They have to do with human consciousness and attitude.

One example relates to how much of the human enterprise on the earth is involved in warfare and just how wasteful and destructive that is. We still think that war is the right way to solve problems. Elgin talks about how Desmond Tutu organized the Reconciliation Commission in South Africa when Apartheid ended. In effect the approach was to say, "We're not here to punish each other, we're not here to take out revenge, we're here to tell the truth, and heal." So anybody who came forward, admitted what they did, and told the truth was not punished. They were forgiven and the healing process began. It was very successful. It was a revolutionary way of dealing with that kind of horror. Elgin said that this is an example of human consciousness rising to another level, above the cycle of revenge and violence. It is really a shift in attitude, and if everybody had that attitude, think of how different the world would be. That kind of thinking can be applied in many areas.

Another one of Elgin's ideas was that there is a shift in the way that scientific people are seeing the universe—as a living universe, not a dead universe. There is clearly an awakening going on in various levels of science, religion, and spirituality that points to reconnecting with the natural world. He said that when that shift takes place you just think differently, approach things differently, and you don't continue destroying nature and consuming resources at an unsustainable rate. It becomes obvious to everyone that that is not the right thing to do.

We often refer to the three E's in sustainability: environment, economy, and equity. Sometimes we approach these problems such as climate change just by looking at how we can solve the problem technically. We tend to forget about people and social responsibility. In the last couple of years, people are recognizing that these things are completely interconnected, and that you cannot just solve environmental issues without solving poverty and indigenous peoples' rights issues.

Paul Hawken, one of the original leaders of the green building environmental movement, recently wrote the book *Blessed Unrest*. He explains that there has been an explosion of nonprofit and community groups growing up around indigenous peoples' rights, social responsibility issues, and environmental issues. Such groups are developing all over the planet by the tens of thousands, almost by the month. When Hawken speaks, he shows an endless list of organizations that have recently appeared out of nowhere. His premise is that this is the immune system for the planet. All of us, like the people in Texas fighting the coal plants, are part of the big immune system; we are the white blood cells. Generally, people who are involved in saving the environment and water quality are also involved in social justice. You can't really draw lines between them, so let's not think of it that way anymore. I think he's right. Hawken said that he didn't see all of this coming. He just noticed that as he spoke about environmental issues that everywhere he turned there seemed to be self-organizing community groups trying to solve problems in all these areas. Most did not travel like he did and often thought they were the only ones doing that work, and yet there were people doing it all over the world. So he set up these big websites to connect people. His website for the environment is www.wiserearth.org, and any like-minded group like this can sign up and connect with other groups around the world doing similar things.

The other book that has really influenced me is *Biomimicry* by Janine Benyus. Benyus is a biologist who has been very inspirational in the green building movement. Her premise is that life has evolved on this planet for billions of years and that human beings are brand new, yet they are about to destroy it. Nature is full of lessons about how to live sustainably on this planet. For example, a spider web is stronger and more resilient than steel, but it's made with no pollution, out of organic material at ambient temperature. The spider web does not require energy-intensive, destructive, toxic processing. She has numerous examples of how nature does things better, gentler, and easier. She inspired a whole segment of the architecture and product design world to look at biological models for design. We have started courses in our architecture program based on that concept. Humans don't have to be so clever and invent their way out of everything. We actually need to wake up, look around, and realize that nature has done a lot of things better than we ever thought of them being done.

In general, I think the biggest mistake people could make is to be timid and shortsighted. We are in a time of huge transformation and people need to be open to lots of possibilities that they might never have imagined before. Part of it is attitude—recognizing that things are always changing. Change won't stop. But we must pay attention to what is happening, learn from the world around us, be ready to respond boldly to it, and, perhaps, make all the difference.

Chapter 14

Partnerships of the Future University

by Nancy L. Zimpher

Nancy L. Zimpher is the president of the University of Cincinnati. She is a widely recognized leader in higher education, civic engagement, economic development, and urban education reform.

Notable achievements by President Zimpher include establishing UC's new Center for the City, designed to facilitate innovative and productive partnerships that leverage university and public expertise to work toward the betterment of the community; chairing the Uptown Consortium, a partnership in neighborhood development that involves five of the largest employers in the UC Uptown area; and founding Strive, a Cincinnati–Northern Kentucky partnership focused on college access and success.

Prior to her arrival at UC, Zimpher served as the chancellor of the University of Wisconsin–Milwaukee from 1998 to 2003 and was the executive dean of the Professional Colleges and dean of the College of Education at The Ohio State University in Columbus, Ohio.

Zimpher is a past chair of the Board of Directors for the National Association of State Universities and Land-Grant Colleges (NASULGC). She chairs the Coalition of Urban Serving Universities (USU). Her publications include numerous books, monographs, book chapters, and journal articles on various topics including university leadership and school/university partnerships.

INTRODUCTION

The concept that higher education shares interconnections with external stakeholders has been a shifting one, yet one that stands to play a critical role in the future success of the American university. I will touch on some

175

historical highlights, discuss emerging trends, and share strategies to guide academic leaders as our concept of partnership takes on a new and central role for our viability in the decades to come.

HISTORICAL HIGHLIGHTS

While the notion of "university partnership" in the true sense of reciprocal and mutual relationships remains relatively new, the idea of engagement is not nearly as novel. I spent five years as chancellor of University of Wisconsin–Milwaukee in a state where "The Wisconsin Idea" dates nearly as far back as the state itself and establishes the principle that the boundaries of the university are the boundaries of the state. The University of Cincinnati, now a state university, has its origins as a municipal university with a history closely entwined with the city, and is currently directly linked to its region's economic and social viability.

Various periods during the history of the United States have strengthened the concept of university partnership while others have not. Although the U.S. Constitution does not confer responsibility for education on our federal government (ACE publication, *An Overview of Higher Education in the United States*, 2006), nevertheless, the actions of our federal government and national leaders have at times forged strong relationships that extended our mission and reach. For many public institutions, their very founding and the grounds on which they stand can be traced to the federal Land-Grant College Act of 1862 (Maryland Paper, Dubb & Howard, 2007) and its goal of providing education to meet the needs of the people within the states. The Morrill Act of 1890 went further by establishing federal funding to these schools, and later the land grant mission expanded to include education, research, and outreach (also called extension). Another influential example of federal partnership, the G.I. Bill arising out of World War II truly changed the enrollment landscape of American higher education and greatly expanded academia's role further outward into society. The Cold War era, the creation of the National Science Foundation in 1950, and our nation's response to the launch of the Russian satellite Sputnik in 1957 not only mobilized the nation in support of more and better science education, but also called upon academia to work more actively to solve national challenges (Kerr, 2002; Dubb & Howard, 2007) and led to shifts in responsibility for scientific advancement from government laboratories and industry to universities.

The "Great Society" of the 1960s and the war on poverty initiatives under the Johnson administration brought about federal policies that would help our nation's growing cities similar to the way the Land Grant Act assisted colleges and universities and agriculture in the nineteenth century.

Many programs were initiated to develop community education, re-search, and service, including some partnerships with higher education. Community service also gained renewed momentum in the 1990s as the Corporation for National and Community Service was created in support of service-learning through the Serve America program and in support of volunteer activities through the Points of Light Foundation. Students seeking to make college more affordable and to become more experienced in community engagement benefited from the Clinton-initiated Ameri-Corps program, which provided student loan forgiveness in exchange for service. In more recent years, the federal Community Outreach and Part-nerships Center (COPC) has financially supported university-community partnerships through a competitive grant program at the U.S. Department of Housing and Urban Development (Dubb & Howard, 2007).

Community engagement returned more prominently to the academic psyche in 1990 with Ernest Boyer's call for higher education to establish a clearer and more prominent role in determining the direction of the na-tion's life—what he termed "a new American college." The Kellogg Com-mission built on that call with its own report calling for "a renewal of the partnership of the public university with the society it serves." The com-mission recognized the contributions universities have made in the past but suggested that even greater service is desirable. It concluded that in-stitutions should go beyond outreach and service to "engagement":

> Engagement goes well beyond extension, conventional outreach, and even most conceptions of public service. Inherited concepts emphasize a one-way process in which the university transfers its expertise to key constituents. Embedded in the engagement ideal is a commitment to sharing and reci-procity. By engagement, the Commission envisioned partnerships, two-way streets defined by mutual respect among the partners for what each brings to the table. (Byrne, 2006, p. 7)

While the degree to which higher education has responded to this chal-lenge is not what many have hoped it would be, one sign of progress is that the Carnegie Foundation has established a new elective classification for community engagement. First developed and offered in 2006 as part of an extensive restructuring of The Carnegie Classification of Institutions of Higher Education, the community engagement classification, as de-scribed by Carnegie consulting scholar Amy Driscoll on the Carnegie website, is "a significant affirmation of the importance of community en-gagement in the agenda of higher education."

In more recent years, the rhetoric of engagement earlier reflected in the response to Sputnik has been echoed as our nation faces the challenges and changing rules of the twenty-first-century economy and society. Our efforts to understand and cope with this shifting reality have resulted in

a myriad of reports in the last few years—a series of wake-up calls—and
action steps to keep the United States "on top." Perhaps the most widely
read of these by higher education is the collaborative report of the National Academy of Sciences, the National Academy of Engineering, and
the Institute of Medicine, "Rising Above the Gathering Storm: Energizing
and Employing America for a Brighter Future."

These reports carry common themes, among them the urgent need for
the United States to maintain its capacity for innovation; to generate more
college graduates in the fields of science, technology, engineering, and
math; to produce better teachers in these areas in our elementary and high
schools; and to improve the academic performance of U.S. students when
compared to their peers around the world. And appropriately, most of these
clarion calls circle back to education, including higher education, and our
need to substantially increase accessibility to college and success for more
American citizens in the new innovation and knowledge economy. While it
remains to be seen what real outcomes and partnerships may arise from
this renewed concern for the country's ability to compete internationally,
one impact is clear: higher education's allies have expanded to include corporate leaders, think tanks, nonprofits, and government officials.

There have, of course, been many occasions when the federal-university
relationship has been strained or nonexistent. An example of the former is
the 1981 *National Commission on Excellence in Education Report, A Nation at
Risk*. While the report found much to fault in the American education system, including higher education's preparation of future teachers, not much
change resulted (Connelly, 1990, pp. 141–168). An example of the latter is the
No Child Left Behind Act of 2001 (NCLB), signed into law in 2002. While
higher education is the pipeline for this act's call for placing more highly
qualified teachers in our nation's elementary and secondary classrooms,
there was little authorization or allocation of funds through this act for
higher education to play a partnership role in the recruitment, preparation,
and retention of teachers who could work effectively with our nation's most
underserved students. Divisions in how education is administered in this
country, both at the federal level and especially at the state level, make it
very difficult for the sectors of elementary and secondary education and
higher education to collaborate effectively to meet the challenges that the
NCLB Act was intended to solve.

THE EFFECTS OF CURRENT DEMANDS
ON EVOLVING PARTNERSHIPS

While university partnerships are nothing new, as the brief history summarized above would suggest, what might be changing are societal needs and

the necessary stakeholders to be involved in these major challenges. These changing needs, along with a demographic landscape that continues to become more urban and metropolitan, call out for some new thinking—some sort of federal-academic response. Perhaps the time has come to reexamine the Land Grant Act to make some amendment to reflect our contemporary realities, such as injecting an urban component that would complement the nutritional and agricultural programs that have resulted from the Land Grant policies as suggested by The Democracy Collaborative at the University of Maryland in its "Linking Colleges to Communities" report (2007).

The demographic shifts showing how urban and metropolitan our nation, our economy, and our world have become are succinctly summarized in The Brookings Institution's "MetroNation" report (2007):

- The top 100 metro areas in the United States generate 75 percent of the Gross Domestic Product;
- Our U.S. metro areas are home to eight in ten Americans and jobs;
- More than half of the world's population is metropolitan;
- And in the United States, the largest 100 metro areas contain 65 percent of the U.S. population and 68 percent of jobs.

In the face of these shifting needs and in an age of rapid change, globalization, and urbanization, the cities where many universities are located have long offered a problem-rich environment for academics to examine and address societal challenges.

If population trends continue, we can expect urban areas of the world to become even more heavily populated. Estimates indicate that 60 percent of the world population will be urban by 2030, with most of this growth occurring in developing countries. By mid-century, we can expect to see cities topping 50 million in population. This mega-urbanization presents a whole host of social and environmental problems at a magnitude never before experienced in history. So it was that in 1998, a small group of leading urban-located public research universities organized themselves into what was then called the Great Cities Universities, and in 2005 evolved into the current membership of thirty-nine institutions in the Coalition of Urban Serving Universities. Its mission is to leverage the intellectual capital and economic power of urban universities, thereby improving urban life and America's competitiveness in the global economy. In addition to their work of legislative advocacy, USU's members partner with cities and metropolitan regions to prompt transformative investment in three key areas, also called "strands":

- Human Capital—to develop and create a workforce ready to compete in the new economy of the twenty-first century;

- Strengthening Communities—to revitalize neighborhoods and enhance economic development; and
- Improving the Health of a Diverse Population—to reduce health disparities and bring about healthier communities.

All of these strands require the modern day invention of new partnerships. In order to graphically depict how modern-day engagements translate "on the ground," I have taken the liberty of sharing a number of partnerships currently underway at the University of Cincinnati, the focus of these initiatives, the disciplines involved, and the key partners in each initiative (see Exhibit B). While these partnerships may differ from those in other like institutions in scope and scale, they are nonetheless illustrative of what an actively engaged university might typically be involved in at the current time.

CHARACTERISTICS OF SUSTAINABLE PARTNERSHIPS

Beyond these shifting trends and historic underpinnings, universities also face a unique reality as "anchor institutions." These "anchors" are what CEOs for Cities has termed "sticky capital"—they work on behalf of cities because of their connection to a particular location (Maurrasse, 2007, p. 2). In other words, they are not likely to pick up and leave and thereby enjoy a special relationship to their city and have a vested interest in the well-being of their community. They impact communities through their landholdings, capacity as large employers, revenue generators, and goods and services purchasers as well as centers of human capital and economic cluster development (Penn Institute for Urban Research, 2007). Universities are not alone in serving as anchor institutions—museums, hospitals, libraries, parks, performing arts centers, and sports facilities can all be counted among them. Yet universities are singularly positioned to offer a wide range of expertise to bring to bear on the challenges their regions face.

That said, my experience in and participation as a true partner have led me to some summary observations about what makes a successful and enduring partnership; and I have written about these characteristics over time. The summary that follows comes from a report of the nation's two leading associations representing public higher education, the National Association of State Universities and Land-Grant Colleges (NASULGC) and the American Association of State Colleges and Universities (AASCU). Their Joint Task Force for Urban/Metropolitan Schools issued a 2004 report, titled *Crossing Boundaries: The Urban Education Imperative*, that addressed the needs of America's urban public schools. This report outlined six characteristics of effective systemic partnerships:

- *Levels of Leadership*: It is necessary to involve a continuum of leadership across all levels of the partnership. This includes university, school district, and community;
- *Attention to Context*: The nature of a partnership must reflect the unique institutions and communities it serves;
- *Shared Responsibility*: All partners involved must recognize their mutual vested interest and take responsibility for shared goals and action;
- *Ambitious Goals*: Wide-scale change should be the only acceptable outcome. This will require interdisciplinary cooperation, community commitment, and leadership with a vision;
- *Shared Accountability*: Partners must create measurable goals together and hold each other accountable for them. Such a relationship depends on mutual trust, clear benchmarks, and defined outcomes;
- *Systemic Redesign*: Strategies and roles must be both visionary and research-based.

As the title of the report implies, the role of both individuals and institutions as boundary spanners is essential to the long-term success of any systemic partnership. The people that fill these roles will be called upon to create their own job descriptions as they move in the direction of innovation. University and college presidents and chancellors have already begun to take on such leadership and their efforts have ignited significant change in their surrounding communities (Howey & Zimpher, 2006).

WHAT WILL UNIVERSITY PARTNERSHIPS LOOK LIKE IN THE FUTURE?

Trying to make predictions about the future has always been a venture fraught with peril and is perhaps even more so in our era of rapid change. So treacherous is this undertaking that experts have crafted the acronym, VUCA—for Volatility, Uncertainty, Complexity, and Ambiguity—to sum up what lies ahead. At least this was the conclusion drawn from the Institute for the Future (IFTF, Palo Alto, California) when asked by the national KnowledgeWorks Foundation to design a futures map with a focus on how teaching and learning would be affected in the future by the mega-trends the IFTF was willing to project. In an attempt to understand the trends that may lie ahead, I, along with many others, took part in the Future Forces conference at Wingspread in Racine, Wisconsin, in December 2006.

As I participated in this conference, I realized that the VUCA future has an impact on one and all, including those of us who are involved in and care about fostering university partnerships. The map acknowledges that the knowledge economy and globalization will

> continue to challenge the basic industrial-era assumptions upon which most public schools, curricula, and evaluation mechanisms are based. New interactive digital media are diffusing rapidly, even in lower-income communities, fostering a youth media culture that is crashing into schools and educators like a tsunami, raising issues of privacy, pedagogical relevance, and equity. Student performance is inconsistent across the country, and the average U.S. performance indicators lag disappointingly behind those of other countries. (2006, SR-986, text from map panel)

Because the Future Forces map examines trends affecting family and community, markets, institutions, educators, and learning, we can look to it for some valuable guidance in identifying who our future partners may be as well as to assess what future needs might be. It is important to consider the Future Forces "drivers of change" that hold valuable clues for higher education. While we can assume that all these forces will affect our institutions in one way or another, I chose for discussion a select few that best illustrate future challenges, specifically in the areas of economics, urbanity, globalism, health care, and teaching and learning as summarized below.

> *Grassroots economics*: This driver of change suggests that we are moving from economies of scale to economies of groups, resulting in an emerging set of rules "for creating value from collaboration more than negotiation, from bottom-up rather than top-down processes, and from shared resources rather than private property."
> *Urban wilderness*: This change force hints that we are shifting from a predominantly rural environment to a predominantly urban one. "As the urban population surpasses the 50 percent threshold worldwide, mega-cities and rapidly growing smaller cities will face unprecedented challenges in managing wealth, health, infrastructure, and social discontent."
> *Local value grows*: As fears of globalism and big business lead to a revival in localism, local engagement will take on new urgency and importance, especially in urban settings with their problem-rich environment. (Possible partners include local segments, business and corporate sector.)
> *It's harder to be healthy*: If we think good health care is difficult to achieve today, it appears that health care will only become more challenging in the decades ahead. Maintaining good health is expected to become more expensive and more difficult as poor urban residents are marginalized with little access to fresh foods, green spaces, and pollution-free environments.

The community becomes classroom: As the boundaries between cyber-space and real space blur and the anywhere/anytime environment of computing and wireless connectivity transforms physical places into "smart" environments, the implications for our partnerships become enormous. "Educational services will be customized to place, making learning increasingly visible in the community."

As we consider these Future Forces trends, universities will want to re-think their approaches to partnering, particularly in the following areas:

I. More Collaboration with State Governments

As the pendulum swings back toward renewed localism, universities' partnerships with their states will become even more paramount. A new spirit of collaboration and cooperation to address issues of the health and economic welfare of the fifty states will become paramount in ensuring healthy local communities. For decades, state public policy makers have placed higher education on the back burner as they grappled with very real and critical budget issues, but a new day has already begun to dawn. For example, in Ohio a new spirit of collaboration is emerging between the governor, legislators, and our public universities. This collaboration has re-sulted in a new plan for growing the college-going population in Ohio by 230,000, retaining more college graduates in the state, and attracting more graduates from other states to live and work in Ohio. This is only a part of a newly articulated ten-year strategic plan for public higher education in Ohio, through Ohio's new chancellor and with the clear support of the new governor. This is a win-win for all sides in Ohio as enhanced college access, affordability, and accountability can begin to pay dividends not only through increasing salaries for Ohio's workers and subsequence in-creases in Ohio's state revenues, but also through reducing dependency on public services and the criminal justice system as more educated residents lead to a more productive and responsible citizenry.

II. More Partnerships with National Foundations and Think Tanks

While universities will work to improve relationships within state boundaries, they may also seek to enhance their collaboration with na-tional organizations that share common goals and agendas. National higher education associations have long been collective resources for uni-versities who share common missions and activities, but our relationships with national foundations, think tanks, and policy-pursuing organizations need to expand and become more strategic. If institutions of higher learning truly want to make an impact, they will need to seek ways to gain a greater voice and greater effectiveness by making alliances with organizations outside the realm of higher education. The previously referenced Coalition of Urban Serving Universities intends to implement and evaluate shared strategies across U.S. cities. By working collectively, the USU can scale up and translate local innovations into greater impact on important national challenges. Furthermore, the coalition has looked outside its own membership to gain the greatest leverage, forming a relationship with the Brookings Institution, in particular on the Brookings' *Blueprint for American Prosperity*. Similar allies such as CEOs for Cities, Living Cities, and other organizations provide possible avenues for gaining momentum.

III. Expanded International Institutional Partnerships

While critics of Tom Friedman's best-selling exploration of the new rules of our global economy can be found aplenty, his book, *The World is Flat*, was successful in focusing our national attention on the twenty-first-century reality that geography does not matter as much as it once did in our world filled with flattened computer screens. While the pendulum of localism foreseen by our Future Forces map may be swinging, it is unlikely that it will propel us backward to a time of total isolation. Our American universities have long been tremendous conduits for the international exchange of people and ideas; however, even in an age of the so-called flattened world, our institutions continue to struggle with how to best become truly international and global. While many of us persist in viewing our international approaches through the lens of the past, I believe a new approach is needed. While student exchanges, international recruitment, and curricular internationalization all have their place and value, the future calls us to be more creative; indeed to think of ourselves as creative enterprises (Leventhal & Zimpher, 2007, pp. 102–108) that seek to pursue international relationships in more well-thought-out and strategic ways. Gone are the days of judging international partnerships by sheer numbers of the memorandums of understanding or partnerships based solely on one faculty member. Rather, in the decades to come, American universities' relationships with international partners will need to be deeper and institution-wide.

IV. Deeper Engagement with Business and Industry

University relationships with business and industry will increasingly embody the spirit of entrepreneurship in all aspects of its functions rather than just in so-called spin-off activities. Thus universities will need to approach businesses differently—more like partners where we are invested in success together. The process of partnership will simply have to be more integrated from the start. Such an approach, already emerging at many universities, will likely reflect the following attributes of entrepreneurship: placing a value on entrepreneurship in tenure and promotion processes, placing high priority on the recruitment of superstar faculty who have track records of entrepreneurial activity as well as scholarly research accomplishments, utilizing technology networks that bring an increasing number of faculty in direct contact with entrepreneurs who operate outside the academy, increased investment in all stages of the commercialization process, and placing a high priority on interdisciplinary cooperation not only outside the institution but, most importantly, within the institution itself. In summary, innovation and collaboration are key in coordinating technology, talent, and financing in order to move the entrepreneurship needle in the future. There are many partners in the private sector, and through our local chambers of commerce, regional and state government organizations, as well as the federal government and Washington-based organizations, all of whom must come to see these important collaborations as not only futuristic, but also necessary to achieving the future that so many national policy makers say we need in America.

V. Education Pipeline Issues

The twenty-first-century age of knowledge, information, creativity, and innovation is one where a college degree has become absolutely essential to a lifetime of career success and quality of life. Yet a myriad of reports indicate that a significant portion of the U.S. citizenry does not complete the education needed to achieve that level of success. As a former schoolteacher and former dean of education, I have spent more than three decades working to bring about true quality education reform to change the dial on this issue. And for the foreseeable future, this is a challenge that will continue to demand our attention. That is why, of all university partnerships, the relationship between higher education and the PK–12 educational community is the one I remain the most passionate about. Further, true education reform is about a pipeline that begins early and lasts for a lifetime. Such improvements require simultaneous change in teacher preparation and systemic school reform.

So in order to create true and lasting change in facing this challenge, we need to undertake more systemic approaches that view education as a continuum from birth through college and career (PK–16) and provide linkages all along the pipeline. Already many universities across the nation are engaged in partnerships that are taking this view, including the membership of the Coalition of Urban Universities cited above. These systemic partnerships require us to make teammates of those we have not often viewed as collaborators. Our potential new partners are in many cases our current "competitors"—our colleagues in vocational school systems, in our community and technical colleges, and at other campuses in our regions.

VI. Workforce Development

Although workforce development is closely aligned to the education pipeline issues discussed above, I list it separately to underscore its importance. Many of the same partners who will need to be involved in the pipeline issues will also need to be collaborators in workforce development. In Ohio, as a part of the new University System of Ohio strategic plan, the chancellor of higher education has proposed the formation of the Ohio Skills Bank to link workforce supply and demand at the regional level, with regional teams to facilitate articulation and transfer between adult workforce centers and community colleges. Potential partners in workforce development include public policy makers, the corporate community, postsecondary education, economic development leaders, PK–12 partners, the arts community, agents of infrastructure, and more.

CONCLUSION

Clearly, many challenges await higher education as we face the future. We may not be able to predict with certainty what may lie ahead, but partnership will be an essential element to help us anticipate and thrive no matter what the future brings.

Some institutions have already moved to make partnership an organizing charter. At the University of Wisconsin–Milwaukee, for example, The Milwaukee Idea created an institution-wide commitment to community engagement. To do so, the institution took a concept long cherished as the Wisconsin Idea—that the boundaries of the university system were the boundaries of the state—and applied a similar approach to the UWM community in Milwaukee. At my current institution, the University of Cincinnati, our UC/21 strategic vision is transforming us into an urban research university for the twenty-first century—hence the "21"—with community engagement as an underscoring principle.

Among our six UC/21 goals is goal four—forging key relationships and partnerships with a newly formed Center for the City that provides a portal for the community to seek university collaboration, as well as vice versa, for the university to seek collaboration with the community.

Similarly, at Arizona State University, President Michael Crow has embarked on the vision for ASU to become a "New American University, where students learn about the world by engaging with it; where a university and the community around it are closely connected to each other; where traditional disciplines merge, collaborate, and redefine themselves; where ideas are pushed to become immediately applicable to the contemporary landscape" (ASU website).

As one of our most esteemed futurists on the American university, James J. Duderstadt writes in *A University for the 21st Century* (2003):

> The most predictable feature of modern society is its unpredictability. We no longer believe that tomorrow will look much like today. Universities must find ways to sustain the most cherished aspects of their core values, while discovering new ways to respond vigorously to the opportunities of a rapidly evolving world. This is the principal challenge to higher education as we enter a new century. (p. 3)

He further suggests that higher education goes beyond simply adapting to change by being leaders in the journey to the future, and that we must:

> [B]roaden the "traditional definitions of teaching and research mission . . . to take on more of a service character." [Not only] is it essential that these research activities be integrated with the teaching mission of the institution, [but] there is little doubt that the need for and the pressure upon universities to serve the public interest more directly will intensify. The possibilities are endless: economic development and job creation; health care, environmental quality; the special needs of the elderly, youth and the family; peace and international security; rural and urban decay; and the cultural arts. There is also little doubt that if higher education is to sustain both public confidence and support, it must demonstrate its capacity to be ever more socially useful and relevant to a society under stress. (p. 135)

And so Duderstadt suggests some "possible futures" for universities as they grapple with the twenty-first century, including the:

- world university
- diversity university
- creative university
- divisionless university
- cyberspace university
- adult university
- university college
- lifelong university
- ubiquitous university
- laboratory university

Amid all of these categories, there is one type that is missing that may mean the most as we look farther ahead in the twenty-first century. It is the one that calls us to define ourselves as "innovation universities." We need to be innovative about becoming innovation institutions!

Appendix: Illustrative Partnerships in a Twenty-first Century Urban Serving University—University of Cincinnati

Focus	Academic Disiciplines	Key Partners
Strive Student access and success PK–16 throughout Greater Cincinnati and Northern Kentucky region, but especially in urban cores. www.strivetogether.org	• Education • Arts and Sciences • STEM	• Urban School Districts • Diocesan School System • Higher Education • Business • Nonprofit • Civic
CincyTech USA Bringing companies, early-stage venture funds, hospitals, universities, and research laboratories together to grow the regional technology-based economy www.cincytechusa.com	• Sciences • Medicine • Engineering • Design • Research • Entrepreneurship • Business	• Chamber of Commerce • Universities • Hospitals • Companies • Early-stage Venture Capitalists • Research Laboratories • Queen City Angels • Incubators—Hamilton County Business Center and BIO/START
Live Well Collaborative New business-university model that firms together with UC students regarding specific product concepts for responding to fifty-plus market segments and building brands	• Interdisciplinary • Design • Engineering • Business • Medicine • Anthropology	• UC • Procter & Gamble Co. • General Mills, Inc. • CitiGroup, Inc. • AARP • Hill-Rom/Hillenbrand Industries • LPK

Partners for the Advancement of Collaborative Engineering Education (PACE)

Top-tier business-university consortium supports strategically selected academic institutions worldwide to develop the *automotive product lifecycle management* (PLM) team of the future

www.pacepartners.org/

- Design
- Engineering

- GM
- EDS
- HP
- Siemens PLM Software
- Sun Microsystems
- Selected institutions in U.S., Australia, Brazil, Mexico, Canada, China, Germany, South Korea, Sweden, and India

Niehoff Urban Design Studio

Interdisciplinary studio initiative undertaken to address urban issues that challenge the quality of life in Cincinnati; it endeavors to engage the community in an urban problem-solving effort

- Urban planning
- Architecture
- Design
- Urban geography

- UC
- Community organizations

Uptown Consortium

Five-way partnership that works to improve the quality of life in the neighborhoods surrounding UC's Uptown campus and to provide the best possible working environment for employees of the partner organizations

www.uptownconsortium.org

Also:

www.uptowncincinnati.org

- Urban planning
- Architecture
- Education
- Social sciences
- Economics
- Health/Medicine
- Transportation
- Public Safety
- Real Estate
- Business
- Community Development
- Finance

- UC
- Cincinnati Children's Hospital Medical Center
- Cincinnati Zoo and Botanical Garden
- TriHealth
- Health Alliance

Center for the City

A portal to connect the community and UC students, faculty, and staff who wish to engage in community interaction and participate in mutually beneficial partnerships.

www.uc.edu/community/cfc/

- All disciplines

- University Relations
- Service Learning
- Center for Community Engagement
- Civic Engagement Council

REFERENCES

Byrne, J. V. (2006). Public higher education reform five years after the Kellogg commission on the future of state and land-grant universities. *NASULGC and the W. K. Kellogg Foundation.*

Connelly, M. (1990). Dueling definitions: A nation at risk and responses thereto. *Knowledge: Creation, Diffusion, and Utilization, 12*(2), 141–168.

Dubb, S., & Howard, T. (2007). *Linking colleges to communities: Engaging the university for community development.* College Park, MD: The Democracy Collaborative.

Duderstadt, J. J. (2000). *A university for the 21st century.* Ann Arbor: University of Michigan Press.

Howey, K. R., & Zimpher, N. L. (2006). *Boundary spanners.* Washington, DC: AASCU/NASULGC.

Eckel, P. D., & King, J. E. (2006). An overview of higher education in the United States: Diversity, access and the role of the marketplace. In J. Forest & P. Altbach (Eds.), *The international handbook of higher education.* Dordrecht, Neth.: Springer.

Joint Task Force for Urban/Metropolitan Schools. (2004). *Crossing boundaries: The urban education imperative.* Washington, DC: AASCU/NASULGC.

Kerr, C. (2002). Shock wave II: An introduction to the twenty-first century. In Stephen Brint (Ed.), *The future of the city of intellect: The changing American university.* Stanford, CA: Stanford University Press.

Leventhal, M., & Zimpher, N. L. (2007). Changing international constructs: How metropolitan universities must engage globally. *Metropolitan Universities Journal, 18*(3), 102–108.

Maurrasse, D. (2007). *City anchors: Leveraging anchor institutions for urban success.* CEO's for Cities.

Metropolitan Policy Program. (2007). *MetroNation: How U.S. metropolitan areas fuel American prosperity.* Washington, DC: The Brookings Institution.

Penn Institute for Urban Research. (2007). *Urban anchors in the 21st century: A commitment to place, growth and community.* Philadelphia: University of Pennsylvania.

Chapter 15

University Governance Beyond 2020

with Larry Gerber and Daniel Mcgee

Chapter 15 includes two sections. The first section by Larry Gerber examines trend concerns and advice for the future of university governance. The second session with Daniel Mcgee focuses more specifically on the ethics and values that impact university governance and the future of higher education.

THE FUTURE OF UNIVERSITY GOVERNANCE
WITH LARRY GERBER

Larry Gerber was first vice president of the American Association of University Professors (AAUP) from 2002 to 2008 and previously served as Chair of AAUP's Committee on College and University Governance. Following twenty-five years of service, Gerber recently retired from his position as professor of history at Auburn University. His particular academic interests are in public policy, political ideology, and the role of government in society.

Gerber is the author of The Irony of State Intervention *(2005) and* The Limits of Liberalism *(1983). He received his Ph.D. from the University of California at Berkeley. Before joining Auburn University, he taught for the University of Maryland's European Division, the University of Arizona, and Brown University.*

This chapter was based on interviews I conducted with Larry Gerber on November 13, 2007, and Daniel Mcgee on September 27, 2007, for this book.

History of University Governance

My current book on the history of university governance begins with the 1870s and the beginning of the modern American research university because there is a direct correlation between the development of the modern university and a more professionalized faculty, the increasing faculty role in the governance of universities, and a movement away from unilateral authority by presidents. As faculty became more professionalized, they played a larger role in having responsibility for governing academic matters.

The appropriate role for faculty in college and university governance was articulated in 1966 with the jointly formulated statement on governance by the American Association of University Professors (AAUP), the Association of Governing Boards (AGB), and the American Council on Education (ACE), which recognized that the faculty had primary responsibility for curricular matters, and in judging their peers in terms of hiring, promotion, and tenure.

Since the 1970s and 1980s, some of the assumptions about the role of faculty and governance came under increasing pressure as more of a business model was applied to the organization and running of universities. There have been a number of trends in the last generation that quite concerned me. I fear that if some of these trends continue into the future, the quality of higher education in America will decline.

Current Governance Issues

One trend is the development of the larger for-profit sector in higher education, which generally does not incorporate shared governance. Most of the for-profit institutions have very few full-time faculty. They do not typically have tenure and they generally operate differently from traditional universities. That is one trend that I believe undermines the practice of academic freedom, as well as shared governance. It would be disastrous as a model for all of higher education.

Another trend that is exaggerated in the for-profit sector and is increasingly coming into play in the nonprofit sector, is the use of contingent faculty. The percentage of faculty who are on full-time tenure track is approximately one-third, and that percentage has been declining quite rapidly over the last twenty years. I see that decline as having very negative implications for faculty governance. I also see it as having negative implications for the future quality of education, if the trend continues. That goes hand-in-hand with the declining professional status of faculty, who are increasingly losing the protection of tenure and expanding the ranks as part-time and adjunct positions and are often treated more like employees in a corporate setting. Consequently, faculty are losing some of their professional status and prerogatives.

Another trend, which could be positive or negative, is the increasing use of distance education. It can have negative implications for faculty governance if it is implemented in a for-profit setting where faculty are simply employees who do not control the curriculum. However, distance education has obvious positive implications as well.

One of the other current trends in higher education is the declining percentage of state support for public institutions. Ironically, while there are increasing pressures from the states for their own measures of accountability and assessment, demanding more oversight, the states are paying less of a percentage of the cost of public institutions.

Future Trends

I am not happy with the current path of university governance. Universities are increasingly heading toward becoming credentialing institutions rather than truly educational institutions. This path does not include many full-time tenured faculty. This contributes to students viewing themselves more as consumers, often with the sentiment of "I paid my tuition, I should get my degree." I don't think it is inevitable that we have to continue on this path without any changes, but I think that if we keep going in the current direction we will see the notions of broad liberal education giving way to a much narrower conception of the role of universities and what students hope to gain by attending universities.

With the decrease in public financial support for higher education, and increasing tuition, there is the growing danger that higher education will become less accessible to many Americans, which could be to the great detriment of the whole country. So, we need a change in direction—a widespread social and political reassessment of where we are heading, one which recognizes public priorities. So much of state revenues are going to other public institutions, such as prisons, which diminishes support for education at all levels. Unless there is some sort of reassessment about the importance of education from kindergarten through higher education, I am somewhat despairing of the future.

Additionally, there is a need for reassessment of higher education's broad vision for a liberal education, which is increasingly being lost. That has paralleled the rise of a broad acceptance of market models, with the market interpreting almost everything and not fully appreciating what economists refer to as "public goods," of which higher education is one. I am hopeful that, in the next twenty years, there will be a broad political, intellectual reassessment by the public of the role of higher education.

If a broad reassessment is to happen, people like me, who believe in a broader mission for higher education, ultimately will have to prove their case to the public about what is being lost by having the increasingly narrow vision of higher education as being simply job training. We must also do a better job of selling the public on the social benefits of investing in higher education: looking at higher education not just purely as an investment in the development of technologies to benefit the economy, but rather as a public investment in terms of a well-informed citizenry and preparing people to be adaptive in an increasingly changing world. The notion of liberal education will have to be updated to the needs of the twenty-first century, but the case for a broad conception of higher education must be made to the public, otherwise it is not going to happen.

In the 1990s, it was touted that Americans in the workforce in the twenty-first century would change jobs six or seven times and, therefore, needed a broad background so they could shift occupations throughout their working lives. There has certainly been a good deal of discussion about education in the last seven years with No Child Left Behind, and now with the arguments about accountability for higher education. But that discussion has become much more narrowly focused on the jobs that students enter immediately after college, or for passing a particular test, as opposed to focusing on the breadth of training. There has been a recent retrenchment, that is, in part, related to the greater emphasis on relying on the market for determining social outcomes.

Consequently, if we rely totally on the market, many of traditional disciplines, like philosophy, would probably completely atrophy and would no longer be options for study. Students are not attending the university simply to buy a product comparable to buying a CD, or choosing a movie they want to see. There should be student involvement in the development of curriculum. However, students new to college and university life are not capable of determining what is generally best for them to study.

Accountability in Higher Education

Accountability is a fairly new phenomenon. Some related aspects about applying a business model at the university are part of an older debate. People commented a hundred years ago about the need to promote the application of business models to higher education. However, those older business models did not include pressure for standardized testing of college students at the end of their careers to try to determine how good an education they had received. So this kind of accountability is a new element. Why it has emerged is a good question.

One of the factors is economic. Since the 1970s, the American economy has not been performing at the same level it had been for the previous generations. There are increasing pressures on state and local governments, in terms of other demands on what limited revenues they do have available. This has created an economic crunch, which is reflected both in lower financial support for higher education as well as demands about tracking how dollars are spent and to concretely see what is produced. When revenues are expanding, there is optimism about the economic future and an assumption that higher education has been quite integral to the expanding American economy. There has been a lot more pressure on accountability measures when state legislators have been confronted with not having enough money to cover all public needs.

The Spellings Commission indicated a need to impose more control on higher education and there has been a fair amount of push back against their approach. Although there are significant elements that would like to see federal intervention, it is less likely to happen in the next five to ten years than intervention at the state level, where the pressure will build even more. This will happen in the private sector as well, but rather than governmental bodies being more involved, it will be governing boards doing more micro-managing than they have done in the immediate postwar decades.

My projection for the near future is that there will be more intervention by state governing boards and state higher education agencies. However, such intervention might prove to be counterproductive. This could lead to a change in the political environment so that, just as No Child Left Behind has produced negative reactions to the possibility of federal government intervention, a similar development might occur in higher education at the state level in a way that then might reverse the trend toward intervention.

The notion that there should be some appropriate standards to show that education is producing a positive result is understandable. The difficulty is in devising appropriate ways to measure success in higher education. The idea that there should be pressure on faculty and administrators at the local campus level to think about whether they're accomplishing what they want to accomplish is a very appropriate pressure to be coming from external governing agencies. The problem comes with external agencies wanting to impose the means by which such measuring is accomplished. It is also inappropriate when the measurement only takes the form of what could be easily quantifiable, or be easily measured by standardized testing. To devise reasonable and reliable ways to measure the level of academic success is a difficult dilemma.

Future Concerns or Pitfalls

One serious problem is the decreasing use of full-time tenured faculty. Tenure came under more direct scrutiny in the 1990s. However, some of the direct challenges to the whole concept of tenure have decreased after the governing board at the University of Minnesota attempted to abolish tenure, which a mobilized faculty successfully blocked. Tenure is being undermined indirectly by increasingly limiting the number of positions that come under the protections of tenure.

The problem is wider than just the smaller number of tenured faculty; it is also the use of contingent faculty. The AAUP certainly recognizes that there are many wonderful contingent faculty and there are many highly qualified part-timers who can be excellent teachers. They may also be accomplished researchers, but the reality is that the typical situation for contingent faculty in American colleges and universities is that many of them do not even have offices on campus. In fact, they are not on the campus on any kind of regular basis, so they are not able to participate actively in governance mechanisms. If they are teaching at two or three different institutions, commuting, and have no offices, they will not become invested in any individual institution. They will not be able to have a voice in or participate in governance. Contingent faculty are less costly salary-wise for the institution, but what are the long-term costs in terms of quality of education? This is one of the most worrisome and dangerous of all recent developments.

The AAUP has general suggested guidelines that recommend that institutions not have more than 15 percent part-time faculty. Clearly that kind of standard has not been met by two-year institutions. Even in many four-year institutions there are not many that will meet that standard. The AAUP then suggested a new standard for an individual department—that there shouldn't be more than 25 percent part-time faculty, but even this more flexible standard is not being met at many colleges and universities.

Governing Boards in the Next Twenty Years

A long-term historical perspective would show that clergy and lawyers were the predominant occupations of governing board members well into the nineteenth century. However, this began to change toward the end of the nineteenth century when people with business backgrounds were becoming more predominant on boards. One of the problems related to the increasing application of business models to running universities is that there is not enough diversity on governing boards. I think that there should be much more occupational, gender, and racial diversity on governing boards so that there would be a variety of perspectives about what is appropriate. It is a sad commentary that people who have university experience as faculty or even administrators at the college or university level are not very likely to actually serve as board members. I would like to see greater diversification of boards as a way of infusing new perspectives.

In terms of current trends, it is most likely that, in twenty years, boards will continue to be dominated by people from the business sector, with maybe a few lawyers. There is a widespread assumption that those who come out of the business world are best equipped to enforce necessary standards of accountability and efficiency on colleges and universities. While I accept the notion that some business expertise is useful and even necessary on a governing board, I fear that insisting that virtually *all* board members come from such a background will overwhelm all other considerations about the purposes of higher education. That too would be disastrous for the future of higher education in America.

I would like to see a degree of faculty representation on university boards, and it does not have to be the faculty from that particular institution, although I do favor representation by faculties on their own governing boards. Even more importantly, it would be highly desirable for governing boards to include representatives who have faculty experience at other institutions who could contribute a faculty perspective that perhaps other board members would not see as self-interested, because they are not members of the faculty that are being affected by the decisions of that particular governing board.

Other representatives also need to be included. Racial and ethnic minorities and women typically have not been as well represented on boards as they should be, especially given the changing composition of the population of American student bodies. Those would be some of changes I would like to see in an ideal governing board. Certainly, I think it's perfectly desirable to have members on a governing board who do have business experience, since one of the important roles of a governing board is to maintain the finances of the institutions. They should not, however, be the exclusive group represented on governing boards.

How to Prepare for Optimal Success in the Future

One point has to do with the preparation of students even before they get into the college or university. Based on anecdotal evidence, I would say that many faculty members have increasing concerns about the quality of the K–12 public education our students are receiving. Leaders of higher education not only need to examine the quality of their own institutions, but also need to explore opportunities for improving the quality of K–12 education so that students coming into colleges and universities will be better prepared in terms of their substantive knowledge base and readiness to work hard and study. It is alarming that so many incoming students have been successful in high school, and yet the majority have no real concept of an appropriate level of academic work. Higher education leaders must become involved in improving K–12 education.

I do have some concerns about many colleges of education. I think that there could definitely be improvement in the way future teachers are both recruited and prepared. Again, looking at my own experience, imposing higher standards and greater expectations on teacher education could help. There is a trend to put more emphasis on content as opposed to method in the training of teachers.

Another area with room for improvement is the articulation of standards for admission. I do not support higher education being purely available to the elite. It should be broadly available to the American public, but should also demand higher standards of admission in terms of preparation. More pressure could be placed on public schools to better prepare their students so they may be admitted to the colleges and universities of their choice.

Advice for Administrators

There clearly has been tremendous pressure on faculty and administrators to make greater use of new technologies in instruction. While on the one hand there are probably many good things about the use of technology in instruction, I think that administrators in particular need to carefully consider a cost benefit analysis as to how useful some of the technological innovations actually are in terms of the quality of instruction. Administrators should examine how much technology contributes to the rising costs of higher education relative to its usefulness in instruction. I use Power Point in my lectures, and I have a Blackboard website for instruction for my classes, so I'm not anti-technology. But I often wonder whether the use of some of these technologies actually is counterproductive in terms of student learning. I would like to see schools of education doing research to try to measure the effects of student reliance on these kinds of technologies. Perhaps they are not necessarily engaged in the most effective way.

When it comes to the curriculum, especially for general education or core requirements, it is beneficial for university and college faculties to periodically reassess whether they are accomplishing what they intended or needed to accomplish. Harvard recently performed a thorough assessment on revising its general education requirements. While I do not have a specific model of what courses ought to be in the core, I do think that core education is extremely important, and that it needs to be periodically reassessed.

There certainly has been increasing discussion in universities and colleges over the last twenty years about interdisciplinary approaches. This is another area that emphasizes the need for flexibility and development of critical thinking skills. An exploration of interdisciplinary programs, and even possibly some modifications in the traditional departmental governing system, is something that university personnel should be open to.

Advice for University Constituents: Federal and State Government, Local Governing Boards, Alumni, Faculty, and Students

I have a general piece of advice for constituents external to the university—which includes governing boards, state legislatures, Congress, and the president: their role can only be setting goals in the most general sense. They do not have the expertise and experience to determine how those general goals can be implemented effectively in the classroom or in the laboratory. A word that has been used often in my own institution—"micro-management"—by any of the external constituents should be avoided.

A primary concern that especially applies to governmental officials is the containment of the cost of a college education. It is necessary to focus on making college accessible and affordable, whether it is by financial aid or financial support for institutions, so that we don't see a decline in enrollment or the quality of American higher education.

I would not be surprised if the list of the top hundred universities in the world twenty years or more from now will include fewer American institutions, especially with the decrease in support. Elected officials need to focus on finances, but they cannot just worry about the cost containment side. They need to be concerned with finding the ways and means of making education at all levels a very high priority for spending.

From very early on, alumni and alumni associations have been more interested in the extracurricular activities of universities, especially sports, rather than academics. I don't think it's healthy to have alumni associations be tremendously involved in the internal governance of institutions regarding academic matters. I do not have any problem with alumni associations having some representation on large governing boards, but I certainly do not think the alumni voice ought to be dominant. Alumni provide financial support for institutions and maintain an important role in their loyalty to the institution, but I don't think they should be too centrally involved in governance.

With regard to the role of students: I was a college student in the 1960s and I certainly argued then that students should have some participatory role in governance matters. They should have some input into the curricula and some other matters, but again, not much input on many academic or governance matters. They should be involved more on an advisory basis.

Theoretically, students can have a voice on governing boards. Auburn has had a nonvoting student representative on the board since the 1970s, yet it was only a couple years ago that we had a nonvoting faculty representative on the board. Students have often been represented longer than the faculty, but having gone to quite a few board meetings at my institution, it has been my observation that the student representative virtually never plays a significant role in the discussions. It is more of an honorary place at the table. However, I predict that there will come a time in the future where a student voice would be more of an active voice than it is right now.

I favor fairly large governing boards, larger than the Auburn board is now with fourteen members, and I believe the Association of Governing Boards supports such a principle. Fairly large governing boards are a good idea for a variety of reasons. Additionally, although I might be hesitant to have a student as a voting member on a seven-person governing board, I would support a student voting on a thirty-person board.

Emerging Issues and Concerns

One thing that has long been an issue for many colleges and universities, and which I think will continue to be an issue that spills over into governance, is athletics. I am a sports fan, but it is tragic the way that so many people identify with their alma mater almost solely in terms of sports. Sports have a higher priority for many alumni than the academic side of the institution. It is often said at Auburn that we would not tolerate having a football team that couldn't be in the top twenty every year, but we're perfectly content to be proud if we are academically ranked in the top one hundred colleges and universities. I think that's symptomatic of many colleges and universities, both an overemphasis on and a commercialization of sports.

Unfortunately, some people are interested in being members of governing boards in large part because of their preoccupation with college athletics. Consequently, there are people with a high priority on athletics making decisions that have to do with academics and the entire university. At times, decisions about such academic matters as admissions policies are shaped more to influence recruiting good athletes. It is definitely a danger. As college athletics has become more and more a multibillion-dollar endeavor, Congress may follow through on removing the tax exemption of the NCAA. This is a pressure that certainly might grow.

I am troubled by the notion that increasingly many more governing boards may look at non-academics to fill the CEO position of the institution. I would hope that that is not a trend which will increase, because I think it is still valuable to consider the president of the university as head of the faculty as well as a representative of the governing board. I would urge presidents and governing boards to take the perspective that the future depends on cooperative relations with faculty, not on top-down management of the faculty.

THE FUTURE OF GOVERNANCE AND ETHICS WITH DANIEL MCGEE

Daniel McGee is the author of more than sixty articles and book chapters on business, environmental, medical, political, and academic ethics. Included among McGee's many honors is the 1970 "Outstanding Educators of America" Award. He served on the National Board of Directors for the American Academy of Religion from 1971 to 1977 and as regional president from 1987 to 1988.

McGee consulted for nearly a decade on various hospital morals and ethics committees and served as president of the Texas Conference of AAUP from 1971 to 1974. McGee earned his Ph.D. in theological ethics from Duke University and was a professor in the Department of Religion at Baylor University from 1966 to 2006.

Constituents, Influence, Power, and Money

Constituents

Overall, there has been a continuing growth of the participants in the academic governance process. Traditionally, there have always been three powers: administrators, the governing boards, and the faculty. Those are still there, and it varies from school to school as to the relationship and the distribution of power among them. However, other groups have assumed important roles in the life of the university within recent decades. For example, there are some universities that include a student who either serves on, or reports to, the governing board.

Another constituency that has a great effect on what happens at a university are the alumni, and that creates its own unique dynamics.

A constituency that often plays a larger, dramatic, and direct role are the donors. Donors may approach a university willing to loan a million dollars for a particular program or chair. This can have significant impact on the institution.

Additional influences include local, state, and federal governments. Colleges and universities have to obey appropriate laws and regulations. Legislators impact state-related schools, and, to a lesser degree, the private colleges and universities of the world.

Power Shift

After World War II, science began to blossom, but this growth has been even more pronounced in just the last two or three decades. The corporate world had a major role in that revolution because scientific advances have become a major source of great economic gains. This has paralleled the dramatic increase in economic power in the United States. Economic power has expanded and those persons, professions, industries, and corporations that are closest to benefiting from scientific development consequently enjoy increased power in the media, government, education, and culture. In the United States there has been a major increase in the relative financial power of the upper class. Most of the power today is concentrated in the hands of 20 percent of our population.

Corporate Influence and Research Funding

The growth of influence that concerns me the most is the role of corporate America through its funding. For example, different corporations compete mightily to obtain university funds to do certain jobs. That becomes quite an exclusive, competitive process within the university. Sometimes corporations lobby their agenda to university administrators.

There are many construction and service jobs on the university campus that are being sought by a number of companies. There is competition in the process, and that sometimes impacts the relative power of various administrators within the university.

The whole research process is a game unto itself. It is a major financial operation, and the pharmaceutical companies, for example, want research conducted by science faculty. Let's not kid ourselves: in some cases, they want favorable reports from the research. Some of the significant disputes within medicine today are about researchers primarily serving their financial supporters or providers rather than those with legitimate, serious health care needs. It is compromising the integrity of some research.

There is clearly a problem, it is being hotly debated, and the public does not hear about that debate. The faculty desperately needs research and the pharmaceutical industry has new drugs that they need to have favorably reviewed. This creates issues. It's a frightening combination.

This problem has increased in recent years in part because of the growth of the scientific revolution and the importance of the unbelievable strides made in science—strides that hold the promise of great blessings for the human race. But those kinds of hopes and dreams can be corrupted by greed. The money and the prestige that surround research opportunities are many times the primary motivators.

The end result is that there may be a hesitancy to report negative outcomes. Government plays a part in this as well. There has been criticism of the Food and Drug Administration for allowing drugs that have not been adequately tested into the marketplace. There are many accomplices in this story. Corporate America parallels the government as a source of funds.

The Important Role of Research

Although there are concerns, research is important and necessary. It also plays a significant role in the economy and lifestyle of a society. Additionally, research is an important function of the American scholarly community. It is important for those who specialize in teaching to realize that if the researchers did not do their job, then teachers would have little to teach.

Future Economic Downturn

There is always the possibility of an economic downturn. For example, under the current federal administration, the funds of the federal government have moved from a rather substantial surplus to a significant deficit. That's going to come home to roost some day. When and how, and the way it impacts us, is yet to be determined.

Initially, government will not become a player in the event of an economic downturn, especially in the private colleges and universities. In the public colleges and universities, that impact might come fairly soon. To prepare, it is important to immediately begin to place some controls on spending. In return, government will have to cooperate and increase the taxes of the wealthy individuals and corporations that have enjoyed reduced taxes in recent years. Administrators need to find ways to retain their funds in a safe place, and maybe back off on projects that would be nice to do, but are not necessary in the immediate future.

Continuing Social Change

Additional areas that need to continue to be addressed, and perhaps accelerated by administration, the faculty, and the governing board, are the trends that have grown out of the Civil Rights Movement. We need to have a broader scope of the larger society reflected in the interest of the administrators—more women, and various races and cultural groups.

As we have increased our numbers of international students and faculty, it might be beneficial to expand that concept to administration and governing boards, to enhance and bring to them some of the insights of international academic communities.

Ethics

Everything that has ever happened, and that ever will happen, involves an ethical dimension, or ethical values and presuppositions. We often conceal the ethical value that prompts our behavior. An example might be a group of people who may wish to conceal the fact that they do not want to appoint a minority or a woman to a position, so they simply do not hire a person from either group.

While preparing for retirement during recent months, I have told many people of my plans for the future. I have taught ethics now for forty-five years. I have teasingly announced that I will establish a consulting firm titled Have Ethics, Will Justify. So for a price, I will invite people to tell me what they want done, and I'll justify it for them.

This game is being played in the real world all the time, so we need to recognize that, when we talk about ethical analysis. We have to be cautious. We need diversity. We have to have room for challenges. We need to examine traditional behavior patterns and goals that have been kind to the human race. We need to do that in an honest way and in a way in which we listen as much as we talk.

It is encouraging that the discipline of ethics has expanded significantly in academia in the last several decades. It has expanded most in the discipline and departments of philosophy and religion. However, in a number of universities, a school or division will have its own ethicist, which can be very good when there is an honest attempt to find someone who is competent in ethical analysis, and in the ethical traditions of our culture. Unfortunately, too often those appointments have been of ethicists who are "owned" by the department or discipline and therefore have no critical assessments to make.

If we fully develop my theory of Have Ethics, Will Justify, the weaker in the society will be damaged most. The more powerful will use the arguments and analysis that promote their own interests. The university and society will suffer.

Ethics should be a part of the training for all. We start off by training human beings in the basic moral responsibilities. First, we must understand that any power we have is primarily a responsibility, not an opportunity for our advantage. As with any power, talent, ability, or wealth, the first question should be, "How am I responsible to use this power or capacity?" It would take some training in education systems, but also hopefully the religious communities of the society will be playing a significant and positive role as well. Then, we must also train our youth and others in what is moral to do and not to do, by looking at the examples of leaders, of parents, of others whose lives impact, influence, and shape them.

Academia is in the information business, but I would add that it has another central purpose, one that is often unstated in higher education, and that is character formation. Academia needs to be honest about that. You do not have to become a Bible school to do this. As a matter of fact, this trend is developing in state-sponsored universities.

Preparing for the Future

Let me identify some of the things that can be done for the future. First, there are a number of interests within most colleges and universities that give students an opportunity, indeed even encourage them, to develop good citizenship habits, such as service programs that help the poor in their community. That sometimes occurs in relationship to a specific academic program, but sometimes it develops in a general context. Student groups do this. Universities have increasingly done this with more consciousness as conflicts have emerged among various student groups, especially those with racial or cultural differences. Universities can find ways of promoting discussion and education about the contributions of these various cultures and include good values of American culture.

We are doing better at this process, but we can still improve. The Civil Rights Movement pointed us in that positive direction, but of course we see that racial conflicts still occur. I think a lot of us are shocked by the examples of racial conflicts within student bodies. We need to find ways to make the university community just and fair.

If there were to be an economic downturn, I think there would be some in academia who would see it coming, and grab all they can while there is still something there to grab. I think there will be others who will see that there is need for more sharing. Both will occur, and those in positions of leadership have primary responsibility to encourage an open and sharing attitude. This will be influenced by example and by either loosening or tightening the purse strings accordingly.

Administrators, faculty, and others need to influence governing boards by their own behavior, and by a demonstration of interests regarding the welfare of the larger community. They are in a position to say, "This is what we should be doing."

There should be more communication between constituents, but first there should be more of the goals and behavior discussed above. Having done that, the values that you want promoted can be addressed.

New Developments

I think most of the trends of the last several decades will continue into the immediate future. I anticipate an increasing diversity in the student body and we should aim for that, and hope that it happens racially, culturally, economically, and internationally.

Another trend that I see continuing is increasing academic diversity. We have seen certain subject areas divided into sub-areas or specializations. That will continue, and that is a good thing, but I also foresee the continuing rise in the interdisciplinary nature of the academic enterprise. There is a danger in specialized disciplines becoming too isolated. There need to be increasing interdisciplinary studies. Some interdisciplinary programs have almost taken the shape of departments, bringing faculty from various specialties together to teach together. It is crucial that this continues to happen, otherwise specialized knowledge will become less and less useful. It has to be understood in relationship to other bodies of knowledge. That is something I think should be pursued by leaders in higher education.

There is a general principle that higher education not only teaches, but also learns. We should be looking into every corner of our society for information, insight, and understanding that can contribute to teaching and character formation. We need to be looking around in those forgotten places of our culture that could teach us something. We do not need to sell our soul in the process, nor do we need to applaud every diversity. We should pass critical judgment on some.

I thought it was very interesting to watch the president of Columbia University welcome the Iranian president to that university. One academic tradition welcomes such guests to campus with nothing but praise for the political leader and his or her country. The president of Columbia did not do that. He made some very explicit criticisms on the Iranian president's leadership, of what was going on in his country, and challenged him to explain. It was clear that the Iranian president had been forewarned and encouraged to respond. I think that is a legitimate form of academic analysis, with the mission of giving that person full opportunity to say anything he or she wants to say, and providing a platform, but not selling our academic souls under the guise of being courteous.

This type of argument also arises in the intelligent design debate. I think there is a place to be critical of that analysis, but I would not want to shut it down completely. There is always a balance that we have to keep.

How to Prepare for the Changes of the Future

Number one in preparing for the future is to not be afraid of diversity and change, while at the same time to become fully aware that the best traditions of academia are where interdisciplinary appreciation has been dominant and where a certain openness is valued. At the same time, it is important to always be prepared for very powerful interest groups that may try to undermine those values and goals within the university. Some people are not aware of their provincialism. They need educating, but beyond that they need leaders who will exercise their power. Leaders must not be afraid to make unpopular decisions. That is always dangerous advice to give to people because there is the inclination among many leaders to think they are not doing their job unless they are "bossing." Hopefully, leaders of the future will not be taking the role of "the handler." Defining every detail of the institution's journey is not the task of any single office or group.

To be a true community, the university must nurture all segments of its body politic so that all can contribute to, and all can receive from, that collective body.

Conclusion
by Mary Landon Darden

Leading a university during a time of great social change is a bit like navigating the Titanic through an iceberg floe in the dead of night. Simply reacting to challenges and opportunities as they arise can eventually sink the ship.

—James J. Duderstadt, *The View from the Helm*

In the end, every expert in *Beyond 2020* agreed that the rate of change in the modern university is escalating. Leading a university will become more complex, more challenging, and more difficult to predict. "It is not a job for the faint of heart," as Trachtenberg wryly notes.

That change will be felt in every area of the university. For instance, the pendulum has long since swung from the *in loco parentis* colonial college, which focused on the moral development and ministerial preparation of individual students, to the moral independence, increased civil rights, and partially broken glass ceiling of the 1960s. However, by 2008, the pendulum, alas, has begun to swing back, as women's salaries that had reached the mid-80 cents on the dollar in the 1990s have plunged back into the low 70-cent range.

Wherever the future pendulum swings, there are many deep concerns on regional, national, and global levels: some old, some new. Elected and appointed leaders alike are grasping for solutions to these problems, some of which may threaten the very existence of mankind.

In these uncertain times, what role will the university play not just in its own future, but in the future of our world? I believe it is poised to play the greatest role of all.

As the university races into this unsettled future, I was encouraged that, along with the many cautions prescribed in this book, I still heard a distinct message of hope and optimism coupled with a genuine encouragement to embrace the adventure to come.

There were other deep and evocative insights revealed as these candid interviews unfolded. The expert contributors were asked to describe the current state of their particular discipline and to project where they thought we were most likely to move in the next twenty-plus years. However, through virtually all of the interviews, I heard an urgency to focus on the external influence of the university as well. They called to the university to guide civilization itself to new levels of health, productivity, integrity, equity, civility, and peace. It was a call to examine not only what the university is likely to be, but also what it could be beyond 2020. Drawing from the collective pool of the wisdom, advice, and knowledge shared on these pages, I wish to speak to what, in my view, is the next step for the university.

The university is no stranger to strategic planning. It is a part of how most successful universities live and breathe. From the interviews in *Beyond 2020*, it appears that planning for the future is just posturing unless it encompasses the *entire* university.

GOVERNANCE

The foundation of any university is the shared responsibility, mission, and purpose of the constituents: the students, faculty, administration, alumni, and board. Trachtenberg says that universities need the active participation of *all* of their members to thrive (personal communication, December 22, 2007). All serve the institution through shared governance in order to insure its optimum productivity and success. Within the shared governance system, there has to be a critical and intricate set of checks and balances, key relational structures, and a sharing of power that insures the institution's stability and maximizes institutional health and longevity. For the university to flourish in 2020 and beyond, certain key points need to be emphasized:

Governance must be shared. Constituents must be collaborative and work as a team. Top-down management has rarely proved successful in the academy. Success in any venture requires buy-in by every constituency in order to realize maximally optimal outcomes.

The board's primary responsibility is the careful selection and hiring of the best possible president for their institution. This would be a president who understands the culture of higher education and of the particular institution, is a good fit, has all of the crucial operational components (such as a need for collaboration) and is capable in all of the many areas of administration mentioned in this book and more. It is then the board's job to serve and support that president as that president serves and supports the institution. On occasion, when it becomes apparent that a president is no longer a good fit for an institution, it is also then the responsibility of the board to remove that president from office.

Presidents are servants of the entire constituency—one of the requirements that makes the job so demanding. It is a president's responsibility to insure that the funds are raised, that appropriate and fair policy is written, that outstanding administrators fill the vice presidencies, that shared governance thrives, and that the members of the academy have what they need to function optimally. Administration serves the faculty so that the faculty can serve the students.

The faculty research and teach, mentor, and serve the students. Faculty chairs are faculty members, selected by the peers in their field to lead the department. Faculty should be selected, promoted, and tenured based on peer review within their discipline and department, by the very people equipped with the increasingly specialized expertise to make such evaluations. Additionally, tenure must be protected not only to insure academic freedom and safety from tyrannical ideology, but also in the hopes that at least some people of the future will still be willing to spend a fortune and spend a decade in college to take a job that may pay less than the entrance salary of some two-year-degreed technicians.

The students, in turn, ideally go out to serve society and, hopefully, return on occasion to support and assist their alma mater—perhaps even as a member of the board.

It is critical among these collaborative relationships that the welfare of the institution be paramount. Ideally, it should be a place of trust, integrity, and mutual respect. If the delicate balance of power and relationships is eroded at any level, it can impair the overall effective functioning of that institution.

Additionally, the lack of genuine equity is still a major concern for the academy, particularly in relation to gender and race. Just as governance must be shared amongst the constituents, it must also be shared equitably. As Van Ummersen notes, only 23 percent of college presidents are women (personal communication, December 19, 2007). This inequity is evident in other areas as well, including within the faculty and boards. Forty years after the Civil Rights Movement, this should no longer be the case. While researching my dissertation, based on interviews with eighteen women college presidents, I discovered that it was particularly difficult to find women college presidents in the South. Our southern states still have a longer journey ahead of them than many of their northern counterparts. Many universities, mostly in the north, have made equity a deliberate priority and part of their mission and strategic plan. The American Council on Education has developed two divisions to assist college and universities in achieving greater gender, racial, and ethnic equity, the Office of Women in Higher Education (OWHE), and the Center for Advancement of Racial and Ethnic Equity (CAREE).

These types of initiatives are vitally important because in order to lead in the future, the university must set the tone and be above reproach. To substantially increase fairness, equity, and justice in the world, the university *must* become a better role model and make these values a priority on every level.

FINANCIAL FUTURE

Financial instability is perhaps the greatest immediate threat to the many universities who do not enjoy the vast endowments of institutions such as Harvard and Yale. Universities must be creative and proactive in finding ways to replace diminishing and limited financial sources with new and expanded ways of insuring the institutions' long-term stability. This includes providing whatever additional funds will be needed to meet the need for emerging new technologies and the many potential new expenses that may emerge from future institutional evolution. It is essential that most universities revisit advancement, entrepreneurism, risk management, and preventive law in order to make a difference in their financial future.

Advancement

When a culture of common values, collaboration, shared governance, and mutual respect exists, there is—as mentioned earlier—buy-in from the constituents. This term is more than a representation of shared philosophy; it can actually become a tangible outcome. As Vanden Dorpel points out, people give to an organization out of a sense of shared values and from a belief in personal philanthropy (personal communication, April 23, 2008). It will be critical to the survival of virtually every university in the future to nurture and develop this kind of environment.

Entrepreneurism

Because there is likely a limit to both what donors are willing to give and to how much tuition can be raised, and because this limit is currently accompanied by radically decreasing public funding and a declining economy, it will become necessary for many universities to increase their entrepreneurism. To stay true to their mission and purpose, one of the easiest areas for the university to move into is Continuing Education. Andrew Meyer's comments on those institutions where Continuing Education has been prioritized, pointing out that the resulting revenues have exceeded those of credit education, should be a wake-up call not just for those in university development, but for all administrators and faculty alike (personal communication, April 22, 2008). It is simple common sense: no institution is equipped to face the future if it is consumed by the daily struggle of paying the bills to keep operating.

Risk Management and Preventive Law

As society becomes increasing litigious and risk continues to pervade the open campus, Robert C. Cloud advises that we must find ways to minimize risk and liability (personal communication, June 3, 2007). Universities should prepare to expand their risk management and legal counsel staffs. There should be a proactive plan to anticipate, prevent, and respond appropriately to the occasion of any mishap. It is a stark reality of today, and probably will be ever more so in the future, that even a few lawsuits based on any form of oversight or carelessness could place most institutions in financial jeopardy.

Again, this is simply prudent use of previous resources to ensure that the university of today is still around to face the challenges of tomorrow.

TECHNOLOGY AND LIBRARIES

Although students of the past were often restricted to higher education options in their region, most now can scour the globe for the best higher education options for their needs. In the future, research and learning will occur virtually from and to anywhere.

As technology continues to break the ties of place-boundness, it will become increasingly more important for universities to establish a unique marketability, with specializations and niche developments that will draw the world market to their institution.

Again, just as we have moved from the one-dimensional, single-purposed colonial college to the mega-dimensional, multileveled, complex system of a wide variety of higher education institutions, so are we likely to continue the journey of further specialization, splintering institutional definitions, and the need for clarification and wide communication of a unique image and mission.

This deepening specification will increase the need for interdisciplinary discussions, to integrate knowledge and the usability of that knowledge, to enhance the ability of our scholars and students alike to develop positive applications and outcomes.

The university that moves too cautiously or not at all in recognizing and adapting to these new realities is unlikely to share in the great successes of the future.

PARTNERSHIPS

As seen by the examples provided by President Zimpher at the University of Cincinnati and Linfield president emerita Vivian Bull, the university must actively seek productive partnerships to accomplish the many and varied goals of not just the institutions, but also the community, state, nation, and the world (Zimpher, 2008; V. Bull, personal communication, February 28, 2008). The collaborative nature of the academy is an excellent tool for developing joint efforts to answer many of the needs and solve many of the problems facing our current civilization. We need to be creative and open in developing these relationships with business, governments, nonprofit institutions, and more. Herein may lie the answers to the most alarming problems facing not just the university, but also the world itself in the decades to come.

THE STUDENT AND EDUCATION

Business schools teach the art of profit-making. Many disciplines define well the individual professional opportunities for students. However, as the problems in the world escalate, perhaps there is a place for renewed emphasis on the net gains for all humanity. Indeed, most disciplines could increase the focus on the other-centered, philanthropic, altruistic, national, and global stewardship potential for both individuals and teams. Addressing these issues specifically and providing opportunities for hands-on experience is fully within the purview of the twenty-first-century university.

Service learning, volunteer work, and travel abroad have repeatedly improved not only communities, but also the lives of those who participate. These values should be enhanced within the missions and plans of future universities and could also be expanded to reach more deliberately into the more profoundly needy regions of the world.

"Students who have opportunities to interact with people from other cultures and races are much more likely to show growth in . . . spirituality related qualities," Alexander Astin writes. "And there is the connection between the discussion on equity issues and the development of the whole person in terms of qualities that are so essential to the survival of the species. They go hand in hand" (personal communication, January 10, 2008).

Despite our affluence, we are in the midst of conflict on so many levels and our potential for accomplishing good is far from being realized.

As we search for ways to prevent famine, disease, pollution, crumbling social structures, war, and replace them with healthy and constructive alternatives, as Carmody says, it is often the students who find the most elusive solutions to our problems (personal communication, April 18, 2008). The students of the future must be equipped with the tools and the values to accomplish that, and be inspired with the heart to eradicate suffering throughout the world.

PROTECTING THE PLANET

There are so many critical issues facing the future university. However, there is one that is so critical at this time that—if a solution is not found—the university may no longer exist. NASA scientist and global expert on climate change James Hansen recently said, "We have at most 10 years—not 10 years to decide upon action, but 10 years to alter fundamentally the trajectory of global greenhouse emissions" (Hansen, 2006).

The earth is currently experiencing catastrophic weather from rising temperatures. Worldwide starvation is epidemic and escalating. We are experiencing a global crisis of epic proportions and there is no assurance that humanity will survive this radical alteration of our planet.

Duderstadt asserts that *global sustainability* is one of the most important emerging new issues confronting presidents, one they especially need to pay attention to. In referring to the *Synthesis Report* from an international group of 4,000 scientists, Duderstadt says, "They concluded that there is absolutely no doubt whatsoever that humankind is changing the planet, that it is much more serious than most people realize, that we can't deny it anymore, that we are headed for big trouble, and it is our universities that will develop the knowledge and hopefully the educated citizens who will grapple with that knowledge. If we don't, we are all in trouble" (personal communication, November 20, 2007).

The leadership and innovation to change the present disastrous course must come from the university. This means that, as they have with so many other human concerns of the past, the great leaders, researchers, and teachers need to make awareness and change a number-one priority for the university. Presidents should speak out, raise awareness, influence legislators, and solicit support for the cause. Researchers need to dedicate themselves to finding the solutions in renewable energy production, advanced technology, and ways to clean and heal our ailing planet. Faculty need to dedicate time to teaching students how to understand what is happening to their world and inspiring them to take immediate action to change this fatal trajectory. In addition, the university needs to find ways to creatively fund this essential work.

SUMMARY

I believe these priceless insights and bold predictions of the academic leaders putting their minds to work on the challenges and opportunities of the future will be an asset to any university seeking to not only survive, but also thrive beyond 2020. It was an extraordinary adventure and privilege to work with these people, for whom I have profound respect and admiration.

If the conclusions are true—and I believe they are—and if the predictions come true—and I believe they will—then we need to make haste in preparing for the university beyond 2020. Even as the university drifted away from the trivium and quadrivium, the place-bound, ivy-covered, ivory tower will increasingly diminish in this new century. The new paradigm will emphasize cyberspace over floor space, electronic data over paper, and virtual instruction will eclipse face-to-face instruction. The university of the past, traditionally linked to community and region, will be of necessity shifting its sights to the global horizon.

There is more work to be done than might have been dreamed of by the colonial college. Many of our world's greatest problems are of a scope and depth that might only have been imagined vaguely in the past. Global warming is just one important example. Universities are the logical place to assemble task forces for environmental intervention. No other single institution in the world is more important, is better equipped, or has more potential to change our world beyond 2020 than the university.

Industry has perhaps an insurmountable conflict of interest in its perspective on seeking solutions, beholden as it is to stockholders whose priority is the highest possible profit with the least initial risk. This has resulted in our prolonged dependence on fossil fuels and polluting energy production.

Government is profoundly influenced by the big-money industries that finance campaigns and constantly loiter in the wings with their tethered agendas. The powerful influence of these for-profit interest groups can paralyze real progress for the future.

Even the churches are wrought with conflict, including diverse views on whether we should intervene to save the planet or not.

At its ideal best, the university stands alone.

However, partnerships with industry and government, accompanied by the wise advice from the academy that, so far, has managed to keep a focus on the original charge of preparing the way for the future, seem the most likely route to global success. The university must be cautious not to collect too many attachments to groups with other agendas. However, just as the university labors to build buy-in internally, it is now being called to build it externally as well.

We are on the crest of a tsunami of change and we need a vessel that can not only survive the impact, but also strategically navigate the dangerous waters and lead humanity into a new world of environmental stability and prosperity, bringing about an end of war, poverty, hunger, and suffering, and providing equal opportunity for education and advancement. It must bring a form of global governance that is based on equity, human rights, and justice; codes of ethics, compassion, and reconciliation; honor, integrity, and civility.

The university is that mammoth ship—and perhaps the only one—complete with tack, cargo, crew, and charts that can set the course for change in the world beyond 2020.

REFERENCES

Duderstadt, J. J. (2007). *The view from the helm*. Ann Arbor: University of Michigan Press.

Hansen, James E. (2006). The threat to the planet [electronic version]. *New York Review of Books, 53*(12). Retrieved June 12, 2008, from www.nybooks.com/articles/19131.

Zimpher, N. L. (2008). Partnerships of the future university. In M. L. Darden (Ed.), *Beyond 2020: Envisioning the future of universities in America*. Lanham, MD: The American Council on Education and Rowman & Littlefield Education.

About the Writer and Editor

Mary Landon Darden's first book, *Beyond 2020: Envisioning the Future of Universities in America*, is the culmination of more than two decades of academic excellence and leadership. During her eight years as a college administrator, she transformed a struggling program into a national showcase, winning the National Exemplary Community Service Award from the National Council of Continuing Education and Training (NCCET). She has also received national media coverage both for her environmental activism and work with evacuees from Hurricane Katrina.

In 2006, Darden received her doctorate in educational administration (Ed.D.) from the Baylor University's Scholars of Practice Higher Education Program. Her groundbreaking dissertation, "Women Presidents of American Four-Year Colleges and Universities: An Analysis of Reported Changeable Attributes Contributing to Their Success," featured interviews with eighteen female college and university presidents.

Darden is currently a consultant for several higher education organizations including the Center for the Advancement of Process Technology, Inc., a National Science Foundation Center of Excellence. Darden works with industry leaders from dozens of international corporations. She is the author of numerous articles and is a popular speaker at conferences, seminars, and rallies.